W9-AQE-728

TWAYNE'S WORLD AUTHORS SERIES

A Survey of the World's Literature

Sylvia E. Bowman, Indiana University

GENERAL EDITOR

SPAIN

Janet W. Díaz, University of North Carolina at Chapel Hill
Gerald Wade, Vanderbilt University

EDITORS

The Poem of the Cid

TWAS 378

The Cid Campeador

THE POEM OF THE CID

By EDMUND DE CHASCA

TWAYNE PUBLISHERS
A DIVISION OF G. K. HALL & CO., BOSTON

Library of Congress Cataloging in Publication Data

De Chasca, Edmund, 1903-
The poem of the Cid.
~~Boston~~ T 76   *139p. 8"*
(Twayne's world authors series ; TWAS 378 :
Spain)
Bibliography: p. 173-79.
Includes index.
1. El Cid Campeador. 2. Diaz de Vivar, Rodrigo,
called El Cid, d. 1099? — Romances — History and criti-
cism. I. Title. II.
PQ6373.D4   861'.1   75-30597
ISBN 0-8057-6194-2

MANUFACTURED IN THE UNITED STATES OF AMERICA

To Edith, Daniel and Edmund

Contents

About the Author

Edmund de Chasca was born in Guatemala where he received his early education at a German school. He attended several colleges and universities in the United States, including the University of Chicago. There he earned the doctorate in 1941 and taught Spanish Literature from 1950 to 1953 before going to the University of Iowa, where he served as Head of the Department of Romance Languages until 1967 and thereafter as Professor of Spanish Literature. Throughout his service at the University of Iowa he was the Hispanic editor for *Philological Quarterly*. In 1972, this journal published a Festschrift for him entitled *Hispanic Studies in Honor of Edmund de Chasca*. Scholars from Europe, Spanish America, Canada and the United States contributed studies which reflect the wide range of Professor de Chasca's interests. In 1972 he was awarded a Guggenheim Fellowship for Comparative Studies of Cid Ballads. The author of five books, published in Mexico, Spain and the United States, and of numerous essays in professional journals, he is considered a foremost authority on the subject discussed in the present book.

Preface

The deeds of Spain's national hero, the Cid, were celebrated not only in the one early epic song we know today; some of his exploits were recorded favorably by a Latin Poem, the "Carmen Campidoctoris," which is known to have been composed in his lifetime, and by a Latin narrative, the *Historia Roderici*, which was written shortly after the Cid's death, probably by a cleric who had participated in his later campaigns. The Christian authors of these works of course sing the hero's praises.

But it is only natural that the pens of the two contemporary Arab historians who give us certain information about the Cid were dipped in venom. These earliest cidophobes were the Valencian Moor, Ibn Alcama, who wrote his account of the siege and capture of Valencia under the title *Eloquent Testimony of the Great Calamity* (c. 1011), and the Portuguese Moor, Ibn Bassam, author of a book entitled *Treasury of the Excellence of the Spaniards* (i.e., of Spanish Moslems), written in 1109.

In striking contrast to the poets who celebrate the Cid, the earlier bards who sang the praises of Greek, Germanic, and French heroes were far removed in time from the fabled exploits described in their poems, and history remembers little or nothing about them. Ruins unearthed by archaeological excavations confirm the existence of Troy, but of Achilles we know nothing; we know that Gunther was a historical figure, but we can only conjecture that Sigfried was; as for Roland, we know that he did exist, but that is all.

We are indebted to Ramón Menéndez Pidal for a masterful historical reconstruction of the Cid and his Spain. Not only did he draw upon the contemporary historical and poetic sources we have mentioned, but by dint of a prodigious effort he has also made known a great wealth of information derived from archival records that he discovered. These records include deeds of donation and endowment, legacies, law suits, marriage settlements, and wills. In the first chapter I have attempted to accomplish the difficult task of condensing the essential parts of Pidal's monumental work, *La España del Cid*, venturing only occasionally to present my own insights.

Perhaps a disproportionate amount of space has been devoted to a review of the historical events involving the Cid. This has been done for two reasons: first, because the historical facts concerning the Cid are thus made most readily available to the general reader and, I hope, more easily understood by him; second, because the thorough consideration of the Cid of history should make possible a more rigorous distinction than has heretofore been made between the historical Cid and the poetic Cid — a distinction which I attempt to make in chapter 2.

In the larger and more original part of this book I have attempted to examine critically certain stylistic and structural aspects of the *Poema de Mio Cid* (hereafter referred to under the siglum *PMC*). I hope the explications will help the reader understand the consummate literary art of our anonymous poet. Because of limitations of space I have not included a chapter on one important aspect of his technique, namely, his moderation in the use of numbers, an aspect which perhaps more than any other demonstrates the controlled but intense realism of his style. This sobriety is especially striking if we compare it to the hyperbolical élan of the poet of the French *Roland*, in which the total number of Christians and Saracens is astronomical. Disseminated numbers in progressive order are also used in the poem as correlatives of significant points in the structural development.

Another omission in this book results from the difficulty, indeed the impossibility, of explaining in English certain devices which are made possible only by the nature of the Spanish language itself: prismatic changes of tense — especially between the preterite and the imperfect — and sounds of words, that is, what the linguists call signifiers. Signifiers include a considerable number of rhymed first hemistiches, an important aspect of the poem's versification heretofore ignored. All these stylistic phenomena have been exhaustively studied in *El arte juglaresco en el "Cantar de Mio Cid."*

Like every Cid scholar I am, of course, enormously indebted to don Ramón Menéndez Pidal. Without the great Spanish medievalist's fundamental work as a historian and philologist my own work would not have been possible.

Preface

I wish to express my thanks to the *Hispanic Review* for permission to reproduce in this book my 1953 article, "The King-Vassal Relationship in the *Poema de Mio Cid*"; to Editorial Gredos for allowing me to draw heavily on parts of my book *El arte juglaresco en el "Cantar de Mio Cid*," and to W. S. Merwin and his publishers, the New American Library of World Literature, for their permission to quote from his fine English translation of the poem.

Chronology

c. 1043   Rodrigo Díaz, known as Mio Cid (*cid* is an Arabic word meaning "lord") is born in the village of Vivar six miles north of Burgos.

c. 1058   Upon the death of his father, Rodrigo goes to the court as the ward of Prince Sancho.

1065   Fernando I dies. Two years before his death he announced the division of his realm. Sancho inherits Castile; Alfonso, León; and García, Galicia and Portugal.

1066   Sancho assigns to Rodrigo the title of supreme captain of the royal army.

1066   Rodrigo vanquishes the Navarrese knight Jimeno Garcés in single combat to decide the disputed possession of the border castle of Pazuengos.

1068   Sancho, whose forces are led by the Cid, defeats his brother Alfonso at the battle of Llantada.

1071   Sancho divides with Alfonso the kingdom of their younger brother, García, whom Sancho had dethroned.

1072   (July) Sancho defeats Alfonso at the battle of Golpejera and captures him. The Cid plays the decisive role in Sancho's victory.

1072   (Oct.) Vellido Adolfo, a Zamoran knight, murders King Sancho. The Cid becomes Alfonso's vassal.

1074   Marriage of the Cid to Jimena Díaz, niece of King Alfonso.

c. 1079   Toward the end of this year King Alfonso sends the Cid to Seville to collect tribute from its ruler, Motamid.

1080   While the Cid carries on negotiations for tribute with Motamid, Count García Ordóñez and King Abdullah of Granada make an incursion into Sevillian border country north of Granada. The Cid defeats the Granadan king and the Castilian count. He captures the latter. According to the *Poem of the Cid* the Cid's enemies accused him of keeping for himself the largest portion of the tribute paid by Motamid.

1081 (July?) The Cid's first exile. While King Alfonso is engaged in his campaign against the kingdom of Toledo the Cid, without authorization from Alfonso, takes it upon himself to attack the Moors who had taken Gormaz Castle, the most important fortress on the Duero river. According to the *Historia Roderici* King Alfonso considered the Cid's initiative an act of *lèse-majesté* and therefore sent him into exile.

1081 (August-September). The Cid goes to Barcelona to offer its rulers, the brothers Berenguer II and Ramón II, his services in subjecting Zaragoza's King Moktadir. Rejected, Rodrigo becomes the ally of Moktadir and, after the latter's death in October, of his eldest son, Mutamin.

1085 (Jan.) Alfonso attacks Zaragoza.

1085 (May) Toledo surrenders to Alfonso after a six-year campaign. Al-Kadir, the weak king of Toledo, who has collaborated with Alfonso, is rewarded for his collaboration. Alfonso makes him nominal ruler of Valencia.

1086 (June) Yusuf Ibn Teshufin, emir of the North African Almoravide empire, invades Spain at the bidding of Motamid of Seville, who could no longer tolerate Alfonso's excessive demands.

1086 (Oct.) Yusuf inflicts a disastrous defeat upon Alfonso at Sagrajas.

1087 Alfonso restores the Cid to his favor.

1089 The Cid's second exile. Alfonso summoned the Cid to Villena to help him against the Almoravides who had invaded the Peninsula for the second time. However, the king bypasses Villena taking a shortcut to Molina. Angered by Rodrigo's failure to join him, Alfonso exiles him again.

1090 (May?) The battle of Tévar. Berenguer II of Barcelona, abetted by Al-Hajib of Lérida and Denia, and by Mostain of Zaragoza, are defeated by the Cid at the Pine-Wood of Tévar. The Cid takes Berenguer prisoner.

1090 (June?) Yusuf's third invasion. His cousin, Syr Ibn Abu Beker, conquers the whole Guadalquivir basin, captures Cordova and Cuenca, and surrounds Seville.

1091   (May) The Cid, upon the urging of Alfonso's Queen Constanza, leaves the Valencian region to join Alfonso's incursion against Granada. To protect the king the Cid advances ahead of him. This offends the king and the Cid returns to the Levant.

1092   (May - June?) Alfonso encamps with his army before Valencia but is forced to withdraw when the fleets of his allies, the republics of Genoa and Pisa, fail to arrive in time to attack the city from the sea. The Cid refrains from fighting his king, but he devastates the lands of the royal favorite, Count García Ordóñez.

1092   (Aug. - Oct.?) The Cid leaves the Valencian region to eradicate pockets of resistance in Zaragoza. During his absence the cadi, Ibn Jehhaf, imprisons the Cid's vizier, Ibn Al-Faraj, brings about the murder of Al-Kadir, and has his treasure seized. He then assumes control of the city.

1092   (Nov.) The Cid lays siege to Valencia. The siege, interrupted by a brief truce, lasts nineteen and one-half months, until 15 June 1094.

1093   (Nov.) Abu Beker, Yusuf's son-in-law, comes to the rescue of besieged Valencia, but he turns back, foiled by the Cid's destruction of causeway bridges, the release of irrigation canal waters, and by torrential rains.

1094   (Oct.) Yusuf sends a huge army under the command of his nephew, Mohammed Ibn Teshufin, to take Valencia. The Cid, taking the Almoravide hordes by surprise, defeats them at the Cuarte plain, three miles east of Valencia.

1095   (May) Ibn Jehhaf is put to trial for regicide. He is found guilty and sentenced to death by burning.

1097   (Jan.) The battle of Bairén won by the Cid against great odds.

1097   (Aug.) Yusuf's general, Mohammed Ibn Al-Haj, inflicts a disastrous defeat on King Alfonso at Consuegra. The Cid's only son, Diego, is killed.

1097   (Dec.?) The Cid takes Almenara after a siege of three months.

1098   The Cid lays siege to the fortress of Murviedro. It surrenders on June 24.

1099   Death of the Cid on July 10.

Abbreviations

See the Selected Bibliography for date and place of publication of books.

BH	*Bulletin Hispanique*
BHS	*Bulletin of Hispanic Studies*
H	*Hispania* (Wichita)
HR	*Hispanic Review*
MP, CMC	Menéndez Pidal, *Cantar de Mio Cid*
MP, CS	Menéndez Pidal, *The Cid and his Spain*
MP, ChR	Menéndez Pidal, *La Chanson de Roland y el neotradi-cionalismo*
MP, EC	Menéndez Pidal, *La España del Cid*
MP, PJ	Menéndez Pidal, *Poesía juglaresca y juglares*
MP, PMC	Menéndez Pidal, *Poema de Mio Cid*
MP, PP	Menéndez Pidal, *Mis páginas preferidas*
MP, TPC	Menéndez Pidal, *En torno al Poema de Mio Cid*
MLR	*Modern Language Review*
NRFH	*Nueva Revista de Filología Hispánica*
PQ	*Philological Quarterly*
PMLA	*Publications of the Modern Language Association of America*
R	*Romania*
RFE	*Revista de Filología Española*
RFH	*Revista de Filología Hispánica*
RH	*Revue Hispanique*
RLC	*Revue de Littérature Comparée*
RF	*Romanische Forschungen*
RPh	*Romance Philology*
RR	*Romanic Review*
ZRPh	*Zeitschrift für Romanische Philologie*

Note: When the *Poema de Mio Cid* (also called *El Cantar de Mio Cid*) is not spelled out, the abbreviations *PMC* or *CMC* are used. Also, only the abbreviated titles of Menéndez Pidal's works without the initials of the author, are frequently given.

CHAPTER 1

The Cid of History

I Rodrigo Díaz of Vivar

RODRIGO Díaz, commonly known as the Cid, was born about 1043 in Vivar, six miles north of Burgos. This ancient capital of Castile and its neighboring village, lie in a high valley of the Duero plateau, a vast region of rolling plains which extend northward to the rugged Cantabrian mountains. The plains are frequently broken by outcroppings and declivities. The climate is severe: "Nine months of winter and three of hell," as the saying goes. Poets of the Castilian mystique depict an agonized landscape of raging sun, a hardworking people of measured speech, of courteous, unostentatiously aristocratic bearing, of sober habits, of self-controlled intensity; *mesura* is a Spanish word for this combination of traits.

Today Vivar is a dwindling village. In a letter written in December 1970 its mayor, Don Pedro Ubierna informed me: "This town has forty-one habitable houses, some of them in a considerable state of deterioration. The inhabitants are for the most part engaged in agricultural pursuits. We do not exceed twenty-four family heads and the total population consists of about 120 inhabitants. . . ." Among the tawny stone dwellings of square simplicity two large buildings stand out: in their midst a squat church, and at their edge the crumbling pile of the convent of Franciscan nuns where the manuscript of the *Poem of the Cid* was kept until 1775. No physical trace of the Cid's ancestral home remains, but the epic that celebrates his deeds evokes a poetic memory of its abandoned halls:

. . . gates standing open and doors without hasps, and bare pegs without fur cloaks and without mantles, and without falcons and without molted hawks.

(3 - 5)[1]

This is the emptiness that made Rodrigo weep as he rode away from his house never to return.

Only untrained hawks still circle the sky above Vivar. Where the Cid's horses ran, a tethered donkey nibbles at a patch. Sheep graze on the banks of the Ubierna. It is called a river, but only in winter does it have enough volume to drive the wheel of the town mill continuously. Its present owner claims it occupies the place of one of the mills that once belonged to the Cid.

II   *The Cid's Ancestry*

In the third canto of the poem the Cid's mills give one of his enemies a pretext to insult him: "Let Rodrigo Díaz of Vivar go back to the mills where he belongs to grind his millstones and collect his toll-corn!" (3779 - 80). The insult was gratuitous. In the eleventh century the possession of mills was a highly esteemed privilege of rank. It is true that Rodrigo Díaz, an *infanzón* — the term used to designate a member of the middle nobility — did not belong to the highest class of *ricos hombres* to which the speaker of the lines quoted above belonged. Nevertheless, his ancestry was honorable enough. On his father's side he was descended from Laín Calvo, one of the judges who according to tradition was elected by the Castilians to govern their county when, at the beginning of the tenth century, they rebelled against the king of León. His paternal and maternal grandfathers, Laín Nuñez and Rodrigo Álvarez were figures of some importance in the court of Ferdinand I (1035 - 1065), but it was the brother of Rodrigo Álvarez who achieved great distinction as a magnate under *el rey santo* ("the holy king"). The Cid's father, according to Menéndez Pidal (*La España del Cid*, pp. 121 - 25), does not seem to have frequented the court, but before retiring to a quiet life at Vivar he won important battles in the war which García of Navarre waged against his brother Fernando.

III   *Rodrigo and Sancho of Castile*

A contemporary of the Cid, the anonymous author of the *Historia Roderici*, informs us that Rodrigo became a ward of Sancho, eldest son of King Ferdinand. Menéndez Pidal surmises that the youth was taken to the court upon his father's death in 1058 (*EC*, p. 127). At court he was trained in arms and letters. He excelled in both.

Prince Sancho, eldest son of King Ferdinand, knighted his protégé when the latter was seventeen. Three years later the young knight participated in Sancho's victorious military expedition to Graus, a stronghold in the kingdom of Zaragoza.

Shortly after his accession to the throne of Castile upon his father's death,[2] Sancho II distinguished Rodrigo of Vivar above all members of his court by appointing him supreme commander of the royal army. The Spanish title for this dignity, namely, *alférez* ("ensign" or "standard bearer"), was the highest rank that the king could bestow on him. A dispute between Navarre and Castile over possession of the border castle of Pazuengos gave the young ensign the opportunity to establish his fame. In his capacity as ensign he was pitted against the famous Navarrese knight Jimeno Garcés, to settle the issue in single combat. Rodrigo's victory earned for him the epithet *Campeador* ("Warrior" or "Battler") by which he was thenceforth known.

IV   *Sancho Repudiates His Father's Testament*

During the two years that the Queen Mother survived her husband, Sancho adhered to the terms of his father's testament regarding the partition, but with her passing he repudiated it. According to poetic accounts as recorded in the *Primera Crónica General (The First General Chronicle)*,[3] Sancho protested the partition, when his father announced it in 1063, on the grounds that the fragmentation of the realm was contrary to the customs of the Goths (*EC*, p. 142). The *juglares* ("epic" or "ballad singers") were probably right. As the strong-minded and ambitious eldest son, Sancho was bound to advocate the principle of an indivisible Hispanic empire established by the Visigoths. This principle could be implemented only by the observance of the right of primogeniture, a right Sancho was denied. His claims, then, were supported by hoary, though by that time supplanted, precedent (Ferdinand followed more the recent examples of French kings).

Sancho was consumed by his ambition to make Castile the dominant power in the Peninsula; this ambition was fanned by Castile's traditional antagonism to León and by his strong dislike for Alfonso, the younger brother whom his father had always favored.

War between Sancho and Alfonso was bound to break out sooner or later. The Cid took the leading part in the battle which finally decided the issue.

V   *Llantada and Golpejera*

The war between the brothers broke out in July of 1068. Observing an old Germanic custom, they agreed to let the result of a single battle determine possession of the other's kingdom. Sancho's and Alfonso's forces, led by their ensigns, Rodrigo Díaz of Vivar and Martín Alonso, clashed at the Llantada plain on the banks of the Pisuerga river which separated León and Castile. The Leonese were defeated, and Alonso took flight. However, the battle was not decisive, for Alfonso refused to abide by the terms of the agreement and was able to make his refusal stand. Indeed, as strong as ever, he subdued the kingdom of Bajajoz later that same year.

After Llantada, rank expediency brought Sancho and Alfonso together long enough to despoil their younger brother, García, of his possessions, Galicia and Portugal.

The issue which the battle of Llantada had been intended to resolve was bound to arise again. For a second time the brothers marshaled their forces, this time on the plain of Golpejera, a few miles south of Santa María de Carrión, the family seat of the powerful Beni-Gómez family, represented in the poem by the Infantes of Carrión. Sancho owed his victory in the long see-saw battle to the superior generalship and intrepidity of the Campeador. Alfonso was captured and dragged in chains through several Leonese cities. Sancho inflicted this humiliation on Alfonso to secure the submission of the latter's subjects. The victorious brother thereupon imprisoned Alfonso briefly in the Castle of Burgos and then sent him into exile.[4]

On 12 January 1072, Sancho was crowned king of León. His reign over the conquered kingdom was short-lived. Ten months later he was murdered.

VI   *Death of King Sancho*

A faction of Leonese nobles, affronted by Sancho's seizure of imperial León, refused to recognize him as their king. Among these nobles the most important was Pedro Anzúrez of the Beni-Gómez family. He had gone into exile with Alfonso to Toledo. Under the lenient custody of King Mamun he easily found means to establish communication with the resourceful Urraca. Pedro Ansúrez and doña Urraca, Alfonso's older sister, organized the movement of resistance against Sancho, with Zamora, the city Alfonso had given her, as their base of operations. Sancho attempted to storm that stronghold but the attempt failed because natural and man-made barriers made it impregnable. He then began a siege that reduced the city to near starvation. The Cid was the driving force and the sustaining spirit of the siege. One day fifteen Zamoran knights took him by surprise. He killed one of them, wounded two others and put the rest to flight. Having failed to get rid of the Cid, the desperate Zamorans decided to resort to an extreme measure: the assassination of Sancho. On 7 October 1072, a Zamoran knight, Vellido Adolpho, stole his way into the besiegers' camp. He caught the king off-guard, pierced him with his lance, and escaped.[5]

Castile was deeply shaken. In one moment her recently won political predominance vanished. Overnight the ruler who had been ideally suited to lead his subjects was replaced by a sovereign who took the Castilian throne, not by right of conquest, but by the right of succession to his murdered brother.[6]

VII   *The Cid, Vassal of a Grudging King*

For a time Alfonso bestowed his favor upon the Cid, notwithstanding the decisive role which Sancho's favorite had played in his defeat at Golpejera. Was Alfonso, exhilarated by his new power, willing to let bygones be bygones? Whatever the answer to this question, it is certain that his most pressing problem was the disaffection of Castile. He solved it by securing the support of the Cid and his party. First, he put the Cid in his debt by making him his vassal. By kissing the king's hand — a symbolic act of loyalty — the Cid pledged himself to serve his liege lord against all enemies in times of war and peace. Alfonso bound the Cid to himself and to León in other ways. One of them was of the greatest importance. In 1074 he arranged Rodrigo's marriage to no one less than his own niece, Jimena Díaz.[7] This was a master stroke of policy, for the marriage settlement, drawn up according to the laws of León, made the husband legally dependent on that kingdom. Other manifestations of favor were not lacking. However, he jealously denied Rodrigo Díaz any and all significant opportunities to exercise the talents that had earned him the name of Campeador. Instead he assigned to him for the most part duties far removed from the field of battle. The Campeador was allowed to take part in the campaign of La Rioja (1076) but only in a minor role. He was excluded from the long-drawn-out war initiated in 1079 against the kingdom of Toledo. The monarch's conduct resulted from the central defect of his character: envy. "He was afraid," Menéndez Pidal says, "lest all the credit for the victory [at Toledo] should be attributed to Ruy Díaz, as it had been by both Hebrew and Latin chroniclers in the times of King Sancho. The answer is to be found in the fact that, *unjustly* moved to anger (Pidal's emphasis), as the *Historia Roderici* points out, he sent the Campeador into exile for the initiative he had taken against the Toledan invaders" (*EC*, p. 269). I will summarize the Cid's unwelcome role against these invaders in due course, but first we should note a less immediate cause.

About six months before the Cid acted in Toledo without previous approval from the king, he also took matters into his own hands in the capital of Andalusia. He had gone to Seville to collect tribute due Alfonso from King Motamid. At the same time, Alfonso's favorite, Count García Ordóñez and four other noblemen, were in Granada on a similar mission: to demand past-due *parias* from King Abdullah Mudaffar. The Spanish ambassadors, either complying secretly with Alfonso's wishes (Menéndez Pidal thinks that Alfonso was uneasy about Motamid's growing power and sought to weaken him by strengthening his bitter enemy, Abdullah), or acting independently, fell in with Abdullah's vengeful desire to undertake an incursión into Sevillian territory (*EC*, p. 259). The Castilian count and the king of Granada ravaged the Sevillian countryside north of the border separating the two kingdoms precisely at the time the Cid was negotiating with Mutamid the delicate business of the tribute that was due. Shocked and alarmed that García Ordóñez should have conspired with Abdullah to attack Alfonso's most powerful and cooperative tributary, the Campeador sent him urgent requests to desist. However, confident that his and Abdullah's superior forces would prevail, the count scornfully rejected these requests.

Having been so long denied the leading role in military affairs to which he was accustomed, the Campeador was straining at the leash. He seized the opportunity to act. Leading the few henchmen who had escorted him to Seville, he rushed to meet the invaders. In the encounter that took place at Cabra, the Cid inflicted heavy losses on Abdullah's routed forces and captured García Ordóñez.

Alfonso was angered by the humiliation his favorite had suffered at the hands of his murdered brother's former vassal; he therefore lent a willing ear to the accusation of his enemies: Rodrigo Díaz had kept for himself the larger portion of Motamid's tribute. Menéndez Pidal surmises that there may have been circumstantial evidence on which the scandalmongers based their accusation. The Moorish king, grateful for all the Cid had done for him, probably rewarded him munificently with gifts or, less likely, according to Pidal, Motamid cheated by paying in debased coin (*EC*, pp. 261 - 62).

In disgrace, the Cid was kept idle for several months. In the summer of 1081, while Alfonso was waging a campaign against the intransigents of the kingdom of Toledo, the Campeador received the news that the Moors had attacked Gormaz, the most important fortress on the Duero river. Again he was unable to contain his impatience. Without consulting the king, he called his knights and led them into Toledan territory. His raid was successful. He scattered the enemy and took many prisoners and much booty. Again the king was furious, and again he listened willingly to the Cid's enemies. They accused him of interfering at Gormaz for one purpose and no other: to betray him to the enemy. This time Alfonso's spite — sinister, baleful, unforgiving — reached the breaking point and moved his hand to fix the royal seal on the decree that barred Rodrigo Díaz of Vivar from his lands.

VIII   *The Cid in Exile*

Both the *Fuero de Castilla* (Legal Code of Castile) and the *Siete Partidas*[8] affirm that against a king's arbitrary power to exile a vassal the latter, if exiled without just cause, had the right to take up arms against the king who had banished him, so that he might have sustenance from his native earth. The Cid did not take advantage of this right. When upon leaving Castile he was obliged to follow a route in territory where the Moors were at peace with Alfonso and under his protection, he said to his followers: "We shall cross that mountain [the Miedes range], rugged and high, and this very night we shall leave Alfonso's kingdom" (422 - 23). Having crossed the mountain he captured Castejón and raided the countryside as far as Alcalá.[9] He did not linger in this border country along the valley of the Henares, because, as the juglar says, "he considered that King Alfonso would send forces to follow him" (508). And the Cid himself declares to his men: "With Alfonso my lord I would not wish to do battle" (538). This well-known line points to the most noteworthy aspect of the Cid's conduct during the years of his exile: the avoidance of any clash with his irate lord, even when the latter's hostile actions imperiled his position in the Levante.

The exile first offered his services to two Christian princes, Counts

Berenguer II[10] and Ramón II of Barcelona. At the time both had designs on the neighboring Moorish kingdom of Zaragoza. Only after being rejected by the Catalan counts did the Cid enter into negotiations with King Moktadir, one of the Peninsula's most powerful and prosperous Arab rulers. Unlike Berenguer and Ramón, Moktadir welcomed the Cid as he had on previous occasions welcomed other Christian expatriates. He considered it a boon to have the Castilian as his ally, for he was continuously threatened by the Christian powers that surrounded him: from the north, Aragón; from the northeast, Barcelona; from the northwest, Navarre; from the west, Castile.

Moktadir died within a month after the Cid became established in Zaragoza. His son, Mutamin, during his four-year reign and, upon Mutamin's death, his grandson, Mostain, during several years of his reign, took full advantage of the Cid's military talents. In 1082 the Campeador took the Castle of Monzón. Then advancing eastward, he occupied Tamarite and stormed the ancient castles of Almenar and Escarpe. He won these victories against the powerful anti-Zaragozan coalition of Al-Hajib, ruler of three small eastern kingdoms,[11] Count Berenguer of Barcelona and King Sancho Ramírez of Aragón and Navarre. It was at Almenar, after a hard-fought battle, that the Cid took Berenguer prisoner. (The count was to suffer the same humiliation eight years later in the battle of the Pine-Wood of Tévar. In the poem the first canto concludes with an account of this battle and with a highly amusing scene in which the previously boastful count is so mortified that he goes on a hunger strike.)

Menéndez Pidal makes two important points concerning the Cid's victories against Mutamin's enemies: (1) the Campeador's brilliant success against enormous odds changed his status from that of protégé to protector; (2) unlike other expatriates who had found asylum in Zaragoza and the opportunity to render important services, Ruy Díaz was no mere mercenary but a man of principle to whom the interests of Alfonso remained paramount (*EC*, pp. 289 - 90). The second point is borne out many times during his exile. I will here adduce one example at the beginning of it. When Alfonso undertook an ill-fated incursion against Rueda in 1082 the Cid did not hesitate to leave Mutamin so that he could return to the side of his king to offer help. Alfonso welcomed him, but only briefly. He soon became envious and suspicious. Aware of his ill will, the Cid turned back to Zaragoza. Mutamin again received him gladly and with his aid renewed his campaigns in the east. Early in 1084 they both raided Aragonese territory. Then the Cid, without Mutamin's aid, took his men into the rugged mountain region of Morella. Alarmed by the Campeador's advance, Al-Hajib and Sancho Ramírez led their armies against him. Again the Cid triumphed. On 14 August 1084 he routed Sancho's and Al-Hajib's forces. He took more than two thousand prisoners, among them notables of Sancho's and Al-Hajib's courts. The few who were not freed were exhibited in Zaragoza. The enthusiasm and admiration of his beneficiaries knew no bounds. The Arab historian Ibn Bassam, a contemporary of the Cid, affirms that his victory against the Aragonese king and Al-Hajib was among his most important (*EC*, p. 298).

Little is known of the Cid's activities for the next four years.[12] In 1088 he renewed his campaigns in the Levante, no longer as the protector of Zaragoza but as the pardoned vassal of Alfonso. During this four-year period the king reached the zenith of his power with the conquest of Toledo and the subjugation of all Andalusia; he also plumbed the depths of disaster as a result of the Almoravide invasion. Alfonso shut out the unhappily inactive Campeador in both victory and defeat.

IX *Alfonso at the Height of His Power*

The most successful period of Alfonso's reign began with the Cid's exile in 1081 and ended with the Almoravide invasion in 1086.

In 1082 Alfonso, to punish Motamid, king of Seville, for irregularities in the payment of tribute, ravaged all of Andalusia to its southernmost point in Tarifa. That same year he renewed his campaign against Toledo which he had initiated in 1079. The imperial city surrendered to him on 25 May, 1085.[13]

The ancient capital of Visigothic Spain was the city most venerated in the Peninsula. With its conquest Alfonso's title of emperor was fully recognized. This is indicated by the unwonted respect with which Sancho Ramírez of Aragon and Navarre usually designates him in diplomatic documents after 1085. Sancho addresses Alfonso as *Adefonso imperatore in Toleto* and recognizes his own lower rank calling himself *"rege Sancio Rademiri"* (*EC*, p. 309).

Possession of Toledo was strategically as well as politically important. Built upon an impregnable rock and surrounded by a river, it provided Christian Spain with a firm new frontier defense.

X *The First Almoravide Invasion*

During the four and a half decades we have surveyed, the following characters have played leading roles on the peninsular stage:
The murdered Sancho II; Sancho's younger brother, Alfonso VI; the
Cid, Rodrigo Díaz of Vivar. Behind the scenes doña Urraca also
played a decisive role.

Another figure, alien and formidable, made his entrance in 1086.
He was the seventy-year-old Yusuf Ibn Teshufin, emir of the North
African Almoravide Empire. Its area, extending from Morocco to
Ghana and from Senegal to Fezzan was larger than all western
Europe. It included the cities and towns on the Mediterranean and
Atlantic littorals, most of the Sahara, and part of equatorial Africa.
Yusuf invaded the Peninsula at the bidding of Motamid of Seville,
who could no longer tolerate Alfonso's excessive demands.

In 1075 and 1082 Alfonso had imposed additional tribute upon
Motamid. On both occasions the Sevillian ruler sent letters across
the strait beseeching Yusuf to free him from Alfonso's oppression.
Yusuf answered that he could not comply until he had subdued
Ceuta and Tangier. In 1085 Alfonso tightened his strangle hold; he
not only increased his demands for tribute but also exacted the surrender of certain important strongholds. Again Motamid, although
with grave misgivings, sent begging letters to Yusuf. Yusuf assented,
having at last completed his conquest of northern Africa.

Motamid was apprehensive for personal and political reasons. As
one of the most refined representatives of Moorish culture in Spain,
this pleasure-loving poet-king looked upon the fanatically ascetic
Yusuf and his followers as barbarians. He also was aware that the
redoubtable zealot from the Maghreb was as much of a threat to his
rule and that of the other Taifas as he was to their Christian masters.
Nevertheless, when his eldest son advised him to seek a *modus
vivendi* with Alfonso, he replied: "If worst comes to worst I would
rather tend the camels of the Almoravides than herd the pigs of the
Christians"(*EC*, p. 329).

Yusuf's fleet landed at Algeciras in June 1086. On hearing the
news, Alfonso abandoned his siege of Zaragoza. Joined by Sancho
Ramírez of Aragón and knights from Italy and France, he led a great
army into the enemy's country and encamped near Sagrajas, five
miles from Badajoz. The Christians, accustomed as they were to
single combat in which the outcome of a battle was determined by
individual valor, could not cope with Yusuf's type of coordinated

warfare. The Almoravide general disposed his forces in compact formations whose individual soldiers acted in dynamic unison to the deafening rhythm of drumbeats that tatooed the valleys and reverberated against the mountains. Alfonso's army was decimated.

The consequences of the Almoravide victory eventually proved to be calamitous to the southern Taifas. Although it brought them together for the first time since the beginning of the century, their unity was not lasting. Yusuf's triumph also made them independent of Alfonso, but only to deliver them into the clutches of the invader. The emir, who all his life had scrupulously and ardently followed the rules of the Koran, could not brook the laxity in religious observance of the peninsular Moslems. Furthermore, this ascetic son of the Sahara, whose fare was only barley bread, camel's flesh, and milk, and whose clothing was only wool, despised their opulence and love of pleasure and disapproved of their cultivation of art and learning. And the flame of his fanaticism was continuously fanned by his counselors, the rabid fakirs. It was they who drafted for him the judicial rulings that justified in his mind the breaking of the promise he had made to respect their titular sovereignty (*EC*, pp. 397 - 98). Fortified by the case the fakirs had drawn up, Yusuf proceeded to liquidate them. In 1090 he threw the Granadan King Abdullah into chains and exiled Temin, king of Málaga, to Africa. In 1091 he took Motamid prisoner and deported him to Agmat in Morocco. In 1094 Motawakkil, king of Badajoz, was killed defending his capital against Yusuf's great Lamtuna chieftain Syr Ibn Abu Beker.

Before his defeat at Sagrajas, Alfonso was on the verge of becoming the master of all Moslem and Christian Spain: Zaragoza was about to fall into his hands; his great captain Álvar Fáñez controlled Valencia; all of the princes of Andalusia except Motamid bowed their heads beneath the yoke of Alfonso's lieutenants; Córdoba's fall was imminent; the king of Aragón and the counts of the March dared not oppose Alfonso's inroads into their traditional spheres of reconquest. "Well indeed," says Menéndez Pidal, "might Alphonso subscribe his Arabic letters as the 'Emperor of the Two Religions,' and those in Latin, as 'Imperator totius Hispaniae' " (*CS*, p. 207). The old poem echoes this consciousness which Spain had of Alfonso's imperial scope when in line 2936 the Asturian Muño Gustioz greets him: "Grace, King of great kingdoms that call you lord!"

The envious king excluded the Cid from the campaigns and the

political dealings that earned him recognition as the emperor of the
two religions. Although Alfonso's success against the inept and
divided Taifas made him overconfident, he must have realized on
the eve of the battle of Sagrajas that Yusuf was the most formidable
enemy he would ever face. Nevertheless, even in that moment of
crisis he failed to seek the help of the best knight in all the land. In
sum, Alfonso ignored the exile both at the height of his power and
on the eve of his greatest defeat.

Would Yusuf have triumphed at Sagrajas if the Cid had led the
Christian forces? Menéndez Pidal answers this question as
follows: "Although the Cid had been content to allow his King
to eclipse him, he had been too successful in dealing with the most
dangerous situations for people to refrain from thinking that, if he
had been in command at Sagrajas, Yusuf never would have established himself as the restorer of Islam in Andalusia" (EC, p. 342).
I agree with this conjecture for, even though the Campeador never
had the opportunity to face Yusuf himself in the field of battle, he
subsequently did demonstrate his ability to overcome tremendous
odds against the Almoravides led by Yusuf's nephew, Mohammed
Ibn Teshufin. Rodrigo exhibited his resourcefulness both in the
pitched battle of Cuarte, west of Valencia, and in the engagement at
the narrow pass between sea and mountain at Bairén, south of
Valencia. On the plain of Cuarte, greatly outnumbered by the
enemy, the Cid must have contended with the kind of compact formations before whose systematic tactics Alfonso had been helpless.
At Bairén, also greatly outnumbered, the Campeador found himself
hemmed in by the enemy, whose thirty thousand troops were drawn
up for battle on the precipitous heights of the landward side while
the crossbowmen aboard the Andalusian and African ships from the
immediate seaward side swept the narrow pass between land and sea
with their missiles.

XI *Alfonso and the Cid Reconciled*

After Sagrajas, did the king, chastened by the great disaster, recall
his exiled vassal? Or did Rodrigo, the ever-loyal subject, hasten to
the side of his lord in time of trouble as he had after the near disaster
at Rueda? Whoever made the first overture, the fact remains that
the king restored the Cid to his favor. As concrete tokens of his
renewed goodwill Alfonso granted the Cid valuable possessions,[14]
allowed many of his knights to serve under him, and gave him free

rein to operate in the eastern part of Al-Andalus, now the only part
of Moslem Spain not dominated by the Almoravides, although their
continuous pressure eastward and northward never ceased to nurse
the hopes of the levantine kinglets that Yusuf would free them from
their Christian "protectors." Alfonso endorsed the concession he
granted the Cid to wage war in the East through a "sealed
privilege" stipulating that he and his heirs would become the
possessors of all lands and castles he might win from the Moors. The
Cid, in turn, vowed that he would hold all he won in the king's
name. When at the end of 1086 or the beginning of 1087 Alfonso ap-
proved this privilege, he did not foresee the extent of the
Campeador's success. If he had, he probably would not have
granted his invincible vassal the above-mentioned concession. I
think this assumption is justified by the emperor's subsequent
behavior.

XII   *The Cid Regains the East for Alfonso*

After spending more than one year in obscurity at Alfonso's side
following the pardon, the Cid resumed his activities in the East.

Zaragoza's King Mostain joined the Cid's incursion against Valencia ostensibly to help him seize the city for Alfonso; his real intention, however, was to take possession of it himself. When Mostain
finally revealed his true purpose and brazenly asked the Campeador
for his assistance in carrying it out — I say "brazenly" because the
Castilian troops outnumbered his by eight to one — Rodrigo
responded that he could not possibly comply because Valencia
belonged to King Alfonso and he was Alfonso's vassal.

In 1086 Álvar Fáñez had abandoned Valencia to join Alfonso at
Sagrajas. Without his strict supervision the city's weak ruler, Al-
Kadir, was unable to control its dissident factions, among them the
all-important castle wardens who refused to continue paying tribute.
Bereft of a strong leader, Valencia fell prey to the greed of its
neighbors.

Among these, the first to attempt to seize it was Mostain's uncle,
Al-Hajib. This was only natural, for his possessions, namely, Lérida-
Tortosa to the north and Denia to the south, were split in two by the
great city. Al-Hajib gathered his forces, which included Catalan
mercenaries, and besieged it. In a countermove Al-Kadir formed an
alliance with Yusuf. It did not bring the desired result. He therefore
appealed to the Emperor Alfonso and to Mostain. It was the latter

who responded promptly; he undertook, with the Cid, the incursion into Valencia to which we have already referred.

When Al-Hajib learned that his nephew and the Cid were pressing toward Valencia, he abandoned the siege. He fled on the Cid's approach because, awed by the living legend of the Campeador's invincibility, he lacked the courage to oppose him.

The Cid was obliged to leave the scene of his operations twice before bringing them to completion. First he returned to Alfonso's side to report the state of his affairs and to reiterate his protestations of loyalty; but he soon resumed his raids, exploring and despoiling the Valencian region. He went back the second time to ratify the previously negotiated agreement according to which all of his gains would be for his liege and lord.

By the time the Cid had returned from his mission to the king, the devious ruler of Zaragoza had broken with him and entered into an alliance with the count of Barcelona. Berenguer surrounded Valencia, encamping at Cuarte, north of the city. In the meantime, the Cid plundered and laid under tribute a wide fifty-six-mile-long stretch between Daroca and Teruel extending northward some sixty miles northwest of Valencia.

Once in possession of this strategically important territory, the Cid marched southward, encamping in the village of Torres, a short distance from Valencia. Berenguer, like Al-Hajib before him, dared not confront the Campeador and withdrew to Barcelona. Once the count removed himself, Rodrigo, easily overcoming all resistance, advanced from Torres and made camp north of Valencia. Al-Kadir sent him costly presents and agreed to pay him one thousand dinars a week. The Cid, in turn, compelled the castle wardens to resume payment of tribute to Al-Kadir.

The Cid's submission of Valencia, capping that of Albarracín and Alpuente, made the position of Castile in the East stronger than it had been under Álvar Fáñez.

XIII   Aledo and Yusuf's Second Invasion

In the South only one pocket of Christian resistance remained: the great castle of Aledo, forty miles northwest of Cartagena, which Alfonso had fortified after Sagrajas and put under the command of his great captain, García Jiménez. From Aledo García Jiménez, secretly abetted by Ibn Rashik of Murcia, devastated the surrounding country. His chief target was the region of Lorca, in the easternmost confines of the Kingdom of Seville. Motamid was so distressed by these depredations that he again begged Yusuf to come to his rescue.

Yusuf acceded to Motamid's request without delay. He crossed the strait for the second time, landing at Algeciras in June 1089. The Almoravide hosts, joined by the auxiliary troops of Motamid of Seville, Abdullah Mudaffar of Granada, Temin of Málaga, Mustain of Almería, and Ibn Rashik of Murcia, laid siege to Aledo. These combined forces first attempted to storm the fortress. Failing in this attempt, they decided to starve it into submission. However, during the long siege the Andalusian Taifas became ensnarled in bitter quarrels. In the most serious of these, Motamid charged Ibn Rashik with treachery, alleging that he had been an ally of Alfonso. Yusuf's fakirs investigated the charge and ruled against the Murcian king, who was seized and handed over to Motamid. The Murcians, outraged by this act, not only withdrew from the siege but did their utmost to hinder it, further weakening the already weakened besiegers. The plight of the besieged, however, was even worse, for their water supply was exhausted. Yusuf, therefore, might have succeeded in forcing their surrender, had he not retreated to Lorca on hearing that Alfonso was marching to relieve Aledo. Yusuf's retreat was not a sign of weakness on his part; the real cause was lack of confidence in his divided allies; he feared that the Andalusians would flee from the enemy as they had done at Sagrajas, where he won in spite of them.

XIV   *The Cid's Second Exile*

While the plight of the besieged Christians was still desperate, Alfonso sent Rodrigo an urgent message commanding him to hasten to Villena seventy miles northeast of Aledo. The Cid left the East at once, but unfortunately he did not succeed in joining his forces with those of the emperor, who, instead of proceeding to Villena as he had promised, took a shortcut to Molina.[15] The Campeador was too late to overtake him there. And so, grieving over the failure, he returned to his camp at Elche. By that time Aledo was safe owing to Yusuf's premature retreat; and Alfonso, having provisioned the fortress, was on his way back to Toledo.

As was the case eight years before, the Cid's enemies poisoned the king's all too receptive ears. Rodrigo purposely avoided joining the expedition, they charged, expecting that without his aid the king and his army would be cut to pieces by the Moors. Again Alfonso was swayed by his baser passions. Enraged, he inflicted the severest possible punishment upon the accused: he not only banished the Cid as in 1081; he deprived him of all the lands and castles he had granted him two years before; he ordered that his estates and riches be confiscated, his houses destroyed. And, following Germanic law, which held the family jointly liable in all legal matters, he went to the extreme of having the Cid's wife, doña Jimena and her three young children, thrown in prison.[16]

The Cid, who was learned in the law, sought every legal means to exonerate himself. But Alfonso was implacable. His injustice went unchecked because in those times the king's power was absolute.

Yusuf returned to Africa after failing to take Aledo. This failure was bound to mortify him, even though he absolved himself of blame for his retreat, justifying it by his lack of confidence in the strife-ridden Taifas who had been a liability in the battle of Sagrajas. Through his great victory in that encounter he became the feared master of most of Andalusia, a fact which his setback at Aledo did not alter. But in the Levante, a region which was traditionally Moorish, the Cid, however precariously, continued to hold his own and this was the real thorn in Yusuf's flesh, for his grandiose plan was to subjugate all of Moslem Spain. He therefore sent back to the Peninsula a great army under his nephew, Mohammed Ibn Teshufin, to dislodge the now vulnerable Campeador from Valencia.

Rodrigo's situation was precarious indeed. As we have·seen, his loyalty to Alfonso was the cause of his rupture with Mostain; he was abandoned by many Castilian knights who feared to incur Alfonso's displeasure; the rulers of Aragón and of Lérida became hostile to him. And Al-Kadir of Valencia, confident that the new wave of Almoravides would overwhelm his protector, no longer would pay him tribute. With one fell stroke Alfonso had undermined the Cid's position both in his relations to the Arab kinglets of the east and the Christian rulers of the northeast.

The Cid set about restoring his former domination of the East by ravaging Al-Hajib's coast country south of Denia. In this region his most important accomplishment was the storming of the castle of Polop, where Al-Hajib kept a great treasure hidden in a cavern. With this enormous booty the Cid had the means to support his depredations of all the country from Játiva to Orihuela, a sixty-five-mile-long region extending north to south almost to Murcia. He so thoroughly devastated and plundered all this area that Al-Hajib had to sue for peace. Having subdued the southern part of Al-Hajib's kingdom, the Cid pressed northward on to Valencia. Al-Kadir, fearing that the Cid would install Al-Hajib in his place as the city's nominal ruler, again became his tributary. The castle wardens also resumed payments to Al-Kadir. Thus the Cid again became master of Valencia.

In the meantime Al-Hajib had fled north from his lost southern domain to his lands in Tortosa. There he busied himself plotting a coalition. He solicited the support of King Sancho Ramírez of Aragón and Count Ermengol of Urgel, but without success, for neither of them dared to confront the Castilian. However, he did find a ready ally in Berenguer of Barcelona, who thought the occasion propitious to settle old scores.

Berenguer, in turn, succeeded in enlisting the support of Mostain, now Alfonso's tributary. Both of them implored the emperor to combine his forces with theirs so that together they could crush the intolerably superior Campeador once and for all. In his appeal to the emperor Berenguer boasted about his own prowess and declared that he alone would drive the Cid out of Tortosa. "But the Emperor was not deceived by the braggart Count," Menéndez Pidal says (*CS*, p. 252). To this we may add that in all probability Alfonso was not deceived because he was only too aware of Berenguer's previous humiliations at the hands of the Cid. We may also suppose that he did not trust the unreliable Mostain who had but recently been the Campeador's ally.

Even without Alfonso's support, however, Berenguer, Mostain, and Al-Hajib gathered their armies and marched to the mountainous country west of Tortosa where the Cid had encamped in the Pine-Wood of Tévar, in a narrow-necked valley which had only three defiles. The Campeador took advantage of the rugged topography because the enemy was too numerous to be confronted in open battle. To divide them he resorted to deception. First he schemed to have some of his men taken prisoners so that when the count interrogated them they would give him false intelligence. The Cid, they told him, planned to flee that same night through the valley's three exits. The deception worked: the three contingents sent to cut off the Cid's forces at the three narrow passes were ambushed and cut down. However, not all went smoothly for Rodrigo.

The Catalans who dominated his main camp from a lofty height above, stole down close to the Cid's tents before dawn and took him by surprise. But the Cid, bestirring his men with frantic haste, succeeded in getting them to don their armor, mount their drowsy horses, and array themselves in battle order before it was too late. The Cid himself was wounded, but his men fought on until they won a great victory, capturing five thousand men and the count himself.

The Cid's extraordinary victory against vastly superior forces enhanced his fame throughout the Peninsula. In concrete terms his success resulted in a pact with Berenguer whereby the latter officially surrendered to the Cid control of the lands of Al-Hajib, who had died in deepest dejection shortly after the battle of Tévar. Abandoned by Berenguer, the guardians of Al-Hajib's young son, Suleiman Ibn Hud, had no alternative but to seek the Cid's protection. In return for it they agreed to pay him fifty thousand dinars a year. Thus Rodrigo became master of the regions whose centers were Lérida, Tortosa, and Denia. About that time he also subdued the area between Buriana and Morella, which included Valencia. The additional tribute which the chiefs of various castles, towns, and cities in this region paid him amounted to the enormous sum of 99,200 dinars (*EC*, p. 390).

XV *Yusuf's Third Campaign*

Yusuf crossed the strait for the third time in the summer of 1090. He was determined to capture Toledo but Alfonso and Sancho Ramírez defended it well and Yusuf had to withdraw as he had at Aledo the year before. This second failure was even more galling to him than the first. After all, at Aledo, the Andalusian kings, though divided, had been his allies; but now they not only refused to help him with troops and money, they collaborated secretly with Alfonso, having at last become fully convinced that Yusuf was their worst enemy.

This feeling, however, was not shared by the majority of Spanish Moslems. They resented the excessive taxes imposed by their extravagant rulers. For this reason they took the side of the traditionally fundamentalist peninsular fakirs, who, fervently saying "Amen!" to Yusuf's holy counselors, insisted that the true followers of the faith should not pay one whit more than the tithe prescribed by the Koran. The nationalism of the southern Taifas, therefore, lacked popular support.

The only hope of Motamid and other Taifas against the African intruders was Alfonso. The Spanish king, however, found it impossible to aid Motamid directly in the defense of his kingdom. Yusuf's first cousin, the formidable general Syr Ibn Abu Beker, rapidly conquered the whole Guadalquivir basin, captured Cordova and Cuenca, and invested Seville. Alfonso sought to divert the Almoravides from Seville by leading an expedition to Granada. It proved to be ineffectual. This stratagem having failed, Alfonso sent a large army under Álvar Fáñez to help Seville. The great captain fought well, but finally his force was cut to pieces. Seville fell and Motamid was taken prisoner and deported with his family to Agmat near Marrakech in northern Africa. One year before Yusuf disposed of Motamid he had dethroned Abdullah of Granada and Temin of Málaga. And shortly after the surrender of Seville the kingdom of Almería also fell into the hands of the Almoravides, as did Murcia and finally the Castle of Aledo. Only Motawakkil of Badajoz, Yusuf's creature, was temporarily spared (he, too, was liquidated in 1094). Thus Alfonso lost control of Andalusia.

One solitary Christian figure remained predominant in Moorish territory: the Cid. While in Andalusia Alfonso's affairs went from bad to worse, his exiled vassal in the East was approaching the zenith of his career. Rodrigo's success was due to his unrelenting initiatives against those who stood in his way.

One of these was the ambitious, untrustworthy king of Zaragoza. Mostain occupied two strategic outposts, one was Yuballa (today Puig), five miles north, the other, Liria, fifteen miles northwest of Valencia. The Cid had never admitted Mostain's right to these two strongholds. He therefore encamped before Yuballa and warned Mostain to abandon it as well as Liria. Mostain refused. Thereupon the Cid surrounded Liria and reduced it to famine and thirst.

After seven months the town was about to surrender, when the Cid received a letter from Alfonso's Queen Constanza imploring him to join the emperor's incursion into Granada. The Campeador, eager to regain Alfonso's friendship, did not hesitate to abandon the siege. He immediately set out with a large body of men. After a strenuous march he met Alfonso at the barren foot of the Sierra Elvira, eight miles northwest of Granada. Then, prompted by the desire to ensure the king's safety and to bear the first brunt of the expected clash with the Almoravides who occupied Granada, the Campeador took it upon himself to advance into the fertile plain west of the city, leaving the king behind. Alfonso took the Cid's initiative as an act of *lèse-majesté,* and the Cid's enemies of course agreed with him. Alfonso's reaction was bound to take the spirit out of his enterprise. He did not attack. And the Almoravides, safe within Granada, wisely did not venture out of its walls to fight. And so, after six frustrating days, Alfonso started back to Toledo, stopping on the way at the castle of Úbeda, which was perched on a height of the Guadalquivir valley. The Cid followed the king there and, oblivious to his ire, paid his respects, only to be greeted with a furious outburst of recriminations and insults. Rightly thinking that Alfonso meant to imprison him, Rodrigo managed to escape to his own camp, only to discover that many of his own knights, unwilling to share the king's displeasure, had abandoned him to join Alfonso. Deeply grieved, the Cid returned to the Valencian region, which he had abandoned at a critical moment to regain the favor of his unjust lord.

XVI   *The Cid Returns to the Levant*

On returning to the East the Cid's chief concern was to establish the strongest possible line of defense against the imminent Almoravide attack from the south. The site he chose, namely, the Benicadell Range, forty-five miles south of Valencia, extends over twenty miles east to west with passes only at its two ends. This barrier shuts off the Valencian plain to the north.

After the Cid ensured his position in Benicadell, his two former rivals, one for Moorish tribute, the other for possession of Valencia, offered to help him hold that city. They were Sancho Ramírez of Aragón and Mostain of Zaragoza. Their about-face was, of course, caused by their fear of the Almoravides, who having subdued all of Andalusia were pressing northward. For the moment, at least, both understood that the one warrior in Spain who had never been defeated in battle was their only hope against the common enemy. Sancho and Mostain also realized that this enemy, if victorious, would give no quarter, as Alfonso's defeats and, especially, the liquidation of the southern Taifas, had shown. I say "for the moment," because their alliance with the Cid was not so unequivocal that they could not rationalize their collaboration with Alfonso as unprejudicial to the Cid when the emperor launched a mighty campaign to take Valencia for himself at the Cid's expense.

From the Poyo de Yuballa, where he encamped, Alfonso sent orders to the wardens of the castles guarding Valencia, demanding payment in advance of five annual installments that they were pledged to pay the Cid. This demand, of course, was calculated to deprive Rodrigo of one of the principal means with which to continue his operations.

Rodrigo could have placed himself at the service of Alfonso, but he did not do so because of the failure of previous reconciliations. Another alternative was to resist the king by force of arms. Never as on this occasion, was the unjustly treated vassal so justified in taking advantage of this legal right. He had been exiled without cause in 1081 and 1089. He had not hesitated to imperil his own position, abandoning his hard-won eastern dominions in order to aid Alfonso. Above all, he must have felt intensely the outrage of his wife's and young children's imprisonment three years before.

All the same, Rodrigo would not fight his king. Again he protested his loyalty; declared he would do nothing directly against his lord, even though the latter had affronted him without cause. Nevertheless, at this critical juncture in his career and, indeed, in the affairs of Christian Spain, Rodrigo, now a potentate in his own right on the strength of his conquests, rightly felt impelled to react with resolution. It was only just, he declared to Alfonso, that he should take revenge against those who were responsible for the king's conduct: his enemies at court who had given the emperor such evil counsel.

The Campeador carried out his threat at once, choosing as the object of his vengeance García Ordóñez. He invaded the lands of the count. Alfonso's inept favorite and chief scandalmonger gathered a great army to repel the Cid's onslaught and advanced as far as Alberite; but on seeing the havoc the Cid had wrought, and probably remembering the defeat he had suffered at the Cid's hands twelve years before at Cabra, García Ordóñez was overcome with fear and withdrew.

Meanwhile Alfonso had succeeded in obtaining promise of help from the two foremost maritime powers in the western Mediterranean, the republics of Pisa and Genoa. But the four hundred Pisan and Genoese ships of the rescuing fleet were late in arriving at their destination. This delay, combined with the defeat of García Ordóñez and Alfonso's inability to continue provisioning his large force at Yuballa, obliged him to break camp. As he retreated, did he dwell bitterly on his recent failures to save Granada, Seville, and Murcia? Was he at last convinced that his vassal was a paragon of loyalty, and' that if he had allowed him to assume a commanding position at his side, those defeats might have been avoided? The letter that Alfonso sent Rodrigo after the Valencia fiasco leads to the conclusion that he did. In this letter Alfonso admitted that he had been at fault, "pardoned" the Cid and restored to him the properties he had confiscated in 1089. In his reply Rodrigo expressed his gratitude, implored the king to turn a deaf ear to his bad advisers, and reiterated his loyalty (*EC*, p. 421).

Alfonso's change of heart, however, came too late. The Cid, with his hands full in the East, could not help the king regain his ascendancy in the South. All of Andalusia was now in the power of the Almoravides against whose new type of warfare Alfonso and his generals were still ineffectual. Indeed, in 1092, the same year that Alfonso had failed at Valencia, he suffered at Jaén a defeat almost as disastrous as the one which, at Sagrajas, eight years before, had overnight deprived him of his sphere of influence in most of the southern half of the Peninsula.

The eclipse of the royal sun had begun in 1086. By 1092 it was complete. Henceforth it was the vassal, Rodrigo Díaz of Vivar, who alone was able to turn the tide of the invaders.

Even before the force of this tide struck Valencia, its approach activated the Almoravide partisans within the eastern sector. In the kingdom of Zaragoza clusters of Almoravidists broke out in open rebellion, confident that Yusuf or one of his generals would soon overrun Mostain's lands.

The Cid spent three months fighting pockets of resistance in Zaragoza, where he remained until October 1092.

XVII   *The Usurper, Ibn Jehhaf*

Dire were the results of the Cid's absence from Valencia. The city was made up of diverse factions, among which the most dangerous consisted of malcontents led by the cadi Ibn Jehhaf. The dissident elements could have been kept under control only by Rodrigo's organizing capacity, skill in government and diplomacy, and fair but stern justice. Furthermore, his record shows that he alone had the indomitable courage and canny generalship to repel attacks from the outside.

Such an attack materialized while he was away. Yusuf's son, Ibn Ayesha, the conqueror of Murcia and Aledo, took Denia and Játiva. And when news reached Valencia that Alcira, only twenty miles distant, had also surrendered to him, the Cid's knights as well as those

of Sancho Ramírez fled their quarter in the northern suburb of
Alcudia taking with them what possessions they could.

Ibn Jehhaf, nicknamed "The Knockneed," was a member of
Valencia's highest aristocracy. He was arrogant, ambitious, ruthless,
greedy, and devious. His scheme was to hand the now seemingly
helpless city over to Ibn Ayesha once he gained control of it. He felt
that in return for his collaboration the Almoravide general would en-
trust its government to him. The Cid's vizier and tax collector, Ibn
Al-Faraj, was fully aware of the cadi's conspiracy, but dared not take
measures to suppress it. He sent letters to the Cid in Zaragoza imploring him to hasten to Valencia's rescue. But before the
Campeador could come, the deafening tattoo of Almoravide drums
reverberated against the Boatella Gate. Their fearful, hitherto un-
heard sound heartened the partisans, terrified the *mudéjares*
(Moslems living in reconquered Christian territory) and leaderless
Christians. The relentless rhythm of the drumbeats produced an unduly magnified psychological effect in the minds of all, for the actual number of assailants was, in fact, very small: twenty soldiers of
Ibn Ayesha and twenty horsemen of Alcira, many of whom scaled
the city's walls clambering up the ropes which the revolutionaries
had lowered for them.

In the alcazar King Al-Kadir, whose feebleness of spirit was now
further weakened by feebleness of body — he was convalescing
from a recent illness — held frantic consultations with the vizier, Ibn
Al-Faraj. Foolishly they decided to summon Ibn Jehhaf. The cadi,
instead of appearing alone, advanced to the palace leading all his
men and forced his way in. He seized the vizier and threw him into
prison. In the confusion Al-Kadir managed to escape in female dis-
guise with the women of his harem. He took with him a chest con-
taining his most precious jewels and, clasped around his waist under
the woman's dress he wore, his most valuable possession: the famous
girdle overlaid with diamonds, pearls, sapphires, rubies, and
emeralds which three hundred years before had belonged to the
wife of Haroun-al-Rashid, the Sultana Zobeida who, according to
the *Arabian Nights*, had dazzled Baghdad with her beauty and
priceless ornaments. Al-Kadir's hoard was as dear to him as his life;
it cost him his life; as we shall see, it was to cost the life of the man
who later had him killed so he could acquire it.

Ibn Jehhaf was consumed by insane avidity to put his hands on
Al-Kadir's treasure. To find it he hired as his spy and fellow con-

spirator a young man belonging to a prominent family, one of whose members had been assassinated at Al-Kadir's bidding in Toledo thirteen years before. This young man, thirsting for vengeance, traced Al-Kadir to his hiding place and killed him. He and his companions then delivered to the cadi most of the treasure, including Zobeida's girdle.

The Cid was still solidifying his position in Zaragoza when he heard the evil tidings from the eastern capital: Al-Kadir had his back to the wall; the knights he had left behind had fled; hordes of Almoravides were advancing northward along the eastern coast. Not until, after a forced march brought him near Valencia, did Rodrigo learn that Al-Kadir had been murdered.

With the loss of his eastern dominions that had cost him so dearly, the Campeador faced the greatest crisis of his career. "Down to four loaves," as he himself said *(EC,* p. 438), he had to contend against enormous odds. The Almoravides, under Ibn Ayesha, were in control in the East from Denia to Alcira; Ibn Jehhaf had usurped the government of Valencia; Valencia now sheltered a considerable number of Almoravides. Last but not least, the emir of all the Muslims cast his gigantic shadow over the city. Yusuf was indeed the political and military colossus of the Moslem world in the eleventh century. His empire encompassed vast stretches of Africa and half of Spain. "Was it not madness for him [the Cid]" asks Menéndez Pidal, "to attempt what the emperor and Álvar Fáñez had failed to achieve at Granada, Seville, and Murcia? So it seemed, and yet, no sooner did he hear of the loss of his eastern dominions than he resolved to march against his formidable enemy" *(EC,* p. 437).

The Campeador's most pressing immediate problem was lack of provisions. To procure them he plundered the Valencian countryside. He then sent a scornful letter to Ibn Jehhaf warning him, among other things, that he would not rest until the murder of Al-Kadir was avenged. In his reply the usurper ignored this warning. Within the limited scope of this chapter it is not possible to give a full account of the diabolically tangled circumstances that complicated the Cid's long two-phased siege of Valencia. The reader is therefore referred to the chapters in *La España del Cid* in which, with unerring sense of direction, Menéndez Pidal leads us through the confusing maze.[17] Here bare mention of the principal events will have to suffice. Between 1 November 1092 and 15 June 1094, Valencia submitted twice to the Christians, the first time briefly, the sec-

ond during the remaining years of the Cid's life and for three years
after his death. Ibn Jehhaf's first capitulation resulted from the
following causes: the cutting off of food supplies by the Cid's
plundering raids in the regions around the capital; the fall of the castle of Yuballa after a siege of eight months, and the Cid's complete
encompassment of Valencia by his occupation of its two northern
suburbs, Villanueva and, east of it, Alcudia.

The terms of the surrender provided for the expulsion of the
Almovarides; repayment for the grain the Cid had left in Valencia at
the time of Al-Kadir's murder; payment of tribute in the amount of
one thousand dinars a week, said payment to be retroactive to the
time the war had begun; the Cid's continued occupation of Alcudia
by right of conquest, and the withdrawal of the Cid's soldiers to
Juballa. According to Ibn Alcama, a witness of these events, the
Valencians did not agree to the surrender in good faith but to gain
time until Yusuf would come to their aid.

They were of course right in thinking that the supreme emir
would be provoked by the Cid's success. Shortly before the
Almoravides were taken out of the city under safe-conduct in com-
pliance with the terms of the first surrender in 1093, Yusuf had dispatched letters to the Cid from Morocco forbidding him to remain in
Valencian territory. Rodrigo not only sent Yusuf a scornful reply; he
also wrote to all emirs in Spain telling them that Yusuf was afraid to
cross the straits to help Valencia. There was probably some truth in
this taunt. However, considering Yusuf's record of grand but never
reckless, indeed cautious, military initiatives, it would not be just to
attribute exclusively to fear of the Cid his decision not to head per-
sonally a fourth expedition. His advanced age and the state of his
health may have been factors. But more important was his feeling
that, having been unusually successful in the past, it would be
foolhardy to tempt Fortune to the limit. "Victories," he is reported
to have said, "are the very special gifts of Allah, and the success I
have gained has already been too great" (*CS*, p. 312). In sum: old,
probably ill, and unwilling to tempt Fortune, Yusuf remained in
Africa. He entrusted the army he sent to Spain to the command of
Abu Beker, the brother-in-law of one of his sons.

The news of the Almoravide landing strengthened the position of
Ibn Jehhaf's Almoravidist enemies, the Beni Wejib. One of them
supplanted him. The new governor, Abu-1-Hassan ibn Wejib,
repudiated the treaty, ordered the gates of the city closed and

prepared to defend its walls (November 1093). Thus cut off, the Cid
was forced to renew the siege.

The Almoravides' return kindled the hopes of the Cid's enemies,
but the Campeador flaunted his confidence by promising the
besieged that if the invaders could drive him out before the end of
August, they would not be obliged to continue living under his rule.
In making this concession Rodrigo followed a custom dating back to
biblical times. Its purpose was to convince those desperate for help
of their helplessness and of the injustice of their cause. The month of
August passed without any signs of the rescuers' approach. Abu
Beker's advance was delayed by illness. Not until he had recovered,
in the autumn of 1093, was he reported to be on the march. By
November his African army, swollen by hosts from Andalusia, was
within striking distance, but it never struck. In preparation for the
onslaught the Cid had the bridges of the causeways destroyed and
the water from the irrigation canals released to flood the fields, so
that the enemy could not advance against him except along narrow
strips of land. The Cid thus helped himself, but Heaven, both
literally and figuratively, helped him even more. On the night of the
attack torrential rains turned the only approaches that were left after
the artificial flooding into impassable morasses. Abu Beker could
have waited until the weather improved to try again, but he turned
back, not only because of the demoralizing effect of the deluge, but
because, as both the Arab historian, Ibn Alcama and the *Historia
Roderici* testify, he and his men were stricken with fear of the Cid
(*EC*, p. 461).

Yusuf's son, Ibn Ayesha, sent the Beni Wejib letters assuring them
that the Almoravides would return to rescue Valencia as soon as the
roads were passable. On the strength of this assurance the Beni Wejib were able to count on enough popular support to stay in power
until news arrived that Yusuf's army had reembarked for Morocco.
Now, without hope for the help they had counted on, the position of
the Beni Wejib became untenable. On the other hand, the *mudéjar*
party of Christian sympathizers gained strength. As the Cid
tightened the siege, the city's inhabitants increasingly suffered its
terrible consequences. On a day in January after six months of
progressive deprivation, a great number of them held a meeting,
then marched to Ibn Jehhaf's house and begged him to take over the
government. The wily cadi played hard to get; he declared that he
would not reassume power unless he were assured of the cooperation

of all parties opposed to him. The spokesmen of the petitioners assured him his wish could be granted. However, those most adversely affected, the Beni Wejib, had second thoughts. Ibn Jehhaf then took matters into his own hands. He had the governor, Abu-l-Hassan ibn Wejib, and his family seized and delivered into the hands of the Cid (CS, pp. 324 - 25). The way was now clear for negotiations.

In the preliminary talks between Ibn Jehhaf and the Cid they agreed, among other things, that in return for the latter's lifting of the siege, the former would resume payment of tribute. In the final negotiations the Campeador, knowing full well how slippery the former cadi was, stipulated further that he should hand his son over as hostage. Ibn Jehhaf agreed and promised to return the next day to sign the treaty. Whether during the personal confrontation he really meant to comply with its terms — especially the surrender of his son — the fact is that instead of returning for the signing, he notified the Cid that he had changed his mind (mid-January 1094).

After going back on his word Ibn Jehhaf in vain sought help from the King of Zaragoza. The Cid, for his part, sent messages to one of the Beni Wejib who had remained in the city. He organized a conspiracy but it failed. The besieged were already desperately short of food by January 1094, when Ibn Jehhaf refused to ratify the peace treaty. During the remaining six months of the siege the city was reduced to starvation. It became a ghoulish scene of famine and death.

Convinced that they could not count on any outside help — Yusuf's army had returned to Africa and Mostain's words of encouragement were not backed by deeds — a group of leading citizens approached the pacifist Al-Wacashi and begged him to do everything in his power to convince the tyrant that all hope was lost. Ibn Jehhaf, who was himself persuaded that he could not count on help from any quarter, listened to reason. And because he realized that he was persona non grata to the Cid, he entrusted the task of initiating peace overtures to Al-Wacashi, a man whose integrity and gentleness of character commended him to Christians and Moors alike.

Just as he had done a few months before, the Cid observed the custom of granting the besieged a period of grace before surrendering: the Valencians were allowed to send messengers to the king of Zaragoza and to Yusuf's son, Ibn Ayesha, governor of Murcia, requesting them to come to their rescue; if their request was not met within two weeks, they were to surrender under the Cid's terms. The two weeks passed. Ibn Jehhaf stalled, but this time he could not put the Cid off. When the cadi's delegates belatedly came to surrender, Rodrigo refused to receive them. They then surrendered unconditionally. The Cid took possession of Valencia on 15 June 1094 after a nineteen and a half months' siege.

XVIII   The Cid, Lord of Valencia

When the Cid again took control of Valencia, he showed two sides of his nature that were henceforth to characterize his conduct toward the conquered: on one hand irreproachable fairness and admirable benevolence in his treatment of the innocent, on the other, extreme severity in dealing with transgressors. His spirit of fairness was demonstrated by the provisions for the government of Valencia as set forth in a speech he delivered four days after the occupation and the first statute of Valencia (EC, pp. 488, 492); his determination to mercilessly punish the guilty was foreshadowed by the first demand he made of Ibn Jehhaf. Before he could recognize him as cadi, the Cid affirmed, he must swear on oath, in the presence of the principal men of both faiths, that he had not kept hidden for himself Al-Kadir's greatest treasure. Furthermore, the Cid declared, should the girdle ever be found in his possession, this would be taken as evidence of regicide, a crime punishable by death and for which he would be tried if the Cid so decided. Heedless of the predictably fearful consequences, Ibn Jehhaf rashly took the oath.

XIX   The Almoravides Attack Again: The Battle of Cuarte

The news of the capture of Valencia filled Yusuf with rage, sadness, and determination to seize from the Cid the prize which he coveted above all others. To this end, operating from Ceuta, he sent contingents of a huge army to the peninsula under the command of his nephew, Mohammed Ibn Teshufin. Mohammed's African hosts, swollen by Andalusian troops, encamped on the Cuarte plain three miles west of Valencia. They greatly outnumbered the Cid's men,[18] who entrenched themselves behind the city walls. For ten days hordes of assailants surrounded the walls, discharging their arrows and filling the air with their deafening yells. Ibn Alcama sets forth at some length the course of the Cid's ensuing surprise attack. The Almoravides were caught off guard because their leader, writes the

Arab historian, "had nothing but disdain for the enemy and believed that his plans for the siege could be carried out in normal fashion" (*EC*, p. 900). One gathers, furthermore, although Ibn Alcama does not spell it out, that Mohammed was unaware of the low morale of his army, many of whose soldiers defected. The general did know that the Cid had sent an appeal for help to King Alfonso and probably assumed Rodrigo would not attempt to break the siege until the royal reinforcements arrived. If this is what he thought he was mistaken. The Cid took time by the forelock; he did not wait for help but resorted to a ruse by which he drew the enemy out into the open while another force of Christians attacked from the rear. "The [Almoravide] horsemen," says Ibn Alcama, "charged against Rodrigo who made as if to retreat before them toward Valencia, and they followed in hot pursuit. He gained the shelter of the ramparts while the Moslem forces pressed him hard, inflicting some losses on him and seeming to have the upper hand. Then the Christian soldiers who were lying in ambush sallied out from their hiding place toward the Moslem camp and attacked it." This rear guard attack threw the Almoravides into confusion. Ibn Alcama writes: "Panic broke loose; everyone believed that it was Alfonso who was upon them. They all took to their heels and fled in every direction" (*EC*, p. 900).

The poem gives an account of the battle which agrees in substance with that of Ibn Alcama as far as the ruse is concerned. "But," as Menéndez Pidal says, "we do not know either through the poem or the chronicler what new formations, what new charging movements or wheeling tactics the Campeador had devised to inflict this crushing defeat on Yusuf's hitherto invincible troops" (*CS*, p. 357).

XX *Execution of Ibn Jehhaf*

After his victory at Cuarte Rodrigo had but one thought in mind: to settle accounts with Ibn Jehhaf. Al-Kadir's treasures must be recovered, the cadi's trial for regicide must be held without delay. First of all, it was necessary to find proof of the crime, namely, the stolen hoard. As he had done eight months before when, to satisfy Rodrigo's legalistic scruples, the accused defended himself through "purgation by abjuration," he again swore that he was innocent of Al-Kadir's death and that he did not possess the treasure. The Cid then ordered a search for it. Enough was unearthed for a jury of Moorish notables to declare him guilty. Under torture, Ibn Jehhaf confessed that he had taken, among other precious possessions of Al-Kadir, the girdle of the Sultana Zobeida.[19] Once the facts constituting the crime were thus established, Ibn Jehhaf was found guilty of regicide and sentenced to death by burning (May 1095).

The Cid's harsh sentence was in complete accord with the legal code of the times, but it was impolitic. It was impolitic, because he did not foresee how intensely negative the public reaction would be not only among Ibn Jehhaf's former partisans but among the cadi's enemies, the Beni Wejib. Most significantly, the Cid's extreme severity was politically unwise because, among the formerly friendly Spanish Moors, many now looked forward to the day when the Almoravides, in spite of previous failures, would yet succeed in taking the city, thus freeing them from Christian dominance. In sum, not only the openly anti-Cidian parties, but also many of the formerly pro-Christian Moors, reacted unfavorably to the Cid's just though ruthless act. Even Ibn Jehhaf's former adversaries now sang his praises. The once generally unpopular, indeed, even hated, official, became a martyr. "In all likelihood," says Menéndez Pidal, "Ibn Jehhaf did the Cid more harm dead than alive. The Moslem spirit of rebellion was now strengthened by remembrance of a martyr" (*EC*, p. 519). In the wake of his death many Valencians broke out in open rebellion. The Cid crushed it by violent means. He went to the length of ordering the execution of one of the rebels, the poet Abu Jafar al-Batti, who had formerly been secretary to the Valencian viziers.

The Cid's violent extremes in suppressing rebellion in the city whose conquest had required an almost superhuman effort and his rapacity in seeking out and seizing Ibn Jehhaf's stolen treasure should be judged in the light of the economic reality of war in his times. "That rapacity," Menéndez Pidal rightly says, "was characteristic of those times. . . . The acquisition of the wealth owned by the vanquished was the chief reward of success for the victor . . . ; the enormous riches he [the Cid] acquired were nothing more than part of the booty, which the Cid divided fairly among his men" (*EC*, p. 517).

If, on the one hand, in taking relentless measures to hold his source of tribute, namely, the conquered city and, if in greedily seizing booty, the Cid was neither better nor worse than barbaric heroes of his and previous ages, on the other hand, his fairness in administering Valencia was exemplary. Ibn Alcama was a Cid hater, but he acknowledged that in dealing with the conquered citizens of Valencia he "was so just and right that no one complained about him or his officials in the least" (*EC*, p. 601).

The Cid dealt fairly not only with the conquered; he continued to be a loyal vassal. He could have acted with the independence and arrogance of a potentate in his own right. Nevertheless Rodrigo's first act when he achieved absolute control of Valencia was to swear fealty to his king and to declare to the conquered that Alfonso was their lord. The eyewitness source of this information is none other than Ibn Alcama himself (*EC*, p. 522).

XXI *The Cid's Last Years*

The condensed account we have given of the Cid's greatest achievement, the conquest of Valencia, supplies the necessary historical background for the military action of the *Poem of the Cid*, which also culminated with the Campeador's conquest of that city. Space does not permit more than an enumeration of the chief events that took place thereafter until the hero's death five years later.

We will first mention those with which he was not directly involved. In November 1096, his long-standing enemy, Count García Ordóñez, collaborated with Mostain of Zaragoza in leading a mighty force against the Cid's young ally, Pedro I of Aragón, who succeeded his father, Sancho Ramírez, in 1094. The count and Mostain were routed. In January 1097, after a thirty-one months' siege, Pedro reconquered Huesca, a city in the middle of the southern part of his kingdom. (Upon bringing this exhausting siege to a successful conclusion he went to the Cid's aid at Peña Cadiella.) In the spring of 1097 Yusuf crossed the strait for the fourth time to attack Alfonso in the region of Toledo. Not daring to leave Valencia, the Cid sent his young son, Diego (he was between nineteen and twenty-two years old), accompanied by a large body of men, to the aid of the king. At Consuegra, Yusuf's general Mohammed Ibn Al-Haj inflicted another disastrous defeat on Alfonso. Diego was killed. Another disaster followed: the king's great captain Alvar Fáñez was defeated by Yusuf's son, Ibn Ayesha, at Cuenca, one hundred miles east of Toledo. While all this was happening, the Cid's hold on Valencia continued to be precarious. However, he not only held on, but won three more remarkable victories; at Bairén and Almenar in 1097 and at Murviedro in 1098. He died on 10 July 1099 at the age of about fifty-six.

CHAPTER 2

History and Poetry: Epic in General and the Cantar de Mio Cid

I The Traditionalist Views of Ramón Menéndez Pidal

RAMÓN Menéndez Pidal always held that the traditional poetry of Spain, which in addition to epic includes later "news-bearing" frontier ballads, was the principal means of informing the people about matters of public interest. For this reason Spanish epic filled a social need. It was not always inspired — although it sometimes was — by great happenings of the past, but by the ". . . common and permanent need of the people to know all about important news of the day. . . . The epic is not a mere poem dealing with a historical subject but a poem that fulfills the high politicocultural mission of history."[1] Epic derives from a direct impression of given historical events, an impression which crystallizes into poetic form when the memory of these events is still fresh. At this stage epic is "veristic"; it retains what Pidal calls its "historical tone"; its historical element remains preponderant. Eventually, however, when epic becomes decadent, "fictionalization" (*lo novelesco*) does away completely with the veristic element which constitutes the basis of primitive epic. Our own Cidian studies confirm this. The final stage of fictionalization is demonstrated by the radical divergence in the character of Rodrigo as he is represented in the poem on one hand and, on the other, as he is portrayed in the decadent epic *Las Mocedades de Rodrigo* and certain Cid ballads two centuries later.[2] As we will frequently note, the Cid of the poem, like the Cid of history, is the epitome of loyalty and respect in his relations with his king; but in the *Mocedades* and some Cid ballads he is rebellious, overbearing, proud, and insolent.

According to Menéndez Pidal, epic tradition flourished with exceptional vigor during the heroic age, which may be defined as that centuries-long period during which oral poetry, in the absence of written historiography, was the only means of divulging public events. We should add that it would be unfair to brand it as illiterate even though it was unlettered. It is true that most people in that age could neither read nor write, but they were cultured in their own way and certainly more closely knit spiritually than in succeeding bookish epochs. The cohesive forces were the church and popular tradition.

The propagators of tradition were epic poets. "Among peoples with a vital, unanimous, national interest and possessed of strongly affective political attitudes," says Menéndez Pidal, "it was through meter, rhyme, and song (in a way more powerful than writing) that matters of common interest were divulged" (*PP*, pp. 44 - 45). Here Pidal refers to "news-bearing" epics. Besides these, oral poets sang what I would call "aorist" epics, that is, traditional tales which, even when composed within memory of the narrated events, modified and even altered history in varying degrees. Our term suggests a greater degree of fictionalization in early epic than Pidal would be willing to admit. Concerning late decadent epic, he rightly declares that ". . . novelesque elements in the end completely replace the veristic element which was basic in earlier epic songs."[3] Before the decadent stage is reached, however, "the traditional existence of a poetic theme . . . through several generations or through several centuries, is kept alive only by means of successive recreations [*refundiciones*], each of which retains something of what preceded . . . and renews it seeking the pleasure of innovation. . . . Through repetition and innovation the poet, the *refundidor*, always addresses the people, the whole nation; his individual disposition and taste are subordinated to the collective spirit."[4] One gathers that since each recreation "retains something of what preceded" the innovations Pidal speaks of are not radical. Our assumption is confirmed by his statement regarding the "verism" of Spanish epic: "*Verismo*," he says, "is not *veracidad*, and it may well manifest itself in subject matter that is not contemporary and which has undergone a poetic or even fictional transformation, provided that such a transformation does not violate the initial historical tone and provided that the historical element remains preponderant."[5]

Whether the epic singer was a veristic informant of recent events or a recorder of fictionalized past events, he was essentially anonymous. Why? We propose the following answer: In the early and late Middle Ages the concept of literary originality, of creative individualism, did not exist among traditional poets for three reasons: first, because they were mouthpieces and sounding boards of collective feelings and attitudes; secondly because the verbal and narrative devices of their art were to a large extent formulistic and, third, because poets lacked the copyright mentality of our individualistic age; they were instead artists who, having inherited techniques from their poetic predecessors, took it for granted that their particular contributions were the common property of their own and succeeding ages. Anonymity, however, should not be equated with uniformity of talent nor with the elimination of unusually gifted singers. For example: the jongleur of the chanson de geste *Raoul de Cambrai*, the only version of which is dated late in the twelfth century, informs us that a valiant poet-soldier, called Bartolai de Laon, witnessed and celebrated in song the battle he is singing about, a battle which took place in 943. "You will never hear a better chanson," the jongleur declares, "it has been heard in many places" (*PP*, pp. 38 - 39).

The jongleur of *Raoul de Cambrai*, retelling a story which had been told two centuries before, is a link in what may be called the traditional chain. This chain is formed by a series of individual creative efforts all of them made akin by the subject which is celebrated and by the habitual devices of oral style and narration which are passed on from one jongleur to another. Our jongleur's unabashed recognition of a remote poet predecessor narrating the same subject illustrates the attitude of poets toward one another: their songs were common property. This attitude was exemplified even by literate poets, most notably by Juan Ruiz, archpriest of Hita, who encouraged all good poets to add or delete from his *Book of Good Love* as they saw fit. "Let it [my book] go from hand to hand: Whoever would so wish./Let any one catch it, if he can, like a ball that ladies toss."[6]

II   *Bédier's Individualist Theory*

From 1904 to 1911, the French medievalist Joseph Bédier expounded at the Collège de France his individualist theory concerning French epic.[7] Bédier's argument is developed so lucidly, forcefully, and brilliantly that it still fascinates the modern reader, no matter the extent to which he may disagree with the author. Bédier's thesis is not now so generally accepted as it was formerly, although it still is equivocally reflected among certain British medievalists. The views of Bédier which concern us may be summed up as follows: (1) A chanson was the product of an individual author, sometimes a poet of genius who was cut off, as far as the past is concerned, from literary predecessors and, as far as the future is concerned, from succeeding poets who would assimilate, renovate, and recreate his work. Thus, *"La Chanson de Roland* began with Thuroldus and ended with Thuroldus," and "each and every chanson de geste has a fatherland, a single author, just as any other literary work." (2) The time span between the poet and the events he celebrates is very long. Hence, (3) epic is a late genre the historicity of which is an evocation similar to that of the modern historical novel whose author consults written historical sources. In somewhat analogous fashion, the jongleur's sources consisted of information made known to him by his collaborators, namely, clerics belonging to a given monastery, who eagerly promoted chansons dealing with a saint connected with it in order to attract pilgrims. Bare mention of a far-off event drawn from a chronicle, from a diplomatic document, or from an oral legend sufficed as a point of departure for a chanson. (4) The lack of exhaustive documentation and the long time span between event and poem accounts for the predominantly unhistoric form of chansons de geste.

Evidence of the kind found in *Raoul de Cambrai*, revealing the existence of a traditional chain which extends from the middle of the tenth to the end of the twelfth century, was intolerable to Bédier. It was intolerable because he held it as an article of faith that chansons de geste were not born until the end of the eleventh or beginning of the twelfth century. How did Bédier explain the above mentioned evidence of a twelfth-century jongleur recalling a tenth-century predecessor? "Bédier," says Menéndez Pidal, "intent on upholding his irreversible hypothesis that clerics consulted monastic archives in order to supply jongleurs with materials for poetic use, resorts to the idenfensible argument of lost documents" (*PP*, p. 41). This argument, though implausible, is still valid if applied to chansons which were composed no earlier than the end of the eleventh century. But what about *Raoul de Cambrai*? Bédier argues that the early jongleur to whom the late jongleur refers based his song on a lost post-tenth-century document. Menéndez Pidal exclaims: "To think that he who brands as unaccpetable the supposition that there can be more than one version of a given poem, must resort to such a supposition himself, provided that the versions do not antedate the twelfth century!" (*PP*, p. 41).

III *Menéndez Pidal's Views Challenged*

In 1972 Professor Colin Smith published his controversial edition of the *PMC*.[8] It is the most important recent edition of the poem.

Paradoxically, it is important both in spite of and because of its strong anti-Menéndez Pidal line, for, whether or not we agree with the challenger's views, the scholarly debate which they will stir up is bound to clarify the questions at issue. In the part of his extensive introduction dealing with the problem of the poetic rendering of history, Smith puts three considerations in place of Menéndez Pidal's view of *historicidad*:

1. Although epic has its roots in a vaguely historical compost, the accurate preservation of history was no concern of the epic poet, still less any duty of his, and was never seen in that way. . . . When the poets do intervene they do so in a poetic way, not in order to preserve historical records.

2. . . . If many poems have a strong air of *historicidad* ["historicity"] about them, it was because the poet, like any other artist, sought to convince his public that he was not offering rubbish but true, worthy and improving material, . . . and more importantly, because the poet sought to create an impression of verisimilitude, of credibility on a human plane, as part of his art.

3. If the *PMC* was not composed as early as 1140 (as Pidal always held), still less in part about 1105, the necessary connection which Pidal discerned between event and poem is much weakened; moreover, a rapid comparison between the *PMC* and what we know or guess about other epics in Spain shows that the *PMC* was untypical in its *historicidad*.

An additional consideration of Professor Smith about *historicidad* is a more subjective one. "Pidal valued *verismo*," he says, "and the exactness with which history was preserved in epic because he was, in his life's work, at least one third historian. Others of different interests and temperament may not share his view. One accepts, with him, that the function of epic was partly an exemplary and social matter. But its function was also an artistic one, and in this, epic is no different from other forms of literature."[9]

IV *Evaluation of the Foregoing Views*

If we delete the last nine words, "epic is no different from other forms of literature," the last two sentences quoted above solve the problem of the poetic rendering of history in epic. The first sentence, to the effect that the function of epic was "partly an exemplary and social matter," halfheartedly admits one of Pidal's central propositions. As for the first part of the second sentence, namely, that the function of epic was also an artistic one, if we may gloss it in Aristotelian terms, Smith is saying that epic was a form of imitation.

This, of course, goes without saying; it is a proposition that applies to all mimetic literary genres, indeed, to all artistic forms. However, is the artistic form of heroic epic, that is, its formal working and power, really "no different from any other form of literature"? We think that it does differ radically from other genres as a class on account of its popular celebrative form, and within its class its congeners differ among themselves because the distinctive character of any given epic hero determines the peculiar nature of his admirable qualities. First of all, if our panoramic view encompasses the *Iliad,* the *Odyssey,* the *Song of Roland,* and the *Poem of the Cid,* we note that epic can celebrate either admirable disasters or glorious triumphs. Furthermore, a closer view reveals the enormous differences of historicity between the non-Spanish works and the Spanish composition. And if we narrow the focus to the two surviving epics celebrating the Cid, we are struck, on the one hand, with the relatively high degree of historical accuracy in parts of the early *PMC* and, on the other, with the complete fictionalization in the *Mocedades de Rodrigo* some two hundred years later. Both the early "veristic" and the late "affabulated" works about Rodrigo are celebrative mimetic compositions. In this sense they are akin. One represents, however, an early manifestation of the popular and collective traditional process, and the other a late manifestation of it.

The formal differences in various kinds of epic do not constitute the chief issue in the divergent viewpoints of Bédier, Menéndez Pidal, and Smith. The crux of the matter has to do with tradition, about which three questions must be raised: (1) Is epic a form of literature propagated by poets who, through a long period of time, created and recreated orally and/or in writing extended compositions which satisfied the need of predominantly unlettered society to keep alive the collective awareness of momentous events? (2) Is a given epic the isolated product of a given poet at a given time and a given place? Or, (3) is epic, as Pidal argues, a form of poetry which fulfills the high politicocultural mission of history?

We are inclined to give an affirmative answer to the first question since, by analogy with modern singers of tales in Yugoslavia, we may assume their counterparts in ancient and medieval times. Epic poets of the oral tradition, both those whose creative activity has been observed and recorded by Parry and Lord and those who lived centuries ago, were the heirs and propagators of poetically rendered historical tradition either in its early relatively veristic stage or in its

late affabulated stage. Also, since Homer, epic poems composed for
oral performance have always been traditional with respect to formulaic style, mythic necessity, and thematic attraction.

It would be an oversimplification to hold that our affirmative
answer to the first question presupposes an unequivocal negative
answer to the second. This is not the place to probe the complex
problem of traditionalism, whether we are talking about the composition of epic in the light of "individualist" or of "traditionalist"
theory. Suffice it to say that those who subscribe to the former
should take into account the sound doctrine of T. S. Eliot, who, in
his essay on "Tradition and the Individual Talent," suggests that
the individual cannot realize his individuality unless he first merges
himself with the tradition.[10]

The third question has no simple answer. We agree completely
with Smith when he suggests that an epic is first and foremost a
poem. But cannot a poem *as a poem*, faithfully render both the
letter and the spirit of history in varying degrees? We believe that in
the case of the *PMC* it does, both because its portrayal of the hero
and the account of his deeds are essentially true and because it is
historically accurate in many matters of detail. At the other extreme,
that of fictionalization, as exemplified by the *Mocedades de
Rodrigo*, not only does this poem *not* fulfill the function of history, it
violates history. Such extreme affabulation, however, is not imcom-
patible with the traditional process; on the contrary, this process,
whether it retains a core of historicity or eliminates it, results from a
preliterate society's need to celebrate national heroes more or less as
they were or as they were imagined to be.

As previously noted, Smith admits incidentally that "the function
of epic is partly an exemplary and social matter." In our opinion he
could have made this admission wholeheartedly without in any way
affecting his admirable aesthetic judgments for, especially in the
case of *PMC*, it is possible to equate the juglar's social function with
his poetic function. He was a *poetic* informant. The adjective as we
use it makes full allowance for fictional elements in the fact-fiction
synthesis. For example, among historical frontier ballads dealing
with the wars against Granada, which Menéndez Pidal equates with
veristic epic, we may observe minimal or maximal poetic license.
Smith cites the case of a well-known frontier ballad which, he states,
"has always been held can be exactly dated and placed in closest
association with the real event." He adds: "It has been recently

shown [by Paul Bénichou] that almost from the start of the ballad's life, the facts of history were being distorted, fictionalized, in the interests of creating drama, poetry, emotion, picturesqueness: such was the *modus operandi* of the poet who made the ballad."[11] Everything Smith says here is essentially true, but he does not take into account the fictionalized ballad's historical *raison d'être*, namely, as Bénichou declares, that it recalls how the kings of Castile kept trying to conquer Granada without success.[12] This lack of success in seizing a great prize by force is presented metaphorically: Juan II of Castile yearns greatly to possess Granada as his "wife." Thus, in terms which without being positively true to the facts nevertheless do not belie them the author of *Abenámar* has poetically conveyed the underlying historical reality of a late phase of the Reconquest.[12a]

Such extreme poetic license is not the only *modus operandi*. For example, among the frontier ballads, one of the best, both with respect to poetic technique and fidelity to history, is the little masterpiece *Álora la bien cercada*, which tells how "on a Sunday afternoon," during the siege of Álora, a town perched high on the percipitous left bank of the Guadalhorce river, twenty-three miles northwest of Málaga, the *adelantado* ("governor") of Andalusia, Diego de Ribera, was treacherously and fatally wounded in the face by the arrow aimed by one of the besieged Moors. This happened in May of 1434. Juan de Mena refers to the death of the *adelantado* in stanza 192 of his *Laberinto de Fortuna* (1444). Born in 1411, Mena was already twenty-three years old when Diego de Ribera was killed. The news of such a nationally important event must have quickly spread from mouth to mouth, and it is reasonable to suppose that the oral diffusion of it included news-bearing ballads, among which the only one preserved was printed in a sixteenth-century *pliego suelto* ("broadside"). Juan de Mena, who was Latin Secretary of Juan II, was bound not only to have become familiar with that incident in his capacity as royal chronicler but also to have heard about it through news-bearing ballads composed while the event was still fresh in the minds of the public.

While it is true, as Menéndez Pidal affirms, that news-bearing ballads like *Álora* "were for their times the one great medium of publicity, something like the journalism of our epoch" (*RH*, II, 4), we should not conclude that Pidal thought of the news-bearing ballad to be a counterpart of the modern news report. Our admonition is gratuitous, perhaps even an insult to the intelligence, but we

venture it because there are those who fail to differentiate with the
necessary rigor the poetic and nonpoetic manner of reporting an
event. The good reporter of our day tries to meet the standards of
what might be called the gospels of plain speech, accuracy, and ob-
jectivity. He suppresses the rhetoric of the narrative voice which,
implicity or explicity, is so important in epic and ballad. The good
reporter works hard to supply reliable answers to the questions
"where?" "what?" "when?" and "how?" In sum, the *desideratum*
is the "bare facts," set forth in detail and in ultraprosaic language.
The composer of the most truthful news-bearing ballads also
related essential facts, but without the scruple of going into details.
Moreover, even the most circumstantial accounts reflected, not a
journalistic, but a poetic criterion. The "story" of Álora is presented
as no modern reporter would "write it up": it is a masterfully con-
structed narration charged with restrained but intense feeling and
having a beginning, middle, and end; it employs with admirable
economy of means the common epic device of systematic enumeration; its language, though plain, is stylized through the use of verbal
formulas, formulas of narrative mode and stylistic patterns; the
music of certain words, even without the melodic accompaniment of
voice and instrument, charm the ear.[13] In sum: the poet of epic or
ballad obeyed, first and foremost, his aesthetic urge and the practical necessity of pleasing his audience. If the poet was good enough
this pleasure was imparted whether he reproduced, modified, or distorted the historical truth. As we will show in the last part of this
chapter, there is a wide margin both for truth and invention in the
Poem of the Cid.

To conclude, let us examine Professor Smith's statement to the
effect that "epic has its roots in a vaguely historical compost." This
is the first of his three arguments against the importance of
historicidad. The sweeping generalization first suggests that it
applies to the *PMC*. However, in the course of his exposition he implies that the poem embodies varying degrees of historical truth.
The best parts of the poem, he contends, "are not those is which
historical facts are conveyed most accurately." Here Smith seems to
admit a high degree of historicidad at least in the parts he has in
mind, that is, those which are not, in his opinion, the best. His tacit
admission about the historical accuracy of said parts, implies, in
turn, that they record events recent enough to be remembered accurately, for he reasonably assumes that the longer the lapse of time

between event and poem, the less accurate the memory of it becomes in the juglar's mind. So much for the side of Smith's thinking that seems to admit a high degree of historicidad in the *PMC*. The other side is brought out when he affirms that "all these views [those supporting the thesis of early thirteenth- rather than mid-twelfth-century composition] except Pidal's harmonize and can be further supported by my own deductions based on the length of time that must have elapsed for certain errors — from a strictly historical standpoint — to creep into the [Cid] legends or to be tolerable in them."[14] Here Smith seems to be identifying the poem with epics which undoubtedly are rooted in a "vaguely historical compost," thus contradicting his implications which suggest that some parts of it are accurately conveyed.

Professor Smith goes a long way toward explaining the implied contradiction of his exposition in the paragraph in which he admits the possibility of a succession of coalesced poems. Referring to Menéndez Pidal and J. Horrent who posit this possibility, he says: "Both Pidal and Horrent may be right, but only — a vital point which neither made clear — if they are talking of poems in an oral tradition which is unknowable." It is true that oral transmission of medieval epic cannot be verified by direct observation but two kinds of evidence may be put forward to make a strong case for it: (1) by analogy to the oral transmission observed among modern singers of tales in Yugoslavia and elsewhere; (2) by the internal evidence of a formulaic style, which uses narrative devices and themes that have characterized oral poetry since Homer. We will deal with these matters at some length in in the fourth chapter.

V *Content of the* Poema de Mio Cid

To facilitate a broad comparison of the historical and pseudo-historical incidents in the *Poema de Mio Cid*[15] with corresponding events set forth in our first chapter, we will summarize its contents. In the summary we will avoid a detailed "synopsis of plot," something that Northrop Frye rightly calls the lowest form of literary criticism. Instead, after stating the subject of the poem in one sentence, its principal incidents will be enumerated (we arbitrarily define "incident" as an action that is indispensable to the system of actions which constitute the whole, as distinguished from "episode," which we define as a supplementary action).

The subject of the *Poema de Mio Cid* is the progressive restitution of Rodrigo's honor through his own efforts following his disgrace which is brought about by the false accusations of his enemies, accusations to which his envious king, Alfonso, lends a willing ear. The Poem is divided into three *cantares* ("parts").

The First Cantar. The Cid is falsely accused by his enemies of having kept for himself the largest portion of the tribute he had been sent to collect from King Motamid of Seville. Believing the scandalmongers, the king sends Rodrigo into exile.[16] To support himself and his followers the Cid fraudulently obtains a loan of 300 gold and 300 silver marks from the Jewish moneylenders Raquel and Vidas. The Cid's first military feats, accomplished with but a handful of followers, take place in border country: he takes the town of Castejón and the castle of Alcocer. Then he penetrates deeper and deeper into Moorish territory, conquering all lands from Teruel to Zaragoza. This series of victories culminates with his triumph over the count of Barcelona in the battle of the Pine-Wood of Tévar in the mountain north of the town of Morella.

The Second Cantar. From Morella the Cid continues his advance southeastward to the shores of the Mediterranean, subjugating the region between Castellón and Murviedro and undertaking raids as far south of Valencia as Denia. These operations are climaxed with the conquest of Valencia and the defeat of King Yusuf of Morocco who was bent on gaining possession of the levantine city. At this point two highborn young men, the Infantes of Carrión, coveting the enormous riches which the Cid had acquired through his conquests, ask Alfonso to arrange their marriage to the Cid's daughters. Before acceding to their wish Alfonso, now favorably disposed toward Rodrigo, pardons him. The pardoned vassal then reluctantly agrees to his daughters' marriage, which is celebrated in Valencia.

The Third Cantar. After two years of pampered married life in the conquered city, the heirs of Carrión show that they are cowards when they hide from the Cid's lion who gets loose and when they are stricken with fear at the battle of Cuarte in which the Moorish King Búcar is killed by the Cid. Mortified by the jibes of which they are the butt, the Infantes, having obtained permission from their father-in-law to return to their lands in Carrión, halt on the way and give vent to their spite by brutally beating their wives at the oak grove of Corpes, leaving them half-dead. The girls would have perished if they had not been rescued by their young cousin, Félix Muñoz, who carries them on his horse to San Esteban de Gormaz.

When the Cid hears of his dishonor, he begs justice of King Alfonso. Alfonso promises reparation and convokes court at Toledo. At the court the Infantes, accused of infamy, are ordered to meet the Cid's demands: the return of his precious swords Colada and Tizón, the return of the dowry of his daughters and a judicial duel to be fought between representatives of the Cid and the two Infantes and their brother, Asur González. In the midst of the heated exchanges concerning these demands, two messengers arrive to ask, in behalf of the princes of Navarre and Aragón, for the hands of the Cid's daughters. Upon the departure of the messengers the dispute between the accusers and accused is resumed. King Alfonso says, "let all this talk end," and orders that the judicial duel take place in the Infantes' own country, the plain of Carrión. The Infantes are defeated by the Cid's champions. Then the second marriage of the Cid's daughters is celebrated, a marriage through which the kings of Spain become the Cid's kinsmen.

VI *Historical Elements*

The most difficult question to answer in the attempt to determine the historical accuracy of certain key incidents in the *PMC* is the following: may the poem itself be accepted as a dependable historical source? Menéndez Pidal gives a more or less affirmative reply to this nagging question. We say "more or less" because in certain instances he ventures a hypothesis or arrives at firm conclusions regarding ostensible historical elements in the poem either on the strength of the air of authenticity of a given part of it, or on the basis of what may be called "the-part-is-of-the-same-kind-as-the-whole" argument. In other words, Menédez Pidal argues that in view of the poem's predominant *verismo*, a given part of it for which there is no documented proof, must be based on fact. He also arrives at conclusions in another way: he marshals incomplete evidence from historical sources and rounds it out in part with what he considers to be evidence found in the poem. For example, the laconic *Historia Roderici* gives only one general reason, Alfonso's envy, for Rodrigo's exile; it does not tell exactly *why* Alfonso was envious (*EC*, p. 268). Pidal gives an answer to this "why" by adducing certain related historical facts. Toward the end of 1079 the king sent Rodrigo to Seville to collect tribute from Motamid (*EC*, p. 255). Having established this fact on circumstantial evidence, he adduces the additional recorded fact that the Cid defeated and imprisoned

Count García Ordóñez, Alfonso's favorite, at Cabra, in 1080. "The Cid's triumph," writes Menéndez Pidal, "had aroused the envy, not only of outsiders and the partisans of Ordóñez, but even of his own kinsfolk. *According to the poem though not to the 'Historia Roderici,'* many false charges against him were made to the monarch, one of which was to the effect that he had withheld the larger portion of the Moorish king's tribute" (*CS*, p. 162; my emphasis).

In answering the question raised at the beginning of the foregoing paragraph, we submit that inferences of the kind that have been pointed out are not only unavoidable but necessary. One might argue that the weak link in Menéndez Pidal's reasoning is the inference he derives from the poem itself. However, in view of the fact that the poem is historically accurate in many fundamental respects, only an uncompromising positivist critic would totally reject it as a possible source of supplementary historical information in the case of complicated events which are only partially accounted for in contemporary historical sources. Such an event was the Cid's exile, the poetic account of which is at least partially true. It is not wholly true because the juglar, in adducing only one cause for it — and not the immediate cause at that — either did so for poetic reasons or was unaware of the immediate cause, namely, Rodrigo's unauthorized intervention at Gormaz in the kingdom of Toledo one year after the Seville affair.[17]

After tricking the Jews, the Cid engages in military operations ranging from raids to pitched battles. One of his two initial successes, the taking of Alcocer, is described in greater and more precise detail than any other warlike feat in the poem. We therefore think it is probably historical even though, in the large context of the Cid's phenomenal accomplishments, history does not record it, presumably because it was relatively insignificant. The juglar does record it and describes it at length, in all likelihood because it took place in his own region, the geography of which he traces with remarkable accuracy.

In contrast to the particularized narration of the conquest of Alcocer, the poet only enumerates in passages of rapid cinematographic technique other military operations of the hero, some of which are recorded by history, others not. We will single out a few among the former. The Cid, in his progress toward the southeast, according to the poem (901 - 11), stayed at a rugged promontory known today as El Poyo,[18] long enough to lay under tribute the whole country from the towns of Daroca to Teruel. This is substantially confirmed by the *Historia Roderici (EC*, p. 358). The Latin history also confirms the Campeador's raid as far south of Valencia as Denia (*PMC*, 1161; *EC*, p. 735) and his occupation of El Puerto de Alucat known today as Olocau (*PMC*, 951; *EC*, p. 291, n. 1). The poetic account also mentions in passing the names of towns and places taken by the Cid, which correspond to fuller accounts in Arab sources. Let one example suffice. The juglar informs us only that the Cid and his men reached Játiva (1160), but Ibn Alcama reports more specifically that between Orihuela and Játiva the whole country was laid waste: "Not one stone was left upon another" (*CS*, p. 249). One could go on and on listing the numerous places that mark the Cid's progress, places which are also mentioned in the Latin history and the two Arab histories. To get the concrete feel of the Cid's irregular course through the territory between Burgos and Valencia, most of it rugged and forbidding, it would be necessary to retrace it step by step, with Menéndez Pidal as our expert guide.[19]

In the panoramic parts of the poem we have pointed to above, the juglar's eye encompasses the sweep of the Cid's irresistible advance. In other parts, besides those dealing with the already mentioned capture of Alcocer, he draws closer to the action and sometimes sharpens the focus so that we can see it before our very eyes. In the following summary I indicate the distribution of these battles and the number of lines devoted to them in each cantar:

I (1,086 lines): Castejón, 437 - 92; Alcocer, 557 - 850; Pine-Wood of Tévar, 985 - 1023. Total: 386 lines, or, 36 percent.

II (1,190 lines): Valencian Moors, 1127 - 54; Yusuf, 1711 - 98. Total: 114 lines, or, 9.6 percent.

III (1,452 lines): Búcar, 2338 - 2491. Total: 153 lines, or, 10.5 percent.

Excepting the already noted battle of Alcocer, three of the four remaining engagements, namely, those against the count of Barcelona, Yusuf, and Búcar, are recorded by history. However, in the poem one of these four is so unspecific about place of occurrence and names of the enemy that it cannot be pinpointed — the enemy is only designated as "Valencian Moors," and their leaders, two Moorish kings who are killed, are not even given proper names. On the other hand, the poetic account of the battle at the Pine-Wood of

Tévar agrees with that found in the Latin History[20] in important matters of detail: the Catalans attack the Cid from a height; the Cid captures the count of Barcelona; the count is held near the Cid's tent but not in it; the Cid offers him food; certain words pronounced by the Cid in the poem correspond to the Cid's words as recorded in the Latin History. Aside from these coincidences, however, the accounts found in the poem and in the history differ radically. This leads Menéndez Pidal to believe that the poet of the cantar was not familiar with said history (*CMC*, pp. 865 - 66). The poetic Cid's victory against Yusuf at Cuarte corresponds to the historical Cid's defeat of Yusuf's nephew, Mohammed Ibn Teshufin.[21] The juglar may have substituted the nephew for the uncle for poetic reasons: the Campeador's triumph would be much more noteworthy over the latter than over the former. The error also could have been the result of faulty memory caused by the lapse of time between the event and the poetic account of it. But whatever the reason, the error of mistaken identity is not a serious one, for the historical Yusuf was the guiding spirit of all four Almoravide invasions. Therefore, any lieutenant who carried out his orders might be taken as his alter ego. The last battle in the poem has a very tenuous connection with history. Búcar, called *rey de Marruecos*, is probably Abu Beker, one of Yusuf's sons-in-law. Yusuf entrusted to Abu Beker the army he sent to Spain to attack and take Valencia. Abu Beker, leading a huge army, tried to carry out his mission but he failed.[22] The juglar is therefore indulging in poetic license or inventing when he represents the Cid as engaging Búcar in battle. The only part of the poem's description which may have a grain of historical truth is Búcar's flight, because the Abu Beker of history, after advancing to within striking distance of Valencia, turned back without fighting the Cid for the reasons set forth in the first chapter.[23]

The historical and semihistorical elements we have surveyed so far are incomplete, because we have limited ourselves to a consideration of those events which may be best understood in the large context of the quintessential summary we have given of the poem. There are other matters of fact that cannot be gone into here. Important as they would be in establishing the extent to which the poem is true to the letter of history, they are not essential for the purpose of conveying an idea of the degree in which it is true to its spirit. The true historical reality is to be sought in the psychological makeup of the persons who shaped events and were shaped by them. It is human motivations that determine the epic action: the envy of an unjust king, the unbreakable loyalty of the wronged vassal, the vassal's demonstration of the fact that, given irresistible will and genius to succeed, nothing succeeds like success — all those human inner drives that unfold in the poem are fully confirmed by the Latin and Arab histories.

VII   *Significant Omissions and Degrees of Emphasis*

Certain significant omissions of things that happened can easily be explained by the juglar's artistic need to be selective. The epic poet must make choices from among the materials he knows firsthand or through tradition. He includes or excludes matter according to his artistic intention which, in heroic epic, is first and foremost celebrative. Thus Alfonso is represented as a character who in the end exemplifies the attributes of a great king. His sovereignty over a united Christian Spain is emphasized several times as one aspect of his greatness even though during the historical period encompassed by the poem he lost all of southern Spain to the Almoravides. Not a word about Sagrajas is breathed in the poem. In the *PMC*, one of whose central thematic ideas is Rodrigo's loyalty and respect verging on reverence (there is one exception),[24] it is inconceivable that the always victorious vassal could have deprecatingly reminded Alfonso of Sagrajas or Consuegra. The juglar could have praised the Cid for going so far as to endanger his position in Valencia in order to help Alfonso. However, such praise for the hero would have been lavished at the expense of the king, something which the intent to exalt Alfonso would not have permitted.

We will now consider the Moslem characters, both those included in, and those excluded from, the poem. One of the most likable is the Spanish Moor Abengalbón, the Cid's good friend, about whom there is no historical record. He plays a memorable secondary role. But no mention is made of the taifa kings of Zaragoza: Moktadir, who gave the Cid asylum after he was rejected by the counts of Barcelona, his son Mutamin, and his grandson Mostain. Having been afforded the protection of Zaragoza, the protégé soon became the protector of his hosts. It is true that the Cid had his troubles with the grandson, so much so at times that the latter could have been taken for one of the Cid's enemies. However, if the juglar had chosen to give the Moors a fair share of his attention, he could have at least mentioned the hero's long association with the Zaragozan kings. Their omission from the narrative, however, is not especially significant. For artistic reasons they are expendable.

But what can be said about the sketchy characterization of the Moslem kings whom the Cid defeated? They are no more than shadows. We have already dismissed as of no serious consequence the substitution of Mohammed Ibn Tushufin for his uncle, Yusuf. However, having made the substitution, why does the poet miss the opportunity to portray the emir of all the Moslems in his full sinister dimensions? This missed opportunity could be alleged by the "personalists" as evidence of what they take to be the weakness of the religious element in the poem. The evidence, though of a negative sort, cannot be brushed aside with undue haste. It should be weighed against the positive proof we will adduce.

VIII *Fictitious Elements*

At this point we will only enumerate the principal fictitious elements in the poem. They are (1) the trick whereby the Cid obtains 300 gold and 300 silver marks from the Jewish moneylenders Raquel and Vidas, (2) possibly the first marriage of the Cid's daughters,[25] (3) the lion incident, and (4) the Toledo Cortes.

IX *Epic and History*

Having summarized the most important views of Pidal, Bédier, and Smith on epic and history, we will venture to set forth our own and to demonstrate their validity concretely through a further analysis of the historical, pseudohistorical, and fictitious elements in the *PMC*.

The epic poet tells a story based on historical, traditional, or legendary events. The extent to which he is faithful to the letter and spirit of history varies greatly. However, the historical matter, whether it is used with considerable fidelity, modified, altered, distorted, or transformed into myth, must yield to the requirements of poetic creation.

The *Poema de Mio Cid*, as we have seen, relates certain historical events with varying degrees of historical accuracy. Compared to other medieval epics, its verismo is indeed so exceptional that in some ways it may serve as a supplementary or confirming source of historical information. Nevertheless, it is as poetic as any predominantly mythic epic if by "poetic" we understand, with the Greek *poiein* ("to make") in mind, the "making" of the whole as a work of art. This Castilian epic, therefore, so poetic as history and so historical as a poem, may serve as no other specimen of its genre to demonstrate how the "particulars" of history may serve the ends of poetic "universals."

Being an artist, the juglar had to be selective; he also resorted to poetic license; he omitted or only mentioned in passing — and then not always accurately — experiences of the greatest importance in the Cid's career after 1081, the chief of these being, as we have noted, his association with three successive kings of Zarogoza. To attain artistic unity he compressed into five years events which occurred during thirteen years (1081 - 1094). The Cid of history was exiled twice and his problems with the envious king Alfonso were never definitively resolved. In addition, in this instance also to facilitate organic unity, the poetic Cid is exiled only once and the king pardons him once and for all so that the story may have a happy ending. The pardon is also made to appear irreversible so that Alfonso, who never quite ceased being envious in history, would exemplify his people's image of an ideal king. It is obvious that the reduction of a time span from thirteen to five years does not seriously impair historical truth; but this truth is, given celebrative epic form, purposely altered in connection with the relations between the Cid and King Alfonso. For Alfonso to pardon his vassal definitively, the juglar had to change his real character much for the better. There is also a modification in the character of the hero himself. It is true that the historical Cid and the poetic Cid were alike with respect to two fundamental traits, namely, magnanimity and loyalty; but it is undeniable that the poet idealizes the protagonist by emphasizing only his unvarying benevolence and by closing his eyes to the extreme severity of which he was capable when only severity would serve the ends of justice.[26] Such idealization is, of course, to be expected in an epic poem whose hero is represented as a paragon of goodness, one whose lack of any self-destructive defect — like the wrath of Achilles and the pride of Roland — makes him the most perfect of all epic protagonists, and the most phenomenally successful.

His success was not more remarkable in the poem than it was in actuality. It therefore demonstrates the following words from Aristotle's *Poetics*: ". . . there is nothing to prevent the things that have happened from being the kind of things that can happen. . . ."[27] "The things that have happened" refer to unaltered particular events. "The kind of things that can happen" refer to the poet's modification or alteration of real events or to invented fictitious matter. These latter things refer to the representation of things "as they should have been"and not "as they were." The idealization of the Cid's character and, even to a greater degree, the alteration of Alfonso's character, fall under this category. In both instances historical matter already at hand is modified and altered. What about poetic figments?

The answer to this question, we think, is that the invented parts may also be considered as representations of what "should have happened," because they are necessary for the organization of a plot, the fictitious elements of which, among other things, make possible the causal connection of incidents, emphasize the Cid's authentic character as well as the king's changed character, and bring out the poetically necessary character of his enemies who represent evil forces working against the irreproachable hero. Rodrigo's economic ruin dictates the trick he resorts to in order to obtain money; the lion incident provides the motive for the vengeful conduct of the Infantes; and, nothing less than the fictitious Toledo Cortes will suffice to exalt the true moral greatness of the hero, for on that solemn occasion the power of his word transcends the power of his sword.[28]

In sum, in the *PMC* fact and fiction are skillfully combined to form a poetic creation with a theme — the Cid's honor — which serves as a unifying principle knitting together a system of actions whose agents are dynamic instruments in the development of that system. Also, in every part, the deceivingly simple thought and style or, to put it in another way, interior and exterior form, serve their formal function which is to tell a heroic story in ringing, celebrative tones. To a considerable extent action, character, thought and diction reflect historical reality, especially the political and religious reality of the times; but in their poetic context these elements exert their working and power in the sphere of art.

X *Conflicting Views on the Political Import of the Poem*

Karl Vossler in his famous *Spanischer Brief* (Spanish Letter) to Hugo von Hofmannsthal sets forth with great firmness his personalist interpretation of the *PMC*. "We do not see [in the *PMC*]" says Vossler, "a pure and simple expression of national, religious nor ethical values as in *La Chanson de Roland* or in the *Nibelungenlied*, but something essentially personal . . . because its subject is the Cid and only the Cid, his honor and his glory is what the poem is about. . . .

Neither does it deal with the hero's intimate problems, nor with deeds and works for the sake of the people . . . ; to be more exact, it deals with his own self-rehabilitation and the defense of his honor."[29] With even more emphasis, the American Hispanist, George Tyler Northup, in an article entitled "The Poem of the Cid Viewed as a Novel," rejects the view that the Cid was the defender of the cross against the crescent and insists that the author of the poem did not have in mind the political and religious importance of the Cid's career. "The capture of Valencia," Northup claims, "is a mere episode, the significance of which is chiefly financial. . . . Much more space is devoted to the little skirmish of Alcocer. The patriotic note is scarcely sounded. If the once used [sic] [30] phrase 'Castiella la gen-til' ["Sweet Castile"] recalls 'la douce France' of the *Roland*, it means little in an age when loyalty to a feudal lord came before devotion to one's native soil. And the religious motive is equally weak in an age of tolerance, when Moors were admired, not hated."[31] Adding his brilliantly articulated argument to the arguments of Vossler and Northup, Leo Spitzer affirms that the *PMC* is not a genuine epic but a "novelized or epical biography" ("biografía novelada o epopeyizada"), whose hero, as a citizen of the all embracing European fatherland, rather than of his local Spanish motherland, does exemplify universal chivalric virtues but not his country's spirit of Reconquest. About the Cid's patriotic motives in refusing to fight his king, Spitzer says nothing; nor is it to be expected that he could admit such motives since, given his "internationalist" point of view, we may conclude that for the eminent romanist the Cid's loyalty does not manifest patriotism, but a generic chivalric virtue that stirs in the Cid's consciousness apart from any political or local motive. If so, Spitzer asks, "how may we explain that one of the greatest ideas of his times, the idea of the European Crusade is not reflected in our hero, considering the fact that the conquest of Valencia accomplished by the Cid of history . . . foreshadowed the conquest of Jerusalem?" He answers his own question with another question: "Was it not because the juglar who wrote the poem forty years later interpreted the historical facts as they appeared to him then and did not wish to glorify the Cid for deeds which did not have a lasting effect?"[32]

Menéndez Pidal does not share the "personalist" viewpoint of Vossler and others. The Cid of history and the poetic Cid, he holds, exemplify loyalty and love of country. The proof of this lies in the fact that though Alfonso was openly hostile to the Cid's occupation

of Valencia, the exiled vassal placed the city under the overlordship
of his lord and king (*EC*, pp. 521, 596). This supreme act of loyalty,
at a juncture of his hard-won gains when more than on any other occasion he had reason to reject his unjst king, "would be incom-
prehensible," Pidal asserts, "if . . . we were to assume that the
motives of the Spanish hero were purely personal. . . . The fact that,
contrary to the custom established in the law and poetry of the time,
neither the Cid of history nor the Cid of fiction makes war on his
king but remains loyal to him, shows the extent to which the hero
subordinated personal motives to love of country, thereby betraying
a spirit practically unkown to the heroic types of older epic poems.
This same patriotism also finds expression in his famous resolve to
reconquer the whole of Spain and even, as the old poem maintains,
to lay Morocco under tribute to King Alphonso"(*CS*, pp. 421 - 22).

In our opinion Menéndez Pidal's nationalist interpretation is just,
notwithstanding the Cid's fabulous personal success. Because he
acquired great wealth and power through his conquests, some
cidophobes have thought that the Cid was nothing more than an
ambitious adventurer. This judgment is unjust, for, once Rodrigo
was exiled, the lawful custom of his times gave him, we repeat, the
right to gain sustenance (*ganarse el pan*) for himself and his
followers. This right did not preclude as something dishonorable the
acquisition of wealth and power; on the contrary, honor was
measured in those times in concrete terms — hence the Spanish
idiom *hombre de bien* ("man of property") an idiom which to this
day designates an honorable man, be he rich or poor. The personalist interpretation would be admissible if the Cid's honor had
been solely commensurate with his material success; it could then be
claimed that the poem is no more than the story of a self-made man.
But the poem, as we shall see, represents him as much more than
that; it is also the story of a man who loved his country and was loyal
to his king. For these reasons he stands high before posterity as a
true national hero.

His expatriation is more than the result of a private discord
between an envious king and an innocent vassal. It is a public question, the consequence of which could have been disastrous for Alfonso and Christian Spain if the Cid had behaved vindictively as he had
every reason to do, not only because Alfonso had probably been an
accessory to the murder of Sancho, the Cid's former lord, but
because after Sancho's assassination and before the banishment

Alfonso excluded him from his most important military action, namely, his war against the kingdom of Toledo. The always favored protégé of the dead king became the vassal who fell into the disfavor of his successor, whose envy rendered him incapable of tolerating superior merit. And the scandalmongers at court, blamed by the Cid and his wife Jimena for the king's ill will, belonged to a common class of political troublemakers in eleventh-century Spain (*EC*, p. 295) and, undoubtedly, one of these troublemakers, the chief one, was the historical rival of the Cid, his *enemigo malo* ("evil enemy"), the frequently mentioned Count García Ordóñez, who plays an important role in the poem as the counselor of the Infantes of Carrión at the Toledo Court. In sum, a king identified primarily with León, who had special motives to be resentful of a vassal identified primarily with Castile and with that kingdom's assassinated sovereign, plus false accusations of political adversaries headed by his most powerful political enemy, the royal favorite Count García Ordóñez — all these things make the Cid's exile politically significant.

And once exiled, the hero's behavior continues to be that of a public figure rather than that of a proscribed man, or a *caballero-bandido* [33] or a "freebooter," [34] as he has been called. At first the king will have nothing to do with the Cid; but the Cid does not respond in kind fighting the king as he had the right to do; instead he shares his spoils with Alfonso and, most important of all, he takes Valencia in the name of the king. Had Rodrigo followed the traditional example of rebellious Castilian vassals, indeed of French vassals at odds with their lord, he would not only have kept all of his gains and claimed for himself the overlordship of Valencia; he also would have waged war against the king as he had the right to do.[35] But as the poem, confirming history, says in line 538, he did not wish to fight with his king: *Con Alfons mio señor non guerría lidiar.* No other line of the *PMC* is more historically authentic than this one; it proclaims more explicitly than any other the Cid's loyalty and his magnanimity, that is, the sacrifice of his personal interest to the greater interest of the king, and the subordination of regionalistic love of Castile to the national interest. Those who joined the Campeador from all parts of Spain undoubtedly wanted to get rich, but the celebrative tone of the poem suggests that it was above all the greatness of Rodrigo that attracted them.

It has been said that the patriotic note is scarcely sounded in the poem because the expression *Castiella la gentil*, is used only once (as I have indicated, it is used twice). However, if we bear in mind the restrained but intense style of the work, it is not necessary that this beautiful epithet be repeated frequently for us to be convinced of the Cid's love of country. Something more eloquent than verbal expression proclaims his patriotism. This is a *cantar de gesta* (literally "a song of deeds") in which *deeds* speak louder than words, and what the hero *does* to signify his grief over his banishment is to refuse to cut his beard even when at the height of his glory at the Toledo Cortes it has grown to an inordinate length.

It is not necessary for the poem to abound in declarations of national sentiments, sentiments that were as natural as the air that Spanish Christians breathed. Even so, certain lines make it clear that the Cid in preparing to face the enemy, counted on national spirit when he recruited men "from everywhere [i.e., Spain]" (119). The juglar says, *grandes yentes se le acojen de la buena cristiandad*, "great numbers gather to him from good Christendom [i.e., from Christian Spain]" (1199). It is true that these men join him *al sabor de la ganancia*, "anticipating riches." However, this does not mean that *ganarse el pan*, by fighting against the pagan enemy, excluded patriotic motivation.

Neither should we expect the juglar, whose thought is so simply expressed, to expatiate on the Cid's historic role as the moving spirit of Hispanic solidarity, nor that the Cid, presented as a man of action, should do so himself. More eloquent than his words are his attitudes and acts: his unshakable sense of duty toward his king; his naming as bishop of Valencia a Frenchman, symbol of universal Christianity; his seeking redress for the affront at Corpes by lawful means rather than by violent personal revenge.

The Cid's behavior shows that however proud he may have been of what in Spanish is designated as his *patria chica* ("his own region"), that is, "Castile the sweet," he prized above all the preservation of the united Christian Spain over which Alfonso ruled and whose very existence was endangered by the disastrous defeat which Alfonso suffered at Sagrajas. If this had not been the case he could have yielded to the spirit of bellicose Castilian separatism like his former lord, King Sancho; he could have made war against his assassinated king's successor and become a second Fernán González, the rebellious vassal who broke with his lord, the King of León. The juglar expresses his own sense of Pan-Hispanic pride when he says of Alfonso:

He is king of Castile and king of León,
and of Asturias as far as San Salvador;
as far as Santiago he is the lord,
and the counts of Galicia serve him as their lord.

(2923 - 26)

Addressing the king in the name of Cid, the Asturian Muño Gustioz says to him: "Grace, king of great kingdoms that call you lord!/The Campeador kisses your hands and feet;/ he is your vassal and you are his lord" (2936 - 38).

As for the Cid himself, according to Menéndez Pidal (*EC*, p. 606), the role he played in the national crisis transcended his regional interests, because it was he, the Castilian hero, who after the assassination at Zamora bowed to King Alfonso of León and after his banishment became the embodiment of the national ideal. "The exclusion of the Cid from the court of Castile," says Menéndez Pidal, "served to accentuate his position as a truly national figure; and it is significant that he should have had fighting side by side with his Castilians, the Asturians Muño Gustioz, the Aragonese knights of Sancho Ramírez and Pedro I, and the Portuguese followers of the count of Coimbra and Montemayor. . . . The fact that knights from so many parts of the Peninsula fought under his banner renders the Cid's campaigns real campaigns for Spain. But neither love of his home land [Castile] nor his wider partiotism [i.e., his Hispanic nationalism] made the Cid narrow-minded. The appointment of a Cluniac monk to the see of Valencia showed that he welcomed Western ideas as an influence that would lift Spain out of her former isolation" (*CS*, pp. 431 - 32).

The Cid's large-mindedness broadens Alfonso's mind in the poem if not in history: Alfonso sends summons to Léon and Santiago, to the Portuguese and Galicians, to Carrión and Santiago, and to Castile, warning the summoned that ". . . whoever should not come to the [Toledo] court, he would hold no longer as his vassal" (2982). Through Alfonso's peremptory order we learn, therefore, that the men who attended the court came from all parts of Spain; that they represented members of the highest and middle nobility (*cuemdes* and *infanzones*); and that they came to the imperial city to witness the resolution of an issue that went beyond mere personal considerations. The issue transcended personal interests because the marriages of the Cid's daughters, the unfortunate consequences of which caused the court to be convoked, had been arranged by Alfonso as a reward for the vassal whose services to the country had been invaluable. This first marriage, which may or may not have been fictitious, a marriage to which the Cid reluctantly acceded, was, then, an act of royal policy promoted by Alfonso to exalt Rodrigo. The second, much more glorious marriage, which did have a historical basis, and with which Alfonso had nothing to do, indirectly raised the relatively lowly *infanzón* to the level of royalty, because through it the native of the insignificant village of Vivar became a kinsman of the kings of Spain. When the messengers from Navarre and Aragón arrive at Toledo to ask for the hands of the Cid's daughters, they address the conqueror and master of Valencia as if he were a potentate; they approach him rightly taking him for what he was, a great political figure — as a matter of fact the greatest at that Court — a figure whose fame, as the poet says, ". . . goes re-echoing even beyond the sea" (1156), whose case was important enough for the Cortes of Spain to be summoned, a subject whom the king received with the highest honors, and a figure before whose presence Alfonso and the highest nobility rose to their feet when he made his grand entrance at the Cortes.

XI *The Religious Element: Conflicting Views*

Owing to the influence of the anti-Cidian prejudices propagated by R. Dozy, it became the fashion among scholarly circles during several generations to deny that the Cid of history was motivated by the spirit of Reconquest. Menéndez Pidal's epoch making *La España del Cid*, in our opinion one of the most thorough and remarkable works of historical research of our times, should have laid to rest the black legend spread wide by the brilliant and prestigious Dutch Arabist. It is true that Pidal's findings are today generally though not universally accepted. The cidophobia initiated by the Arab historians, nurtured by the Catalan Jesuit Juan Francisco Masdeu, and made respectable by Dozy, is no longer virulent, but it still persists, in certain quarters, in the form of an antiheroic interpretation of the poem. According to Gerald Brenan, the *PMC*, unlike the French chansons de geste, is totally devoid of the crusading spirit. The Cid's driving motive, he insists, is to acquire *averes*, that is, lands and money.[36] And in an article dealing chiefly with the religious element in the *PMC*, Carmelo Gariano holds that it lacks the ideal of a Holy War which inspires the poet of *La Chanson de Roland*. "The motive of the Cid's enterprises," he says , "is territorial conquest and the booty to satisfy his instinct for domination and to restitute his honor in the eyes of the king. . . ." Gariano

does not see in the Spanish expression *moros y cristianos* more than
an idiom meaning "everybody." Concerning the expression *la limpia cristiandat* ("clean Christendom"), he affirms that "it does not
at all indicate a Christian world as opposed to a Moslem world, but
is a simple designation of Castile without religious implications." As
for the Cid's attitude toward the Arabs, he assumes that because the
Cid and the Spanish Moors were friendly toward each other,[37] he
did not consider the fanatical Almoravide invaders a grave danger
to Christendom. Gariano does not fail to notice that the king of
Morocco is the Cid's enemy (laisse 88), but he does ignore the lines
in which the Christians fervently express their joy on receiving the
news that at last Valencia has a bishop. In support of his viewpoint
Gariano quotes the opinions of Dozy, Fitzmaurice-Kelly, Northup,
and Spitzer, all of them opposed to those of Menéndez Pidal, but he
completely ignores the latter.[38]

Today only those who disregard Menéndez Pidal's reconstruction
of eleventh-century Spain can deny that the historical Cid's conquest of Valencia was wanting in religious motivation. And only by
failing to grasp the meaning of the poem as a whole and by failing
also to take into account certain key passages, is it possible for
modern Cidian criticism to deny that the Cid of poetry is close to the
Cid of history. In defense of this judgment we will again depend in
part on Menéndez Pidal for documentation, but first we will reca-
pitulate the argument of an American Hispanist whose knowledge
of medieval Spain is wide and deep.

In an important article, Thomas R. Hart, Jr. [39] studies the poem as
a product of its times, that is, he considers it within the framework of
medieval values in the Christian world. In Hart's opinion it was the
crusading spirit of the age that motivated the Cid to take Valencia.
He supports this view by showing that the Spanish war against the
African enemies of the faith was equated with the pilgrimages to
Jerusalem by the highest ecclesiastical authority. In 1089 Pope Ur-
ban II offered those who contributed their personal effort or their
wealth to the restoration of Tarragona indulgences equal to those
given persons who made a pilgrimage to Jerusalem. And in 1100 and
1101 Pope Pascual II, fearing that the Almoravides would subdue
the west, forbade Spanish knights and clerics to abandon Alfonso's
kingdom for the crusade to Jerusalem, granting indulgence for their
sins to those who remained to fight in Spain. Another significant
aspect of the Cid's campaign against Valencia as it is related in the
Cantar, is the absolution which Bishop Jerome, following the exam-

ple of Bishop Turpin in *La Chanson de Roland*, gives the soldiers who perish in battle. Finally, with respect to the Cid's much discussed acquisition of wealth and possessions, Hart insists that we must not see in Rodrigo a self-seeking, ambitious man without special interest in the high cause he serves for, being a warrior, he must meet the material demands of war. And if the Campeador's success is measured by his material gains the reason is, above all, because his success pleases God as the means by which His Will is done on earth. Hence, Hart points out, every victory won by the Campeador and his men is always acknowledged to have been made possible by God's help (792 - 93; 1102 - 03; 1118; 1157 - 58; 1334).

Having reviewed the controversial arguments of others regarding the religious question, we will now set forth our own views.

In a literal sense the word *reconquista* means "the recovery of Spanish territory held by Moslems." The Cid's successful military activity culminating with the conquest of Valencia agrees, therefore, with the letter of the word. Does it also agree with its spirit, in the larger sense of fighting zealously for the preservation of the Faith? There cannot be any doubt about the answer if we take into account the events that occurred after 1086. Before that year, relations between Christians and Moors, in spite of Christian domination and exploitation of the Taifas, had been, on the whole, relatively harmonious. However, thereafter the sinister Yusuf and his African hosts gave the intense Christian effort to resist and vanquish them the character of a Holy War. Is this reflected in the poem? It is, implicitly and, although to a lesser extent, explicitly. We agree with the following judgment of Menéndez y Pelayo: "The sentiments which motivated the heroes of that kind of poetry [cantares de gesta and more specifically the *PMC*] are as simple as their actions. They were undoubtedly produced by the great impulse of the Reconquest; but we must not think they felt it in abstract terms which lend themselves to a modern historical synthesis or to ostentatious discourse; instead of thinking in such terms, the men of the early medieval age derived their strength not from conceptualization of a lofty ideal, but from the continuous struggle for the possession of concrete and real things."[40] In the light of this penetrating statement, we must give full weight to the many deeds and to the few but sufficient words which confirm it.

The magnitude and enormous difficulty of the Cid's accomplishment is conveyed in the following lines: "And I shall stay in Valencia, whose conquest has cost me so much. / It would be a great folly to abandon her now" (1470 - 71).

The Cid could have spoken more hyperbolically, but his *mesura* restrained him. According to the great Aragonese historian Jerónimo de Zurita (1512 - 1580), the conquest of Valencia was the most extraordinary achievement ever performed in Spain by anyone but a king (*EC*, p. 609). It would be unjust to Rodrigo to suppose that what he fears if he leaves Valencia is the possible loss of its tribute. "Dozy," says Menéndez Pidal, "in likening the conquest of Valencia to a mere marauding expedition, is greatly in error" (*EC*, p. 609). And having conquered Valencia, we should add that the Cid's efforts to remain in control were exerted to keep it from falling into the hands of the Almoravides. This was the reason why the Campeador thought it would be a great folly to abandon the city whose conquest had cost him so much. The hero's true motive is revealed before winning it when the juglar says: "He [the Cid] would now lay siege to Valencia to give it to the Christians" (1911). According to John H. R. Polt this line does not express any religious motive on the part of the Cid because in the preceding lines the poet says that the Campeador promises those who will join him the opportunity to get rich.[41] Like Gariano, Polt admits only the acceptations "people" or "followers" for the word *cristianos* (1191) to support his point of view.[42] We, on the contrary, without denying that the Cid takes advantage of the human desire for gain to attract recruits, reject the simplistic notion that the only thing he offers them is wealth; he also offers them the opportunity to recover, for those who profess the religion of Christ, the city so long possessed by those who professed the religion of Mohammed. To reduce the term *cristianos* to one single acceptation is to ignore the semantic shades of meaning of a key word which, as well as designating "everybody," connotes the physical, psychological, and social circumstances of the time and place that determined its usage. The same criticism may be made of Polt's giving to the phrase "Moors and Christians" the single meaning of "everybody." Even if we admitted this acceptation and no other for the twinned expression, the fact remains that it reflects the way of life of a society in which two religions coexisted sometimes in relative harmony, at other times in strife. One of the reasons so many recruits sallied to the Cid's cause is given by none other than the Arab historian Ibn Alcama: "A great number joined him," wrote the first of the cidophobes, "*because they learned that he wished to invade Moorish territory"* (my emphasis).[43] Ibn Alcama did *not* say "because they wanted to get rich." In light of this testimony given by a contemporary *enemy* of the Campeador, we may conclude that the Christians of the poem to whom the Cid wishes to give Valencia respond to his call not only on account of promised gains but also because they were bent upon recovering for Christian Spain a great city so long held by Moors. Confirming the words of line 1191, the Campeador says to Minaya, immediately after seizing the great prize: "I wish to ordain a bishopric in the lands of Valencia" (1299). And when Jerome of Périgord is appointed to the see, the poet exclaims: "God, how great was the rejoicing in all Christendom/for in the lands of Valencia there was a lord bishop!" (1305 - 6).

Precisely: in *all* Christendom.

Later, when the fighting bishop accompanies the Cid and his army to confront the Almoravides and helps defeat them, the Campeador gives him a great share of the spoils, so great, that the juglar says: "The spoils that fell to him [the bishop] also were enormous" (1796). Such generosity signifies more than the joy of sharing good things with an invaluable ally; it is also a concrete acknowledgment of the bishop's importance as a living symbol of the Reconquest and corresponds to the liberality with which the Cid endowed the new episcopal seat in 1098. In the diploma setting forth the terms of the endowment, its fervent exordium declares the Cid to be heaven-sent to propagate the religion of Christ and to avenge the Christians' long servitude to the Moslems. This diploma contains one of the very few extant signatures of Rodrigo: *Ego Ruderico, simul cum conjuge mea, afirmo oc quod superius est (EC*, p. 551).

It has been said that the religious motive was weak in the Spain of the Cid, where Moors were not hated but admired.[44] Let us consider what is true and what is false in this simplistic generalization. It is true that Spanish Arabs had become lax in their religious observance. However in 1086 Yusuf and his holymen brought back an intense fanaticism which fanned the never diminished zeal of a peninsular Moslem minority that had always disapproved of the softness and hedonism of their coreligionists. As for the Spanish people and their leaders never, in spite of political rivalries, had they felt the unifying force of religion as strongly as when they faced this new threat. The second declaration we have cited, namely, that Moors were not hated but admired also needs to be rectified. Certainly, in the Spain of the Cid the culture of the Arabs was much more refined than that of the Christians and therefore admired. In the poem the friendship between the wealthy and — it may be assumed — cultured Moor Abengalbón was representative of the harmonious relationship on the human plane of the two races. But this *amigo de paz,* "peaceful friend," (1464, 1528, 2636) of the hero stands for a Moorish element radically different from that personified by the outsider Ibn Yusuf Teshufin, a deadly enemy against whose type of warfare the Cid was the only successful defender. Valencia fell to the Almoravides three years after the Cid's death. Not until 1238 did another heroic figure, King James I of Aragón, recover Valencia for good. It was fitting and symbolic that James' favorite sword was Tizón, which the Cid had taken from Búcar; he preferred it because it "brought fortune and success to those who used it" (*EC*, p. 616). We have said that the use of this sword by a Christian king almost a century and a half after the Cid's death was symbolic because it represented concretely the enduring power of the Cid's heroic precedent and of his exemplification of a changed attitude toward Spanish Moslems who threw in their lot with the Africans (*EC*, p. 636). Whether the poem was composed in part as early as 1110 or in its entirety as late as 1140 or even much later, the juglar and his living audience celebrated the victories of "clean Christendom" well aware of what these victories meant. Neither the simple style of the poet nor the moderation of the Castilians of the heroic age made for prolix expression of the religious and patriotic feelings which moved them. But what they say sparingly and, above all, what they do, are enough to convey unequivocally the religious and patriotic import of the poem.

CHAPTER 3

Composition and Authorship

I Oralist Doctrine

MILMAN Parry and his disciple Albert B. Lord, in Yugoslavia, and other scholars elsewhere,[1] have observed firsthand a basic phenomenon of the composition of epic songs: the modern singer of tales does not depend on a written text to memorize the tale which he delivers before a living audience. In fact, he cannot use a text because he cannot read nor write. For this reason he must rely on his auditory memory, an extraordinary memory developed during a long period of training. The outstanding cases of poets who have exhibited a phenomenal development of their auditory memory would be incredible without the testimony of impeccable investigators. Lord adduces, among other cases, that of the most gifted of all South Slavic singers, Avdo Mededović. Avdo hears the recital of a two-thousand-line song once and then elaborates his own twelve-thousand-line version of it.[2] The most extraordinary cases are those of two singers, one from Uzbek and the other from Kirghis, whose memories were capable of retaining songs of twenty thousand and two hundred thousand lines respectively.[3] Singers of this sort cannot be conceived of as possessing text-bound memories intent on reproducing memorized matter verbatim, like the modern actor who notwithstanding the wide histrionic margin he enjoys as an interpreter, is nevertheless no more than an oral and mimic executant of the playwright's script. The epic singer is, in spite of his anonymity, an independent creator, a recreator, an improvisor within the strict discipline of traditional verbal, thematic, and narrative techniques. If the song, his or another's, is exceptionally good and especially appealing to the public, its traditional life may be extended over a long period of time. Hence, by its very nature oral transmission does not permit identical reproduction of a particular song, whether it be recreated by the same singer or by different singers.

It follows that the very life of an oft-repeated and enduring song depends on the variants through which a given oral poet vitalizes it; its form is protean in varying degrees, elaborately embroidered and reshaped by the improvising bent of certain modern singers of exceptional merit like Avdo Mededović, but moderately changed by the medieval juglares who adhered more closely to original versions but not so closely as to completely forego amplification, ornamentation, or more emphatic treatments of certain parts.[4]

The auditory memory of the oral poet largely relies on powerful mnemonic aids: verbal formulas, stylistic patterns, formulas of narrative mode,[5] clichés of common speech. Therefore, formulaic style is inseparable from epic. (We use the term "formulaic" in a general sense to designate all of the above mentioned categories, and the terms "formulary," "formulistic," to designate verbal formulas.) Lord affirms that oral poetry of formulaic style, "even the most mediocre, is as much a part of the tradition of oral epic singing as is Homer, its most talented representative." Homer, declares Lord, "represents all singers of tales from time immemorial and unrecorded to the present."[6] And his teacher, Milman Parry, who in his first book, written within the walls of his study, insisted only on the traditionality of Homer's style, was led to conclude on the strength of his fieldwork among oral poets in Yugoslavia, that a formulistic style such as that of Homer must not only be traditional but also must be oral.[7] Parry's position implies Lord's explicit declaration to the effect that what is true of Homer is also true of all epic traditional poets of all times and places.

In the light of this doctrine and in view of the formulaic techniques of the *Cantar de Mio Cid*, may we assume that it is an oral poem pure and simple? We believe that before venturing an opinion we should consider (1) the theory, which still persists, of monastic — and therefore learned — influence in the composition of the poem; (2) the role of "written tradition" which, according to Menéndez Pidal, functioned as effectively as oral tradition; (3) the nature of the medieval juglar, and the possibility of equating him with modern singers of tales; (4) the three Lordian tests, namely, formulas, enjambment, and themes, in regard to (a) their validity and (b) their application to the *Poema de Mio Cid*.

II *Theories of Monastic Influence*

Conjectures about monastic influence in the composition of the *PMC* date back to a series of articles published by Jules

Cornu between 1881 and 1898,[8] and to an 1898 study by Rudolph
Beer.[9] In the middle of the present century the possible influence
of Cardeña in the composition of the poem has been proposed
by the Oxford University Hispanist P. M. Russell in two important articles. In the first[10] Russell affirms that in view of the
attention given legal matters and lay documents in the PMC, it
is possible that a clerical author composed it.[11] This literate
author heeded the authority of the written word, probed archives to find the forgotton name of a legal expert attached to
the Cid, and familiarized himself with legal matters which could
not have been generally known. In his second article Russell
suggests with less firmness that the "CMC, in the state in which
it has come down to us, possibly shows more signs of the influence of Cardeña than accepted theories allow. . . ." He adds,
"an attitude of Pyrrhonism is probably the right one to adopt
towards this question."[12]

The validity of Russell's arguments depends on his late dating of
the poem. A date later than 1140 — the one proposed by Menéndez
Pidal — is fundamental to his thesis because only after the up-
heavals of 1142, the year during which Alfonso VII made known his
intention of turning over the monastery of Cardeña to the Abbot of
Cluny, were the threatened monks, once free of the danger of dis-
possession, able to dedicate themselves to the task of recording
Cardeña's legendary role in the history of Castile. The Cid's connection with the monastery of course became one of its important
legends. And if a Cardeña monk had anything to do with the composition of the parts of the poem dealing with his institution's
hospitality to the hero and his family, he could not have made his
contribution until the Cardeña-Cid legend was recorded, namely,
after 1142.

We will not here attempt a searching discussion of Professor
Russell's arguments, all of them adduced with learning, skill, and
acumen. Suffice it to say that he does not include in his reasoning a
consideration of *style* (apart from content) as an indication of
authorship. Is the style that of cleric? Of a juglar? Does it reveal
both clerical and juglaresque characteristics? From our point of view
the stylistic evidence is more fundamental and conclusive than the
historical evidence, because the latter abounds in unknowns. These
force us at every step to choose between one or another hypothesis,
none of which is absolutely verifiable.

III *Monastic Influence and Written and Oral Tradition in the Theory of Menéndez Pidal*

In the first volume of his monumental edition of the *CMC*, Menéndez Pidal flatly rejects the theory of monastic composition, but, like Russell, he does not take style into account. Therefore, notwithstanding the importance of his arguments against the thesis of monastic composition, we will not discuss them; we will instead review that part of his writings dealing more explicitly with the problem which concerns us, namely, the function of traditional style in the composition and transmission of epic songs.

Traditional epic style, according to Menéndez Pidal, is propagated both by written and oral tradition: from pen to pen, so to speak, as well as from mouth to mouth. Both the poet who composes orally and the poet who composes or transmits a song in writing react to the "poetic tension," which exerts its force on the agents of tradition: poet vis-à-vis poet, poets vis-à-vis the people. Another, more exact term which we think may be used for "poetic tension" is "traditional empathy," that is, the dynamic, mutually responsive contacts interacting generation after generation between the "initial signified and signifier" and the "final signified and signifier." These are linguistic terms, introduced in Hispanic criticism by Dámaso Alonso, designating (a) the meaning (interior form) and (b) the acoustic conveyors of the meaning (exterior form) on the part of the speaker and on the part of the listener. Both the poet who composes orally and the poet who does so in writing are governed by a twofold awareness: on the one hand, they are aware of tradition as a shared treasure that is transmitted by poets past and present, on the other they are aware of tradition as an individual possession permitting renovation and recreation.

"Traditional matter that is preserved in manuscripts," says Menéndez Pidal, "presents characteristics that are identical to that which is purely oral."[13]

What these words, written in 1924, do not make clear, is whether or not in such manuscripts a juglar writes down his own song in the act of composition. Put more simply: does the epic poet compose as he writes? It seems that what Pidal was thinking of was rather the process of diffusion and recording than of actual composition, because on the same page he declares that the diffusion is mixed, that is, it is effected by oral and written transmission, although "essentially *it has to be oral* and sung" (my emphasis). In spite of

the words I have emphasized, the sentence in which they are found
is not devoid of ambiguity. The eminent scholar had not as yet made
a clear choice between oral and written composition. His position
was also equivocal thirteen years before and twenty-nine years later.
In his 1908 edition of the *CMC* and in his *Romancero hispánico* of
1953 he frequently stated that juglares memorized the long poems
which they sang and that they memorized from manuscripts; in
Poesía juglaresca y juglares[14] he repeatedly says that the *PMC* was
written, without specifying whether the manuscript he has in mind
is a dictated text or an on-the-spot transcription of an oral performance. Neither did Pidal, during these years, advance any
hypothesis about the kind of writer who might have been the author
or the copyist of the manuscript.

Not until 1965, with the Yugoslav singers in mind, does Pidal, in a
lecture read before the Real Academia de Buenas Letras of
Barcelona,[15] show full awareness of the "extraordinary powers of
memory which abound to an astonishing degree among those
singers who dedicate themselves to oral transmission."[16] For the first
time in his writings — as far as I know — he leaves no doubt that a
primitive text of the *PMC* (not Per Abad's copy of 1307 but a lost
manuscript of the end of the twelfth or the beginning of the
thirteenth century) was dictated by the juglar who knew thoroughly
the lines of the old poem and who through various repetitions introduced revisions, improvements, and additions (p. 233).

The oral memory which preserved this *Urtext* until the beginning
of the fourteenth century was a most faithful and conservative
memory, comparable to that of the medieval clerics who knew the
New Testament to the letter, a memory that was very different from
that of the Yugoslav poets who "improvise a new version of the
original every time they sing it . . ." (p. 223).

Obviously Pidal is here referring to the transmission, rather than
to the composition, of the *PMC* as a whole. Why does he overlook
the initial creative act? A partial explanation is provided by his implied belief that the poem had fairly small beginnings, in other
words, that it blossomed into full-blown shape over a period of time.
"Every hero," he says, "first becomes famous on the strength of his
newsworthy exploits" (p. 215), those of the Cid being his victories
over proud and arrogant counts, victories which were celebrated in a
short Latin poem, the *Carmen Campidoctoris*, known to have been
composed during the Cid's lifetime and, it may be assumed, in short

epic songs in the vernacular, orally composed "al calor de los hechos," that is, while the celebrated events were still fresh in the public consciousness.

IV *Written and Oral Tradition According to the Oralist School*

The oralist school does not even bother to consider the hypothesis of clerical authorship and it roundly rejects the theory of written composition for which Menéndez Pidal made allowance before 1965. It also rejects Bowra's "transitional" theory. According to the eminent author of *Heroic Poetry*, writing not only aided, it also perfected, Homer's style. Writing, furthermore, facilitated a transition from improvised oral poetry to poetry which up to a certain point depends on writing.[17] But according to Lord, such a transition is not feasible because the techniques and mental processes of the writer and the oral poet are mutually exclusive: "The written technique," Lord says, ". . . is not compatible with the oral technique, and the two could not possibly combine, to form another, a third, a 'transitional' technique."[18]

Lord bases his categorical conclusion on his observations of oral composition in Yugoslavia; he suggests that even very exceptional singers who have learned to write confirm his conclusion, because when they are asked to write down a song they try but do so with great difficulty; what happens is that, when attempting to record in permanent written form the ideas which they express spontaneously within habitual metrical and melodic units during an oral performance, they are shackled by the unaccustomed means of expression. Metrical and musical rhythm are all important mnemonic aids whose impetus depends on oral performance. This impetus is halted when the poet abandons his oral and musical medium and undertakes instead the use of the pen, which for him is awkward and unnatural.

V *The Modern Singer of Tales and the Medieval Juglar*

Are the modern and medieval singers of tales comparable? We should, first of all, note certain great differences: (1) To begin with, we should emphasize an obvious fact — the social milieu of the epic poet has changed enormously; formerly the juglar addressed himself to all social classes and the singer of heroic songs especially to the highest aristocracy. His modern counterpart, the South Slavic

singer, addresses a predominantly peasant audience. (2) For this
reason modern singers, with rare exceptions, have been reduced to a
single class of plebeian entertainers. In medieval times there were
many kinds of juglares, from the roguish street singers to highly
placed poets who chanted heroic songs in the palaces of kings. (3)
The singer of this century, no matter how important his cultural
function, has been forced to yield to modern social conditions; but
the juglars of old were the most effective informants of traditional
matter in society. (4) As Menéndez Pidal asserts in his 1965
study, "the Slavic-Turkish oral poem is closely related to the fictionalized
folk-tale . . ."[19] in contrast to old epics reflecting history, tradition,
or legend.

So much for what we think are the chief differences. We will now
list the fundamental similarities: (1) The role which from time immemorial, from Homer to Avdo Mededović, the singer of tales has
played as the conveyor of tradition either in the first stage as in the
PMC, which celebrates a hero's recent exploits, or in a very late
stage when the patina of centuries surrounds epic with a mythic
aura. (2) The medieval and modern audiences are very different, but
what remains unchanged in principle is the relationship between the
singer and his audience during the act of oral performance; this is a
critical, dynamic relationship even though we make allowance for
the distraction of an unstable audience some of whose members
move about and come and go — distractions which actually require
the singer to exert his utmost effort of concentration. (3) With more
caution we venture the hypothesis that medieval singers, like
modern singers, were unlettered. However, whether or not a given
medieval juglar could read and write, he thought and performed
orally. (4) The medieval juglar and the modern South Slavic singers
observed by Parry, Lord, and others had at their command, thanks
to their remarkable auditory memories, a great repertoire of epic formulas, of verbal formulas, of clichés of current speech, and of
narrative techniques. (5) Because of the nature of oral transmission
resulting not from an effort of rote memory but from a disciplined
capacity for recreation, there is no such thing as a fixed living text,
for the very life of a song pulsates with variants which may differ, in
the case of conservative renditions, in matters of detail or, in the case
of bold departures, in degrees of elaboration, ornamentation,
modification, and alteration. The more conservative manifestation
of this phenomenon has been demonstrated by Menéndez Pidal in

his study of some six hundred versions of the ballad "Gerineldo," all of which vary from each other in minor ways without being essentially altered in their traditional content. What Pidal showed in connection with a short ballad he thinks is true also of long epics, which in his 1965 study he unequivocally calls "orally transmitted poetry and therefore [with respect to variants] identical to the short song."[20] (6) The most fundamental similarity of all oral poems since Homer is formulaic style.

If this last proposition is true, the abundance of formulas in the *Poema de Mio Cid* is proof that the poet, or rather the poets who composed and recomposed it, reacted to the same cultural and creative imperatives which have governed all oral poets. We may therefore believe with a considerable amount of confidence that the *PMC* is clearly an oral composition (a) if it contains a proportion of formulas and formulaic language comparable to that of traditional Spanish ballads the oral character of which is indisputable, (b) if formulaic style in the full sense of the word characterizes epic to a much greater extent than it characterizes written medieval compositions, and (c) if oral techniques are different from written techniques.

VI *Lord's Three Tests*

The questions we have raised bring us now to Lord's three tests of oral composition, applied to our poem: themes, enjambment (i. e., run-on lines) and, the most important, formulas.

In the *Poema de Mio Cid*, which poetically narrates fairly recent events, themes are not as abundant as in epics that relate legendary events of a remote past or in modern oral tales replete with folkloric motifs. Nevertheless three of the most common epic themes form an integral part of the poem's structure: the family quarrel, the vengeance brought about by the quarrel, and the assembly. But beyond these manifestations of what Lord calls "thematic attraction," thematic and mythically potential elements emanate from the poem[21] in a more subtle way. We perceive myth in the making in connection with one of the Cid's swords, even though it cannot be grouped with the magic swords of Germanic and French traditions as we have demonstrated elsewhere.[22] But what previously escaped our attention notwithstanding its significance as an embryonic beginning of myth, is that in laisse 151 (a laisse is an epic stanza of varying length with uniform assonant rhyme) the sword Colada ap-

proaches the supernatural by terrifying one of the villainous Infantes of Carrión as it flashes its dazzling light upon the duelling
field.

Parataxis — the placing of related clauses, etc., in a series without
the use of connecting words — is perhaps more characteristic of epic
and ballad style than of any other form of literary expression,
because epic formulas, the formulas of current speech, the
repititious expressions, etc., which are the juglar's stock in trade,
consist of self-contained syntactic units of expression limited to a
certain number of syllables by the exigencies of exact meter in
ballads and of irregular but not rampant meter in the old Castilian
epic. The paratactic style of epic, for obvious reasons, does not lend
itself to enjambment; it may therefore be said that a minimal
proportion of run-on lines is the hallmark of epic and ballad style.

The only study of enjambment in the *PMC* is that of Orest R.
Ochrymowycz.[23] The results of his analysis are as follows: (1) Lines
that form a completely independent grammatical unit total 64 percent; lines that belong to a string of what might be called "verbal
beads" (unperiodic enjambment) total 28.8 percent. In unperiodic
enjambment metrically neat segments of a thought sequence follow
one another line by line with pauses between lines. Only a minimal
proportion of lines of the poem, 7.2 percent, exemplifies the modern
concept of enjambment, namely, what Parry calls "necessary enjambment." Within this percentage only eight-three lines, 2.2 percent, may be classed under the category of "strong necessary enjambment," that is, cases in which no pause whatsoever is possible
between one line and the next. This kind of enjambment occurs two
times less frequently in the *PMC* than in the oral poems studied by
Parry, a significant fact, because, we repeat, the low frequency of
necessary enjambment is a special characteristic of oral style.

We have analyzed for good measure a sampling of enjambment in
the highly regular *mester de clerecía*, since, on first reading, this
type of medieval clerical verse conveys the impression of a style
which is as paratactic as that of the *mester de juglaría*, that is, the
"manner of the minstrel-poets." Confirmation of this impression
would, of course, invalidate Lord's enjambment test. Our analysis of
three hundred lines of the *Libro de Alexandre*, whose anonymous
clerical author boasted about his *curso rimado* ("rhymed sequence")
and his *sílabas cuntadas* ("exactly counted syllables"), shows, however, that necessary enjambment is three times more frequent in
the *Alexandre* than in the *PMC*.[24]

VII   *Formulistic Content*

At this point we will consider only verbal formulas, those which comply with Parry's definition, namely, ". . . a group of words which is regularly employed under the same metrical conditions to express a given essential idea."[25] There are other kinds of formulas, both verbal and nonverbal,[26] which an all-embracing study of formulary content should include. We do not do so here, because what particularly interests us for the time being is to compare the frequency of verbal formulas in the *PMC* with that of the only kind, verbal formulas, which Ruth House Webber has exhaustively studied in the *Romancero*.[27]

In a fifty-page monograph[28] and in the second, 1972, edition of *El arte juglaresco* . . . (pp. 332 - 82), we have listed and analyzed the fifteen-hundred-odd verbal formulas in the 3,730-line-long poem, each line consisting of two half-lines or hemistiches. These correspond to the odd and even octosyllabic ballad line, each even line rhyming with the same assonance throughout a given ballad. Since Mrs. Webber's final statistical results in her valuable study of formulistic diction in the *Romancero* are based on the octosyllable, we will present ours on the basis of the hemistich. According to Mrs. Webber's calculation, 10 percent of the 22,210 lines she has examined are formulistic. Our results show that 17 percent of the poem's 7,460 hemistiches are formulistic.

It may be objected that our results are not comparable because we consider the occurence of the same three or more habitual expressions sufficient to classify them as formulistic. Mrs. Webber, on the other hand, has been satisfied with no less than five or more occurrences. However, we do not think the objection would be valid because the same minimum of occurrences should not apply to 7,500 epic hemistiches as to 22,000 ballad lines. Only a discrepancy showing a considerably lower proportion of formulas in the *PMC* would be important. What is significant is that the traditional Spanish ballad, the oral composition of which is indisputable, meets Lord's principal test. *The Poema de Mio Cid*, whose oral composition has not been generally accepted, also meets that test.

VIII   *The Weight of Evidence Favoring Oral Composition*

Finally, in light of our exposition we present certain conclusions. Is there monastic influence in the *PMC*? If, with Lord, we consider written and oral composition incompatible, the cleric accustomed to write within the lonely walls of his *scriptorium* could not express himself with the spontaneity of a juglar who has instantaneous command of his formulistic techniques and who performs under conditions of poetic tension, reacting to the stimulus of a live audience and to the traditional example of poet-minstrels past and present.

If a cleric did compose the poem it would have had to be one turned public entertainer. This would not have been impossible. Such clerics, to be sure, were not generally true juglares but, for the most part, persons who, having left their Order, became vulgar goliardic jesters and minstrels. However, in 1160, only two or perhaps a few more decades after the composition of the *PMC*, a certain Peire Rogier of Alvernia, a learned canon of Vermont, abandoned his canonry and became a wandering minstrel, traveling from court to court, including the courts of Castile and Aragón.[29] Could not such a cleric have recited heroic songs? Could his Cardeña counterpart be conceivable? We think this could be possible but not probable. We know through the documented history of *juglaría* ("minstrelsy") that there were juglares who frequented royal and seignorial courts where they could have become familiar with the activities of chancellors, notaries, and scribes.[30] Besides those wandering poets, we should keep in mind "those who were supported by and paid in seignorial households, as well as those attached to the palaces of kings since ancient times. . . ."[31] On the strength of the evidence we have that juglares frequented and, indeed, formed part of the households of kings and lords, we may reasonably suppose that even an unlettered juglar could have acquired through his contact with lettered officials in chancelleries, the kind of knowledge which, according to Russell was within the reach only of the latter. Is "written tradition" identical to "oral tradition" as Menéndez Pidal believed in 1924 and as late as 1953? We prefer to subscribe to his unequivocal conclusion of 1965: the written texts of epics were dictated texts.

In conclusion we affirm that the incompatibility of oral and written techniques observed among Slavic and Turkish singers of tales has been definitively proved. It is true that this incompatibility cannot be positively demonstrated with respect to the composition of medieval epics, but we believe it may be inferred by analogy. If our deduction is valid, the formulistic style, the minimal proportion of enjambment, and the thematic content of the poem all tend to prove its oral composition.

IX *Authorship*

In an intricately dialectical and forceful monograph published in 1961, more than fifty years after his monumental three-volume edition of the *PMC*, Ramón Menéndez Pidal declares that quite contrary to his first opinions, he eventually arrived at the conclusion that the poem was the product of more than one author.[32] He bases his definitive thesis of dual authorship on a searching examination of the poem's historical content. This content is remarkably accurate in the parts he attributes to an early juglar from San Esteban de Gormaz, who narrates events shortly after they took place; but it is erroneous in parts which he attributes to a juglar from Medinaceli, who reworked his predecessor's version much later. Pidal notes, in addition, differences in style, as we have.[33] Considered apart from their poetic function, the stylistic differences might be ascribed to separate authors. Nevertheless, we confess that given the undeniable organic unity of the poem, the thesis of two separate authors, each exhibiting his own distinct style, would be aesthetically repugnant to us if, in order to defend it, one would have to grant a concomitant structural and stylistic dichotomy.

Menéndez Pidal does not suppose any such thing in spite of the fact that in his examination of positive data and historical details he finds the early juglar much more accurate than the later one. Consideration of these divergences is important for the solution of problems of the literary history of the poem but not for an aesthetic appreciation of it. Menéndez Pidal himself suggests this:

In our *Mio Cid* we observe, finally, how two authors, so distinct, so divergent as far as epic verism is concerned, are found to be very much akin at the level of literary creation. The poetic genius of the author from San Esteban de Gormaz attracts and gives impetus to the genius from Medinaceli who creates his predecessor's work anew. This continuity of inspiration in collective art through spans of time is a great truth, a great aesthetic phenomenon which modern traditional criticism observes, affirms, and proposes . . . : continuity of inspiration based on common taste, purpose, and cultural milieu.[34]

This artistic affinity, which manifests itself through shared traditional techniques, explains why variations of stylistic devices may be explained by showing that they are poetically felicitous, in-

deed, even poetically necessary, rather than by alleging dual
authorship. Such variants undoubtedly may reflect, within a general
resemblance, distinct stylistic inclinations on the part of different
poets. However, if, as in the *PMC*, these poets are poetically akin
and equally talented as Pidal rightly claims, their differences are
never incompatible; on the contrary, they merge and they complement each other. The collaboration of oral poets cannot be compared to that of modern writers. The latter work together at the
same time. The former assimilated the song of another juglar and
recreated it independently. This individual recreation of a work of
traditional art is corollary to the continuity of inspiration which
Pidal emphasizes, a continuity which implies repeated renderings.

We conclude, therefore, that it is inevitable to think of *more than
one* author as far as the extended traditional life of an epic composition is concerned. But with respect to a particular rendering of such
a composition it is equally inevitable to think of *only one* juglar.

In the extant *Mio Cid* the original composition of an early juglar is
assimilated and enhanced with unusual success by a later juglar who
makes his predecessor's creation his very own. On the whole their
techniques are so well integrated that it is impossible to differentiate
unequivocally between them. Nevertheless, one device of epic style,
namely, parallel series or laisses, is handled so much more
elaborately in at least one instance of the last part of the poem than
in the first part, that a comparison of said laisses in our opinion may
demonstrate dual authorship.

X *Two Styles in Two Pairs of Parallel Series*

In comparing a pair of parallel series (laisses 50 and 51, which will
be designated A, A') in the first cantar with another pair in the third
cantar (laisses 128 and 129, hereafter B, B'), we will note striking
differences in the disposition and elaboration of the stylistic
elements.

What distinguishes the style of the above pairs of laisses is the
regular and symmetric conformity of the corresponding elements in
A, A', versus the irregularity and asymmetry of the corresponding
elements in B, B':

A		A'	
¡Dios, cómmo fo alegre	926	¡Dios, cómmo es alegre	930
todo aquel fonssado		la barba vellida,	
que Minaya Álvar Fáñez	927	que Álbar Fáñez	931
assí era llegado		pagó las mill missas,	

diziéndoles saludes	928	*e quel dixo saludes*	932
de primos e de hermanos,		*de su mugier e de sus fijas!*
e de sus compañas,	929	*¡Dios, cómmo fo el Cid pagado*	933
aquellas que avien dexado!		*e fizo grant alegría!*
		¡Ya Álvar Fáñez, bivades	934
		muchos dias!"

God, how they rejoiced, all
that company/that Minaya Álvar Fáñez had returned, thus/
bringing them greetings from
cousins and brothers/and
from the families they had
left behind!

God, how he rejoices, he, bearded
handsomely,/because Álvar Fáñez
had paid the thousand masses/
and had brought him greetings from
his wife and his daughters!/God,
the Cid was pleased and rejoiced!/
"Ah, Álvar Fáñez, may you live
many days!"

In the above pair the arrangement of syntagms (sentence units) is almost identical in the first three lines; in both hemistiches of two of these three parallel lines (926 - 927 and 930 - 931) the sentence units and their order match each other almost perfectly. In one of the paired lines (927 and 931) the first hemistich is almost identical ("que Minaya Álvar Fáñez" and "que Álbar Fáñez") and the second hemistich, while different in sense, is a complement of the first; the number of lines in A and A' is comparable, four lines and five lines respectively if we do not include in A' the extra sixth line, 934b, which Menéndez Pidal has added.

Let us now consider B (70 lines) B' (5 lines):

B   B'

41 lines: 2675 - 76, 2681 - 2719

Allí les tuellen	2720	*Leváronles los mantos*	2749
los mantos e los pelliçones,		*e las pieles armiñas,*
páranlas en cuerpos		*mas déxanlas marridas*
y en camisas y en çiclatones.		*en briales y en camisas*
		e a las aves del monte
		e a las bestias de la fiera guisa.

13 lines: 2722 - 34

Essora les conpieçan a dar   2235
   ifantes de Carrión
con las çinchas corredizas
   májanlas tan sin sabor;
con las espuelas agudas,
   don ellas an mal sabor,
ronpien las camisas e las carnes
   a ellas amas a dos;
limpia salie la sangre
   sobre los çiclatones.

Ya lo sienten ellas   2740
   en los sos coraçones.
¡Quál ventura serie esta,   2741
   si ploguiesse al Criador
que assomasse essora
   el Çid Campeador!
Tanto las majaron   2743
   que sin cosimente son;
sangrientas en las camisas
   e todos los çiclatones.
Canssados son de ferir   2745
   ellos amos a dos,
ensayandos amos
   quál dará mejores colpes.
Ya non pueden fablar
   don Elvira e doña Sol,
por muertas las dexaron   2748
   en el robredo de Corpes.

Por muertas las dexaron,   2752
   sabed, que non por bivas.
¡Quál ventura serie   2753
   si assomas essora el Cid Roy Diaz!

Then they stripped them of their cloaks and furs; / they left nothing on their bodies but their shirts and silk undergarments./

. . . .

Then the heirs of Carrión began to lash them;/ they beat them without mercy with the flying cinches,/ gored them with sharp spurs, dealing them great pain./They took their shirts and the flesh of both of them,/ all over the silken cloth the clean blood ran,/ and they felt the pain in their very hearts./ Oh it would be such good fortune if it please the Creator/that the Cid Campeador might appear now!/They beat them so cruelly, they left them senseless;/the shirts and the silk skirts were covered with blood./ They beat them until their arms were tired,/ each of them trying to strike harder than the other./Doña Elvira

They took away their cloaks and their furs of ermine, / and left them fainting in their shifts and silk tunics,/left them to the birds of the mountain and to the wild beasts.

They left them for dead,

| and Doña Sol could no longer speak;/they left them for dead in the oak grove of Corpes. | you may know,with no life left in them./What good fortune it would be if the Cid Ruy Díaz should appear now![35] |

In B, B' the lines that resemble the neat parallelism of A, A' are 2741 - 42, vis-à-vis 2753, but the two lines of B are more affective than the one line of B' because the juglar expresses the wish that it might have pleased God to have the Cid come to the aid of Dõna Elvira and Doña Sol. (The same wish is also expressed in B' but not in the same context.) This additional line in B illustrates how, in contrast to A, A' (the parallel lines of which are neatly paired), the parallel lines in B as opposed to B' are enhanced by a great number of additional lines. The corresponding elements of B, as against B', are intensified by preceding and following narrative and dramatic development suffused throughout by the emotion of the narrator. Through this development in B the poet of Medinaceli is able, in his description of the outrage at Corpes, to exert the full power of his poetic genius in creating such details as the blood running over the white silks of the brutally beaten young wives (2739). Other lines which are parallel by virtue of similar word order and meaning are 2720 - 21 in B and 2749 - 50 in B', but the parallelism is not as precise as it is in two of the paired lines of A, A'. In two instances, one in A, A' (928 - 29) and one in B, B' (2750 - 51), one parallel line is followed by another, nonparallel line; but in A the nonparallel last line is just an extension of the meaning of the preceding parallel line, whereas in B' the last, nonparallel line, although the meaning complements that of the preceding line, opens a new, fearful perspective, that of the Corpes setting with its birds and its wild beasts.

It is not enough to show how the lines of B' differ from their parallel counterparts in B, nor how those of A' are more precisely paired with those of A, to demonstrate the enormous formal difference of the paired elements of A, A', as against B, B'. In the short laisse B' the five lines which correspond to lines in B are recapitulations of only certain points of it. The most merciless details are described only in B, the movement of which may be compared to a surging wave. The crest of the wave is line 2746: "each of them trying to strike harder than the other!" And in the final lines, "Doña Elvira and Doña Sol could no longer speak;/they left them for dead in the oak grove of Corpes," the wave has spent its fury.

Given the consummate development of B, the summary character of B' seems not so much repetition of preceding matter as the wake of the wave that crested in the last two lines of B. The moans of the defenseless women have ceased. The Infantes leave them for dead. Because of the distance of twenty-nine lines separating the first two lines of B' (2749 - 50) from the corresponding lines in B (2720 - 21), the former, more than analogues that move hand in hand in pairs seem like analogues that move in a long line, each separated by temporal distance. But this distance, traversed by repetition, is not sufficiently extended to weaken the connection between the explicit *allí* ("there") of lines 2720 - 21 (reechoed in 2749 - 50) and the implicit *aquí* ("here") of the brutal act's reverberation in the inhuman world of nature, a reverberation suggested in line 2751 by "the wild beasts," for the almost lifeless women are bound to be the prey of these wild beasts. Distance is shortened between lines 2741 - 42 of B and the last line of B' and it is almost completely eliminated between 2748 and 2752.

Finally, we may conclude from the above analysis that B' is an intensely affective, partial recapitulation of the long, detailed, heart-rending contents of B, not a complete, slightly varied repetition of it. On the other hand, A' is almost a counterpart of A. In this instance the poet is much more conventional, resorting as he does to the kind of precisely balanced parallel series found in *La Chanson de Roland*. The formulistic repetition, line for line, in A' is an effective emphatic device, but the conclusive effect of the partial repetition in B' has greater impact. The poet's technique in A, A' is neither more nor less effective than its application in other instances, as in laisses thirty-five and thirty-six. It may be compared to the regular variations of the same melodic theme in classical music, the delight of which is produced by limpid balance. The poet who composed B, B', on the other hand, was carried away by his opportunity to do justice to the most powerful scene in the poem. The usual *système de bascule* technique would not do; he therefore elaborates the first of the two parallel series in order to convey the full measure of the Infantes' monstrosity. The setting for their depraved lovemaking before the torture is a wild mountain with a thick oak grove whose branches touch the clouds (2698).

Is Menéndez Pidal right in saying that "this scene of Corpes belongs to the poet of Medinaceli who, in his use of lyrical devices, shows himself to be much superior to the poet of Gormaz"?[36] There can be no doubt that we are dealing with very distinct techniques, that the purported second poet is more creatively resourceful and that he produces a more intense effect. We say "purported" because it is possible that the *same* poet availed himself of both techniques; he could have purposely employed the usual device of more or less exactly parallel repetition for the initial phase of the narration and then augmented that device in order to meet the challenge of a climactic incident. We believe that our correlation of line-end imperfects in laisses with *a-a* assonance and of line-end preterites in *ó* assonance with the preliminary and final phases of the structure has shown that poetic reasons fully justify the predominance of the *a-a* assonance in the unfolding phase and of the *ó* assonance in the conclusive phase of the work.[37] This does not mean, however, that distinct poets could not have yielded to the same poetic exigence. The analysis of the parallel laisses A, A' and B, B' leads us to the same conclusion. In other words, we do not mean to refute the thesis of dual authorship. On the contrary we believe that given the circumstances of oral composition, it was inevitable for more than one poet to have created and recreated his version of the poem during the five-odd decades that elapsed between one or several early brief versions and the long version of 1140 which Pidal identifies with the poet of Medinaceli.

XI   *Did a Late Juglar Revise Laisse 128?*

As is the case among modern singers of tales observed by Parry, Lord, and others, there must have been, in medieval times, outstanding juglares who revised and added their own contribution to epic songs already in existence. In our own times Lord tells us about the 2130-line-long version of the Yugoslav song "The Wedding of Smaigalic Meho" (copied in 1886 by Friedrich Krauss) which notwithstanding thirty additional lines remained essentially the same as late as 1925. But some ten years later a singer of genius, Avdo Mededović, learned this later version, and he expanded and adorned it to almost seven times its original length.[38] In French epic a second version of *Moniage* is more than twice as long as the first. In the Spanish Romancero, we have observed, among many examples of amplification and elaboration, the ballad dealing with the slaying by the duke of Berganza of his wife. In the version published in the *Silva* of 1550 the ballad consists of thirty-four lines; in the *Cancionero llamado Flor de Enamorados* it is seventy-eight lines long. The first, earlier, version is confined to a bare but powerful account of the incident; it omits the sword blow described in the second. Furthermore, in the latter, the dramatic dialogue consists of eleven speeches instead of five, as in the early version. Finally, the adorned version introduces a young Castilian page who does not figure in the other version.

If in the oral poetic practice of the Spain of the Cid the amplification of short epic songs was a common phenomenon, we may suppose with some confidence that, in the 1140 or later version of the poem, laisse 128 that we have examined is the expanded form of an early version of the laisse. This laisse well might have consisted of lines 2720 - 21, 2748, 2741 - 42. Let us place this earlier hypothetical laisse beside laisse 129, which the later juglar probably left intact:

Allí les tuellen	2720	*Leváronles los mantos*	2749
los mantos e los pelliçones,		*e las pieles armiñas,*	
páranlas en cuerpos	2721	*mas déxanlas marridas*	2750
y en camisas y en çiclatones.		*en briales y en camisas,*	
Por muertas las dexaron	2748	*e a las aves del monte*	2751
en el robredo de Corpes.		*e a las bestias de*	
¡Quál ventura serie esta,	2741	*la fiera guisa.*	
si ploguiesse al Criador		*Por muertas las dexaron,*	2752
que assomasse essora	2742	*sabed, que non por bivas.*	
el Çid Campeador!		*¡Quál ventura serie si*	2753
		assomas essora el Cid Roy Díaz!	

Then they stripped them	2720	They took away their cloaks	2749
of their cloaks and furs;		and their furs of ermine,	
They left nothing on their	2721	and left them fainting	2750
bodies but their shirts and		in their silks and tunics,	
silk undergarments.		left them to the birds of the	2751
They left them for dead	2748	mountain and to the wild beasts	
in the oak grove of Corpes		They left them for dead	2752
Oh, it would be such good	2741	you may know, with no	
fortune if it should please		life left in them.	
the Creator		What good fortune it would be	2753
that the Cid Campeador	2742	if the Cid Ruy Díaz	
might appear now!		should appear now![39]	

In the abbreviated form in which we have presented laisse 128 it is well matched with laisse 129. The balanced syntagms and the equal number of lines of these two series comprise a counterpart of the technique of the parallel series fifty and fifty-one of the first cantar, a technique that is highly regular and symmetrical.

In the light of what modern traditional and oralist criticism has shown, we believe, on one hand, that in its earliest form the two series could have stood side by side as we have presented them above. On the other hand, we think it is reasonable to suppose that in the extended version of laisse 128, the juglar of Medinaceli, carried away by his lyric impetus, floods the narrow channel that was ready for him with the great volume of his creative resources.

We present this hypothesis as one of two possibilities. The other is that one single poet could have converted his spare technique of the first cantar into the exuberant narration of laisse 128 in the third cantar for poetic reasons. In any event, what interests us primarily from the viewpoint of aesthetic criticism is to understand how the extant version exerts its marvelous working and power. We will not assume the role of a literary detective bent on examining minutiae in order to trace duality or even multiplicity of authorship. From our point of view, therefore, the epic we are examining is the work of one particular poet who, stimulated by the empathy which binds him to his poetic precursors and to his living audience, not only recreates what belonged to a fellow artist, but what through his individual contribution belongs to him exclusively. How far removed in time, space, and social circumstance is the written transcription which saved the Castilian masterpiece from oblivion. However, even if this transcription cannot reproduce the recited original faithfully, it still reflects the act of creation and recreation of the poet of Medinaceli.

CHAPTER 4

Style

I Salient Stylistic Aspects

THE *Poem of the Cid,* like all oral epics, abounds in habitual devices of style. Besides verbal formulas as defined by
Parry, it includes systems of stylistic patterns and formulas of
narrative mode. Other stylistic aspects are internal rhyme,
numerical precision and the structural importance of numbers, the
frequent violation of conventional grammatical logic in the use of
tenses — a violation which far from confusing us, dynamically conveys the psychological complexity of time perception. A particularly
important aspect of the use of tense is the predominance of the imperfect indicative in the first part and of the preterite indicative in
the second part. Considerations of space and the difficulty of ade-
quately elaborating in English a stylistic commentary of an old
Spanish text compel us to limit this final chapter to a brief consideration of the most typical aspects of its formulaic style. We regretfully
omit even a summary of our findings of the poet's use of internal
rhymes (an aspect of the versification heretofore unnoticed),
number, and temporal forms.[1]

II Formulistic and Formulaic Content

May we say of the *Poem of the Cid* what Lord says of the twelve-
thousand-line-long *Song of Bagdad,* namely, that "there is nothing
in the poem that is not formulaic?"[2] The answer may be affirmative
if we take into account not only the strictly epic formulas, but also
(1) stylistic patterns which, without necessarily expressing the same
essential idea, manifest an habitual expressive tendency in the disposition of verbal elements; (2) formulas of narrative mode, like
abrupt transitions and direct discourse introduced without a verb of
saying; (3) parallel series; (4) concluding lines of a laisse linked by a
repetitive word or words with the initial line or lines of the following
laisse; (5) the regular recurrence of certain choices of word order

100

calculated to accommodate a lively paratactic style; (6) the ever-present tendency to express thought in a parallel or polar manner through repetition of the same idea with different words or through the coupling of normal opposites; (7) tripartite enumeration.[3] To demonstrate these stylistic aspects would require an exposition of monographic length. In this condensed chapter we will only present a succinct review of our findings, beginning with an analysis of the formulaic content of sixteen lines of the poem. These lines have been chosen at random, not tendentiously chosen to prove our point. In the line by line analysis, the solid line or lines under a given hemistich or hemistiches indicate: (1) a verbal formula, that is, a habitual expression occurring three or more times in the poem; (2) a broken line represents a stylistic pattern, that is, a line showing a marked tendency to dispose verbal elements in a certain way without expressing the same essential idea: and (3) a line consisting of a string of *x*'s stands for the expression of an idea that is not habitual but required in context (hence the designation "contextual line").

Formula Analysis of Lines 778 - 793

Contextual expression: xxxxxxxxxxxxxxxxxxx
Stylistic Pattern: -------------
Verbal Formula: ⎯⎯⎯⎯⎯⎯⎯⎯

778   *A Minaya Álbar Fáñez* / *bien l'anda el cavallo,*
      For Minaya Álbar Fáñez / well rides his horse for him,
      --------------------- / ----------------------------

779   *daquestos moros* / *mató treinta e quatro*
      of these Moors / killed he thirty-four
      ------------- / ⎯⎯⎯⎯⎯⎯⎯

780   *espada tajador,* / *sangriento trae el brazo,*
      his sword sharp, / bloody is his arm,
      xxxxxxxxxxxxxxxxxxxx / xxxxxxxxxxxxxxxxxxxx

781   *por el cobdo ayuso* / *la sangre destellando,*
      his elbow downward / the blood dripping,
      ⎯⎯⎯⎯⎯⎯⎯⎯⎯⎯⎯⎯⎯⎯⎯

782   *Dize Minaya;* / *"agora so pagado,*
      Says Minaya: / "now I am satisfied,
      ⎯⎯⎯⎯⎯⎯⎯⎯⎯⎯⎯⎯⎯⎯⎯

783   *que a Castiella / irán buenos mandados,*
      that to Castile / will go good tidings,

784   *que mio Cid Roy Díaz / lid campal a arrancado."*
      that My Cid Roy Diaz / a pitched battle has won."

785   *Tantos moros yazen muertos / que pocos vivos a dexados,*
      So many Moors lie dead / that few alive has he left,

786   *ca en alcaz / sin dubda les foron dando.*
      for in pursuit / they fearlessly kept striking them down.

787   *Yas tornan / los del que en buen ora nasco.*
      Now return / those of him [i.e., his men] who in a happy hour
      was born.

788   *Andava mio Cid / sobre so buen cavallo,*
      Rode My Cid / on his good horse

789   *la cofia fronzida / Dios commo es bien barbado!*
      his coif rolled back / God, how splendid his beard!

790   *almófar a cuestas, / la espada en la mano.*
      mailed cowl on his shoulders, / his sword in his hand.

791   *Vió los sos / cómmo se van allegando:*
      He saw his men / how they are gathering:

792   *"Grado a Dios, / aquel que está en alto,*
      "Thanks be to God, / He who is on high,

793   *quando tal batalla / avemos arrancado."*
      because such a battle / we have won."

A full discussion and defense of the above analysis is also beyond the scope of this presentation which is intended for the non-specialist. However, the specialist may verify our analysis by examining the lines or half-lines which are the same as, or similar to, the half-lines and lines of our sample. These hemistiches and lines are listed in the accompanying note.[4]

A glance at the analysis will show that almost one-half of the thirty-two hemistiches form stylistic patterns, about one-fourth of the half-lines verbal formulas, and over one-fourth of the full lines verbal formulas. Only 6 percent of the thirty-two half-lines are contextual, that is, not formulistic nor formulaic. As previously stated, (the statement bears repeating) we arbitrarily designate as "formulaic" all habitual verbal devices which do not necessarily express the same essential idea and as "formulistic," or "formulary," groups of words which do so. For example under the first category, the stylistic pattern in 778AB results from the singer's conscious choice of a given word order: the line is launched by the preposition *a* which in Spanish precedes a direct or indirect object when the object is a person or a personified thing:

778AB   *A MINAYA ÁLBAR FÁÑEZ / bien l'anda el cavallo.*
         For Minaya Álbar Fáñez / well does his horse ride for him.
  66AB   *A MIO ÇID E A LOS SOS / abástales de pan e de vino*
         My Cid and those of him [his men] / he provides with bread and wine
815AB   *AL REY DON ALFONSO / que me a ayrado*
         quiero enviar en don / treinta cavallos.
         To King Don Alfonso / who has turned his wrath on me I wish to send to him / as a gift thirty horses.
914AB   *A SARAGOÇA / metuda la en paria*
         Zaragoza / has he forced to pay tribute
1009AB   *AL COMDE DON REMONT / a preson le a tomado*
         Count Don Ramón / has he taken prisoner
1599AB   *A LA MADRE E LAS FIJAS / bien las abraçava*
         The mother and the daughters / warmly he embraced

As the examples below show, the stylistic pattern demonstrated above may become a full-fledged formula:

2628A   *A DIOS VOS ACOMENDAMOS*
         to God we commend you
 372A   *A DIOS VOS ACOMIENDO*
         to God I commend you

2154A   A DIOS VOS ACOMIENDO
         to God I commend you

Both in the case of the stylistic patterns we have listed and of the related formulas, the poet elects not to use the subject-verb-object sequence; he prefers to start the line with the direct or indirect object which he wishes to emphasize.

If stylistic patterns are as important as formulas in the analysis we have presented and if we consider such patterns an integral part of the singer's style, a broad definition of his techniques should include both. It should also include nonverbal formulas of narrative mode and take into account the metrical irregularity of the *PMC* which is not unique in this respect.[5]

III *Toward a Redefinition of Epic Formula in the Light of the* Poema de Mio Cid

The oral poet's fundamental techniques consist of (1) verbal formulas, namely, groups of words forming an identical or similar pattern which are used in the same or similar or dissimilar metrical conditions to express a given essential idea whose connotative meaning and intensive force are often determined by the extent to which they are modified by poetic context; (2) stylistic patterns which do not necessarily express an idea common to them all but constitute expressive systems that follow a given syntactic arrangement; (3) nonverbal formulas of narrative mode consisting of the customary but variable manner in which the verbal matter is arranged to tell the story.

IV *Possibilities of Aesthetic Reference of Epic Formula*

Albert B. Lord affirms that the essential idea of the formula is what is in the mind of the singer, almost as a reflex action in rapid composition, as he makes his song. "Hence it could, I believe, be truly stated," he says, "that the formula not only is stripped to its essential idea in the mind of the composing singer, but also is denied some of the possibilities of aesthetic reference in context."[6] We now propose to raise certain questions about Lord's statement on the strength of a stylistic analysis of the poetic function of certain formulas which, in the case of the *PMC*, at least, shows that the possibilities of aesthic reference and of the flexibility of the essential idea in the singer's mind are much greater than the distinguished leader of the oralist school supposes. This is especially true of the most frequent traditional expressions, namely, the epithets.[7] Especially noteworthy are *el buen rey* ("the good king"); the epithets which the king addresses to the Cid; those which the Cid directs to the king; designations of the king's vassals.

The most frequent and the most simple designation, "Mio Cid" is not an epithet in the strict sense of the word but an honorific title; nevertheless I adduce it as an epithet because it was originally used among Moors as a celebrative appositional noun with adjectival force in the denomination "Ruy Díaz mio Cid" ("Ruy Diaz My Lord"). It is true that "Mio Cid" is used so frequently that it acquires the familiarity of ordinary address (but always on the plane of epic dignity). However, there are notable exceptions to this rule: the casual designation acquires ususual force through immediate repetition at the end of first hemistiches where it produces internal rhyme,[8] as in lines six and seven:

> *Sospiró MIO ÇID, ca mucho avié grandes cuidados*
> *Fabló MIO ÇID, bien e tan mesurado*

> (He sighed, MY CID, for he felt great affliction.
> He spoke, MY CID, well and with great moderation.

The immediate reiteration of the simple name in this and other cases (153 - 54; 802 - 3) occurs at points of intense affectivity. Substitute another designation of the Cid like Campeador in line seven and you lose the intensive effect. And if we suppose, as we are probably justified in supposing, that the signifiers *Cid* in these lines are musically emphasized by extending the one syllable into a prolonged pattern of several notes, it cannot be doubted that in this case the reiterated simple name has acquired great expressive power.

Perhaps the most significant instance of a formula that is repeated throughout the poem is that which demonstrates how an epithet may serve as a structural correlative. I refer to the increasing frequency of one adjective to reflect a psychological change, namely the adjective *bueno* ("good," "worthy"), which is applied to the king fifteen times. Our conclusion from an examination of the incidence of this adjective is that the increasing frequency and affective intensity of its use manifest a gradation in the attitude of the narrative and other voices from the implicit negation of the king's goodness to the emphatic affirmation of his excellence. This gradation corresponds to that which takes place in the sentiments of the king toward his vassal, sentiments which, as they change, also change his moral character. No sooner is the recitation launched than the Burgalesans implicitly deny Alfonso's goodness exclaiming in the famous twentieth line:

> *Dios qué buen vassallo, si oviesse buen señore!*
>
> God, what a good vassal, had he but a good lord!

During the whole first third part of the poem, that is, during the period of royal displeasure, the adjective *bueno* is used only once but in the contrary sense, "bad," since, as we have seen, it is found in the conditional clause "if only he were good!" From line 20 to line 1323, he is not called either good or bad. This is a diplomatic silence. It is not until we are well into the second cantar that Alfonso gives unmistakable indications of goodwill; thereafter the adjective is used frequently. The juglar calls the king *bueno* for the time when he pardons the Cid's family. Here the adjective signalizes the turning point of the king's attitude from grudging envy to benevolence. The pardon of the family foreshadows that of the father.

The long positive phase of royal goodwill which unfolds in the last two-thirds of the poem is also accompanied by a rising feeling of admiration for the changed character of the former persecutor of his best vassal. And it is during the final, culminating stage that the adjective is pronounced most fervently and with the greatest frequency (six times out of the total of fifteen).

Rita Hamilton has written an excellent study of epic epithets in the poem.[9] Her consideration of the epithets that designate Martín Antolínez is especially illuminating. Among these, Mrs. Hamilton singles out *burgalés de pro* ("the excellent man of Burgos"), *el burgalés leal* ("the loyal man of Burgos"), and *burgalés natural* ("the son of Burgos"), in support of Professor P. E. Russell's thesis of a Burgos audience.[10] More in line with our approach, she makes a penetrating stylistic commentary of the epithets that emphasize Martín's loyalty to the Cid. However, she misses entirely the noun *membrado* ("clever," "prudent") in the epithetical adverbial phrase *a guisa de menbrado* ("like the shrewd man he is"), which, used in the sand-chest episode, is applied to that clever citizen of Burgos with a pointed intention. Especially attractive I think, and as far as I know totally new, are Mrs. Hamilton's penetrating observations regarding the epithets which with great pride proclaim the Cid to be a citizen of Vivar. These epithets, which had escaped my attention, occur with extraordinary frequency up to line 1728 in order to (1) extol the insignificant village that gave birth to a national hero, (2) to bring out the greatness of his triumphs, contrasting the humbleness of his birthplace with the importance of the territory he conquered but especially with the importance of the great city of Valencia, and (3) to refute the pretensions of the Infantes when they boast that they are *Comdes de Carrión* ("Counts of Carrión").

Among the names that are modified in degree or altered in kind to reflect a change of attitude on the part of the speaker the most notable are those used by the king to address the Cid. These range from branding him as a man in disgrace, in line 882, to the declaration in line 3510 that the Cid is the best vassal in the realm. In this span the king names the Cid forty-seven times using nineteen designations. The first designation, *omne ayrado* (i.e., a banished man who has incurred the wrath of his lord), and the last, *en todas nuestras tierras non ha tan buen varón* ("in all our lands there is no better man"), are extremes of an epithetical scale that marks the transformation of Alfonso's feeling toward his vassal in the course of the poem.

In contrast to this gamut, the names with which the Cid designates the king manifest only positive gradations of affectivity, never a shift from one pole to another. He loyally calls him *Alfons mio señor* ("Alfonso my Lord") when, during the blackest period of his relations with him, he abandons Castejón which was a protectorate of the monarch, instead of fighting against him as he had every right to do according to the *Fuero Viejo de Castilla*. And when, during the most glorious stage of his career, he receives the royal pardon, he addresses Alfonso in the same way.

What distinguishes the king from the Cid as speakers with respect to the epithets they address to each other, then, is that the former varies the tone of those he uses according to his change of attitude, whereas the latter never alters his. He does not alter it because his loyalty is inalterable.

Finally let us observe how two of the common formulas in the poem, namely, *besar la mano* ("to kiss the hand"), and *ceñir la espada en buena hora* ("to gird on one's sword in a happy hour"), undergo contextual modification. Martín Antolínez has just drawn up the contract with Raquel and Vidas for the 600-mark loan. "Ah, you should have seen how they rejoiced when they tried to lift the coffers," the juglar exclaims addressing the audience directly. "They cannot get them on their backs," he continues, "although

they are both strong men! Raquel and Vidas are happy men, they
will be rich so long as they both shall live!" (170 - 73). At this point
Raquel kisses the Cid's hand and says:

> *Ya Campeador, en buena cinxiestes espada!*
> Ah, Campeador, who in a happy hour girded on sword!

   The hand-kissing homage and the epithet are, of course,
celebrative, but in this case I do not think we can possibly interpret
the act or the epithet as simple, unadulterated, unconditional expressions of obeisance and admiration as they are in every other instance in the poem. In the context the celebrative formula is sugared
and syrupped with the officiousness of Raquel who sees the Cid as
the source of enormous wealth, who looks upon him with the eyes of
greed.
   When Lord declares that "the formula not only is stripped to essential idea in the mind of the composing singer, but also denied
some of the possibilities of aesthetic reference . . ." he is thinking of
what he calls "the artistically weighted epithet," especially the kind
that exemplifies what he calls the "pathetic fallacy," namely, that of
critics who attribute to the "innocent epithet an irony or pathos felt
only by the critic, but not acknowledged or perhaps even dreamed
of either by the poet or his audience" (p. 66).
   If Lord is correct, my interpretation of the formal meaning of *besar
la mano* and *en buena cinxiestes espada* are pathetically fallacious.
Nevertheless, I have ventured to demonstrate the capacity for
aesthetic reference and degrees of emphasis of these formulas, rely-
ing, first, on a principle which I think is inductively demonstrable
and, second, on the strength of a clear and generally shared intuitive
impression, namely, the impression produced by the impact of a
phenomenon on the sensibility. The principle is the following:
words are a dynamic not a static, a complex not a simple, a flexible
not a rigid, element within any linguistic context, except in a context
of scientific exposition. For this reason the habitual use of a phrase
in an epic poem does not always cause it to lose its expressive flexibility, its capacity for aesthetic reference or for ironic reversibility.
   The oral poet may, and does, at times, vary the degree of
emphasis and the shade of meaning of the same word or phrase in
different parts of his composition. He can do this because the word
is a sign charged with potentialities of meaning and because he is a

conscious artist both at the level of line formation and at the level of structure. And as for clear intuitive impact, I believe the scene in which the Cid and Martín Antolínez trick Raquel and Vidas is highly amusing to all. As Dámaso Alonso has shown in a masterful study, the juglar, a combination of poet, musician and actor, knew what he was about: to delight his audience with the tonic of laughter. Every mischievous touch of the comic devaluation of Raquel and Vidas was, I am sure, accompanied by a corresponding inflexion in the tone of his recitation. And in delivering the line on which I have commented his tone was, I believe, delicately ironic.

The gist of our argument, then, is that the formula may, indeed, combine its essential idea with its possibilities of aesthetic reference.

V *Formulaic Narrative Devices: Repetition*

A constant device throughout the poem, ranging from the smallest unit to the thematic parallelisms of the two large divisions of the organic whole, is the repetition, with or without variation, of related meanings. In ascending order these parallelisms occur in the half-line, in the whole line, in the laisse, and in the interior form of the entire poem:

Half-Line

Penssó e comidió

He thought and reflected

(1889)

Whole Line

Mucho pesa a los de Teca   e a los de Terrer non plaze

Much it grieves those of Teca   and those of Terrer it pleases not

(625)

Laisse

a: Minaya to the Cid:

"*Vos con çiento   de aquesta nuestra conpaña,*
"You with one hundred   of this our company,

pues que a Castejón   sacaremos a çelada,
now that Castejón   we will lay under ambush,

en él fincaredes   teniendo a la çaga;
there you will remain   holding the rear guard;
a mí dedes dozientos   pora ir en algara."
give me two hundred   to go ahead on the vanguard,"

(440 - 41B)

a': The Cid to Minaya:
"*Vos con los dozientos   id vos en algara;*

"You with the two hundred   go ahead on the vanguard;

(442)

E yo con los çiento   aqui fincaré en la çaga,"

And I with the hundred   will here hold the rear guard,"

(449)

The Poem

a The theme of the Cid's honor in the political sphere
a' The theme of the Cid's honor in the domestic sphere

Besides the juxtaposing of like elements, many related or normally opposite elements are placed one beside the other. In a hemistich: *de noch e de día* (222), "night and day," *moros e cristianos* (968, etc.), "Moors and Christians"; in a whole line: *el día es exido, la noch quierie entrar* (311, etc), "day has gone, night is about to come." There are also antithetical juxtapositions like *e yo faziendo a él mal, él a mí grand pro* (1891), "and I doing him great harm, and he doing me great good." In the most subtle contrast of opposites the same adjective, *bueno*, "good," expresses, in line 20, a contrary idea, because it is found in a contrary-to-fact condition: *¡Dios, qué buen vasallo, si oviesse buen señore!* "God, what a good vassal, had he but a good lord!" This line with its emphatic signifiers VASÁLLO and SEÑÓRE and signifieds "vassal" versus "lord" expresses quintessentially the central idea of the poem's thematic complex. At times the twinning is agglomerated:

       a   *a'*   *a*   *b*
e me ayude e me acorra   de noch e de día!
and may it aid and sustain me   by night and by day.

(222)

      a   *b*
besóle la boca   e los ojos de la cara
he kissed his mouth   and the eyes in his face

```
      a                 a`
todo se lo dize   que nol encubre nada
he told him everything   nothing keeps he from him
```
(921 - 22)

```
      a               b
Grado a Dios   e a las sus vertudes santas
Thanks be to God   and to his Holy Grace
```
(924)

In the above examples the clustered pairings serve to intensify the affectivity of the speaker. The words in line 222 are addressed by the Cid to the Virgin Mary when he sadly leaves the Cathedral of Burgos. Lines 921 - 922, 924 express the Cid's great joy when Minaya returns to Castile after having presented to King Alfonso Rodrigo's first gift of thirty horses. Here the gladness of the Campeador and his men is even greater than it is on succeeding similar occasions when the value of the gifts is multiplied because the first light of hope when the task ahead seems overwhelming is more precious than when, after overcoming initial obstacles, each success assures additional successes. Not until this first favorable change in the relations between the Cid and the King takes place, and Minaya brings back news of the exiles' relatives, does the juglar present the first "twin series" (Menéndez Pidal's term), the poetic function of which we will now analyze:

Laisse 50

The Joy of the Exiles at Receiving News from Castile

> ¡Dios, commo es alegre   todo aquel fonssado,
> que Minaya Álvar Fáñez   assí era llegado,
> diziéndole saludes   de primos e de hermanos,
> e de sus compañas,   aquellas que avien dexado!

> God, how they rejoiced,   all that company,
> that Minaya Álvar Fáñez   had returned thus,
> bringing them greetings   from cousins and brothers,
> and from the families   they had left behind!

Laisse 51

The Joy of the Cid

> ¡Dios cómmo es alegre   la barba vellida,
> que Álbar Fáñez   pagó las mill missas

e quel dixo saludes   de su mugíer e de sus fijas!
¡Dios, commo fo el Çid pagado   e fizo grant alegría!
"Ya Álvar Fáñez,   bivades muchos días!
más valedes que nos,   tan buena mandadería!

God, how glad he was,   he of the handsome beard,
that Álvar Fáñez,   paid for the thousand Masses
and had brought greetings   from his wife and his daughters!
God, how pleased the Cid   and how he rejoiced!
"Ah, Álvar Fáñez   may you live many days!
You are worth more than any of us,   you have done your mission so well!

To understand the poetic function of the above laisses we should
first point out that they are not "twinned series" (*series gemelas*) as
Menéndez Pidal calls them. We prefer the term "parallel series,"
which allows for greater variation. The most obvious change is that
of assonance, which in epic poetry can be, as it is in this case,
analogous to a change of key in music (perhaps the singer accompanied the change of assonance with melodic variation). Furthermore, each of the laisses presents the essential idea from different
viewpoints; the first emphasizes the joy of the vassals, the second
that of the Cid. The common denominator of both series is Minaya.
We see him first focused at some distance against a crowded
background, then closer up, face to face to the Cid who, toward the
end of laisse 49, "kissed his mouth and the eyes of his face."
In the structure of the poem this parallel series functions as the
culmination of a surging movement, forming the crest of a wave.
Not long before the king has given the first signs of good will (laisse
48) when he tells Minaya that all good and valiant men of his
kingdom who wish may go to the aid of the Cid, he adds "I will not
forbid them, nor seize their possessions." When Minaya com-
municates this message, the Cid cannot contain his joy, joy which
the poet emphasizes by intensifying the affectivity of the signifiers
through repetition within the laisse: $a + b$ in line 921; $a + a'$ in line
922; $a + b$ in line 924, as we have noted in our graphic presentation
of binary devices on pages 109 - 110. The spare but intensive iterative
techniques of these lines foreshadow the more elaborate repetition
with variations of the two parallel series we have examined. The intensive function of a parallel series is even more striking in laisses
128 and 129 which we have already examined in the third chapter.
Only a complete index of parallel expressions within a hemistich

a line, or in clusters of lines in the same laisse would fully demonstrate the juglar's ever-present tendency to dispose his formulaic presentation in a binary manner. However, even without such a concordance of parallelisms the reader is struck by their frequent occurrence in almost every part of the poem both in the form of corresponding and complementary elements on one hand, and of normal opposites and occasionally of antithetical extremes on the other.

The metrical unit — a line of two hemistiches — provides a dual manner of expression which favors the disposition of ideas in neat pairs. How lucidly the poet displays the dual arrangement of similar or antithetically related ideas, from the smallest unit, the hemistich, to the largest, the poem in its totality! The basis of the structure is the king-vassal relationship; Minaya, if not a second protagonist, is nevertheless presented as the Cid's right arm; the Cid overcomes two obstacles to his honor, one in the political, the other in the domestic sphere; his two daughters marry first two highborn heirs, then two princes.

VI *Affinity of Parallelistic and Enumerative Devices and Parataxis to Epic Style*

The epic poet's bent for parallelistic and enumerative techniques goes hand in hand with his paratactic style,[11] which characterizes not only the *PMC* but all oral literature since Homer.[12] Parataxis lends itself to epic style for the following reasons: (1) verbal formulas are self-contained units, easily juxtaposed; (2) parataxis is the natural style of spoken language, which, stylized and metrically regulated, is integrated into the epic composition, especially into dialogue; (3) parataxis lends itself to the rhythmic repetition of equivalent, complementary, or antithetical ideas, devices which, as we have noted, serve to emphasize the affectivity of the narrator or speaker; (4) parataxis lends itself particularly well to the stringing together of independent verbal syntagms, and for this reason it does not lend itself at all to enjambment, run-on lines being minimal in epic because, in presenting a recreated song in varied form (a singer never repeats a song by rote, without variations) the juglar can remember and recite self-contained lines more easily than run-on lines; (5) parataxis favors musical presentation, which progresses from measure to measure. Finally, oral epic style, as a manifestation of the history of language, reflects its early development, before grammatical coordination and subordination became fashionable among literate poets.

Contrary to the opinion of Notopoulos[13] parataxis does not incline the oral poet to think episodically either at the line level or at the level of structure. At this level, according to Notopoulos, the need to improvise prevents the singer from attempting to put together a well-organized whole. As we have emphasized elsewhere,[14] if many epics, especially French chansons de geste, are loosely structured, this defect is due to the singer's lack of talent, not to parataxis, which in no way prevents the logical connection of parts of speech. The Spanish grammarian Gili Gaya[15] explains the reason for this as follows: ". . . through simple juxtaposition we constantly imply the same connections that we express by means of conjunctions and relative words. . . . Those who claim that in parataxis clauses are separable and independent, while in hypotaxis they are inseparable, have in mind only grammatical structure, but they misrepresent expressive reality [i.e., the reality of spoken language]." He illustrates his point with the following enumerative sentence: "*The clouds darkened the sky in the north, the humidity was suffocating, gusts of wind announced the approaching storm.*" If we added the conjunction "and" before the last term of the enumeration ("*and* gusts of wind") we would grammatically indicate its end; without the conjunction we are left in suspense about what is to follow. However, the lack of the connecting word "and" can be supplied by inflection: spoken aloud, a lowering of the voice in enunciating the last term would suffice to indicate that the enumeration has been completed.

It is true that today we do not have the full advantage of those who once listened to the singer, because his oral recitation with its inflections and his acting ability supplied the connections not grammatically provided in paratactic pairs or series. The modern reader, nevertheless, had no trouble in sensing the implied connections. A good paratactic style is very satisfactory both for the reader and the listener; it is enough that the grammatically unconnected parts follow each other in logical order for their connection to be understood.

VII *Enumeration*

The poet enlivens his narration at points where it is necessary to accelerate movement, by supplementing neat twinned expressions with rapid asyndectic series. Among the many passages which demonstrate this enumerative dynamic technique, we will quote lines 715 - 18 (repeated in lines 3615 - 18): which describe a charge of the Cid's knights against the enemy:

Laisse 35

> *Embraçan los escudos   delante los coraçones,*
> *abaxan las lanzas   abueltas de los pendones,*
> *enclinaron las caras   de suso de los arzones,*
> *ívanlos ferir   de fuertes coraçones.*

> They clasp their shields   over their hearts,
> they lower their lances   swathed in their pennons,
> they bowed their faces   over their saddletrees,
> they made ready to attack them   with strong hearts.

The four lines are grammatically independent — in fact each one is a sentence — nevertheless they are integrated into a four-unit period by virtue of their logical, if not syntactical, connection. The passage is an excellent illustration of paratactic unity which may be as organic as hypotactic unity. Furthermore, it demonstrates that parataxis is the most effective means of describing a series of rapid movements. To show its efficacy it is enough to gloss the enumeration hypotactically: "[the Cid's men, charging to come to the aid of Pedro Bermúdez] *first* clasped their shields over their hearts, *and then* they lowered their lances, swathed in their pennons; *and finally*, bowing their faces over their saddletrees, they made ready to attack them with strong hearts." In this gloss, the italicized words specifying the temporal sequence and connection of the independent sentences of the period, diminish the force of the verbs and spoil the rhythm which is the palpable link between signified and signifier. Relieved of the intrusive linking adverbs "first," "then," and the conjunction "and," what is the effect of the untrammeled paratactic style? It permits launching each line with the most dynamic word of each sentence, namely, the verb, the effect of which cannot be fully rendered in English because in Spanish verbs do not require a personal pronoun and, especially, because, whereas the translation can shift from the more vivid present to the past, it cannot convey the prismatic effect of the shift from the preterite to the imperfect. In Spanish the imperfect is a simple, not a compound, tense, as it is in English. It would be absurd to translate the last line "*they were going to make ready* to attack them."

In the following series (laisse 36), the poet uses the kind of anaphoric enumeration which is found in *La Chanson de Roland* and in Spanish ballads:

Laisse 36

Veriedes tantas lanças   premer e alçar,
tanta adágara   foradar e passar,
tanta loriga   falssar e desmanchar,
tantos pendones blancos   salir vermejos en sangre,
tantos buenos cavallos   sin sos dueños andar.

You should have seen so many lances   lowered and raised,
so many shields   perforated and pierced,
so many coats of mail   broken and dented,
so many white pennants   held high red with blood,
so many good horses   running riderless.

The change of word order between laisses 35 and 36 and the change from the active to the passive voice are very effective. Because of the shift to the passive voice the focus is moved from the dynamic impulse of the agents to their effect on the object of the agents' force. The poet could have continued using the stylistic pattern of laisse 35 saying: "they lowered and raised so many lances, they perforated and pierced so many shields," etc., but such duplication would have sacrificed the effect of variety and contrast produced by the change of focus and the shift from the active to the passive voice. This shift also subtly divides the action between the Christians and Moors but with a decided advantage to the former, because, since they win the battle, it goes without saying that it was the Moors who suffered the greatest damage to their arms and whose blood flowed most freely. Menéndez Pidal heads laisse 36 with the words "they [the Christians] destroy the enemy ranks."

The device of juxtapositional technique that best shows the connecting capacity of parataxis in the poem consists of linking lines expressing the same idea. Such lines are found at the end of one laisse and at or near the beginning of the next. For example, laisse 28 ends with the line *el castiello de Alcocer en paria va entrando* ("the castle of Alcocer begins to pay tribute"), and the following laisse begins *Los de Alcocer a mio Çid yal dan parias* ("Those of Alcocer to My Cid now pay tribute").[16]

In certain series frequent repetition of the same word could be monotonous. However, monotony is avoided in such cases because the repetition is an intensive device, as may be confirmed in laisse 82, in which the epithet *Campeador* is so frequently repeated.[17]

The humor of the sand-chest trick is largely the result of the identical reactions of the moneylenders, Raquel and Vidas. The Jews move like puppets pulled by the same string. The adjective *amos*, used three times in seven lines of laisse 9 emphasizes the idea of two in one: *Raquel e Vidas en uno estavan amos* (literally: "Raquel and Vidas were both in one," i.e., "together"). Another example among the many which could be given is the repetition of the verb *comer*, "to eat," (three times in three verses) in laisse 62, in which the Cid mischievously insists that the captured count of Barcelona, who has gone on a hunger strike, should eat:

> *Dixo mio Çid: COMED,   COMDE, also,*
> *ca si non COMEDES,   non veredes cristianos;*
> *e si vos COMIÉREDES   don yo sea pagado . . .*

> Said my Cid: COME, COME, COUNT, EAT something,
> for unless you EAT   you will see no Christian soul;
> and if you EAT   so will I [!] be satisfied . . .

Here, besides the repetition of the verb, the alliteration *comed, comde, algo*, which I have translated freely "Come, come count, eat something," to preserve the original effect, emphasizes the mockingly solicitous tone of the Cid.

VIII   *Formula of Recommencement*

The only formula of recommencement in the poem is found at the beginning of the second cantar:

Aquí s compieça la gesta   de mio Çid el de Bivar.
Here begins the song of the exploits   of My Cid, the Son of Vivar.

Why "begins" instead of "continues?"[18] The poet is not beginning another story, nor even a new phase of the story he started to tell one thousand lines before. At the end of the first cantar we left the Cid and his men rejoicing at the booty they have taken from the count of Barcelona and his defeated forces. We have seen the count, suspicious and shamed, depart when the Cid generously frees him. The first cantar has an inconclusive ending; it lacks concluding lines such as the two at the end of the second cantar ("The verses of this song are almost ended. / May the Lord be with you and all His saints.") and of the third ("Such are the tidings of My Cid the Campeador, / and here this account of his deeds is ended"). The first laisse of the second cantar starts where the first left off; it continues narrating in a straight line the series of incidents launched in canto I, with the information that as a result of the victory won over the count, the Cid establishes himself firmly in the lands of the King of Lérida (See MP, *PMC*, n. 1087).

If there is no clear dividing line between the first and second cantos, why does the poet open the latter with a formula of commencement (really not of *re*commencement)? One possible explanation is that he recited the first cantar during one session and the second during another and that he announced a new story to assure those in the audience who had not previously been present that the matter he was going to recite, although preceded by other matter, had an inceptive beginning — in other words that he was not beginning in *medias res*. This explanation may account for the singer's practical motive, but the basic consideration which keeps us from accepting literally the verb "to begin" in line 1085 rests on our analysis of the poem's structure. In this structure canto I narrates the incident that gives rise to following incidents and initiates the series of victories by which the Cid retrieves his honor. This first cantar also contains two fervent lines (282 - 82b) to the effect that the Cid hopes to bring about an honorable marriage for his daughters. His hope is fulfilled, albeit with dire results, in the second cantar, and gloriously fulfilled in the third. Almost at the beginning of the poem, therefore, the decisive incident of the whole composition is foreshadowed.

The foregoing explanation, based on the fact that the poem is an organic whole, does not preclude the possibility that in the course of its oral evolution one of several poets could have composed a short, contemporary news-bearing song celebrating the Cid's defeat of the proud count. This short song could subsequently have been incorporated into the long version as composed in the integrated form of the poem we know today.

There is another piece of evidence showing that the second cantar is a continuation of the first. Immediately after the so-called formula of recommencement the poet brings his listeners up to date: he tells them how the actions initiated previously at Zaragoza, Huesa, and Montalbán (951 - 52) have ended, thus recapitulating what happened and elaborating it. Not until he has linked what he proposes to tell with what he has already told, does he rapidly in-form us about previously unmentioned conquests, those of Jérica, Onda, Almenara, and Burriana (1092 - 93).

IX *Abrupt Transitions*

Sometimes the juglar quickly changes the course of his narrative. In laisse 101 Álvar Fáñez and Pedro Bermúdez have just kissed the king's hand after the latter thanked them for the Cid's last and most generous present. Then the singer abruptly addresses his audience with the words: "I now wish to tell you about the Infantes of Carrión" (1879).[19] Such sudden shifts occur in other parts of the poem also. In laisse 48 the speakers are the king and Minaya, but in laisse 49 we are told of the Cid's raids from El Poyo. In laisse 87 the scene is the alcázar of Valencia from which the Cid's wife and his daughters view the surrounding region. At the end of the laisse, the juglar says: "I would now tell you news from across the sea, / of that King Yusuf, who is in Morocco." In the first line of laisse 131 the juglar says, "thus boasted the princes of Carrión, one to another." He shifts in the next line, saying, "But now I will tell you of Felix Muñoz. . . ."

The above breaks in the juglar's usually straight storytelling technique, breaks which may be considered to be formulas of narrative mode, result in a pleasing change of direction. Such formulas provide one more example of the poet's varied technique.

X *"With the Blood Running Down his Elbow"*

One of the most notable examples of the juglar's selectivity in the utilization of verbal formulas, showing that they do not occur to him "almost as a reflex action,"[20] is *por el cobdo ayuso la sangre destellando*, "With the blood running down his elbow" (501, 1724, 1781, 2453). Among battle formulas this is the one which most strikingly proclaims a warrior's prowess. Because it is applied to Minaya three of the four times it occurs in the poem, the expression becomes a formulary emblem of the most important of the Cid's men, Minaya, the Campeador's right arm. The formula is particularized in a very special way by one meaningful repetition. In laisse 24, Minaya solemnly vows not to accept any part of the booty won at Castejón until he has fully demonstrated the strength of his arm. He says to the Cid that he will not take from him a wretched farthing until he has joined battle with the Moors in the field "with the blood running down my elbow." And the formula is repeated precisely when Minaya, in laisse 40, fulfills this vow. In fact, not

only is the formula repeated; it is intensified by a preceding line
which reads "his sword cut deep, his arm was bloody."

XI   *Scenic and Plastic Elements*

Words designating scene provide visual background and those
designating objects fashioned by human hands — some of them of
great plastic beauty — are usually seen close up: their formal effec-
tiveness varies since the designation of a place or of a thing may be
included in the narration primarily for practical reasons or to intensify a poetic effect.

The most elementary function of scene is to situate characters in
physical and psychological space (the latter in the inclusive sense
proposed by Wolfgang Kayser).[21] Scenic background may also place
historical characters in time, when its man-made objects, like the
Parthenon or a medieval cathedral, belong to a certain period. The
poetic function of scene is to provide an atmosphere, an ambience,
which is appropriate to the emotionally charged human actions that
take place within it. Or perhaps it may be said — since man and his
environment are so interactive — that it is such actions that impart
to scene at least a share of its tonal effect.

In the poem landscape and inhabited places usually serve to
provide background for characters. Rarely are they an object of
special interest in themselves. Fields and places file by without
arousing special interest, but providing, nevertheless, essential
background. They also serve a specificative purpose. The juglar
takes pains to orient his listener so he knows exactly where he is. If
he mentions an anonymous place, he does not fail to situate it near a
known place: "and he halted at an eminence that is near Mont
Real" (863).

When the poet would have us see a place more distinctly, he
describes it sparingly with formulary adjectives: the rugged terrain
of the Miedes region is *maravillosa e grand* (literally, "marvelous
and great," freely, "high and forbidding"). The ". . . *e grand*" formula is used with *maravilloso* five times (427, 864, 1084, 1648,
2427), with *fiera(s)* ("wild") twice, and with *fuerte* ("strong") and
espessa ("thick,") once. In these instances the neat, evocative
simplification of the descriptive clause without specification of
plastic dimension, depicts a wild place conventionally. But when the
juglar sets the stage for the most violent scene of the poem, the outrage at Corpes, he discards the formula even though he could have
used it. Instead he says:

Into the oak wood of Corpes   the Infantes have entered;
the mountains are high,   the branches rise to the clouds
and there are wild beasts   that roam all around.

(2697 - 98)

To the conventional adjectives "high" and "wild" he adds a hyper-
bole "the branches rise to the clouds." The juglar has reserved one
of his few hyperboles for one of the climaxes of the poem, thus giving us one more example of his economy of means and of his virtuosity within the limited metaphorical scale of his restrained but intense epic style.

XII *Objects, Accouterments*

Américo Castro has noted "the singular value inherent in every
detail of dress."[22] He is right, of course, but not only pieces of
clothing acquire in context a definite formal significance. From the
very beginning, certain other objects possess an extraordinary sym-
bolical significance, for example, the doors standing open, the gates
without fastenings, and the empty porches of the Cid's house as he
abandons it to go into exile. The emptiness of his house corresponds
to the Cid's empty heart as he bids it adieu, weeping. Objects,
usually inanimate, are animated in context. The pennants carried
high and the weapons borne by Christians and Moors are not inert
and independent objects but living extensions of the warriors' arms.
The raised pennons are hyperaesthetic correlatives of the soldiers'
battle cries; cuirasses, helmets, and lances are projections of the
breasts, heads, and arms that bear them. Articles of clothing and
other objects function poetically in other ways: in one instance as a
key factor of strategy; in many others as decorative and ostentatious
appurtenances; and on one notable occasion a new white hat worn
by an innocent youth symbolizes the purity of his heart and his
naivete.[23]

In laisse 29 the Campeador takes Alcocer through a stratagem involving military paraphernalia:

> When My Cid saw that Alcocer   would not yield to him,
> he thought of a stratagem   and wasted no time:
> He left one tent standing,   he carried off the rest;
> he went down the Jalón   with his banner raised,
> his men in their armor   with their swords girded,
> shrewdly   to take them by ambush.

"Very clever," suggests the juglar between lines, "was the Cid because he made the enemy believe that he was abandoning Castejón armed with armor and with his sword *girded on*," not *unsheathed*, or *in his hand*, or *bloody*, as at other times when he was about to attack.

The poetic function of various luxurious objects and articles of dress are especially striking in the lines which describe the jeweled and gold-wrought tent poles of the king of Morocco (1785 - 91); those which enumerate the mounts, attire, and weapons of King Alfonso's men when they make ready to meet the Cid at the shore of the Tagus river (1965 - 71); those describing the bloodstained silks of the Cid's daughters at the oak grove of Corpes (2738 - 89); those which give an account of the instructions the Cid gives his men about how they should dress for the Toledo Court (3073 - 79); and, most brilliant of all, those describing the attiring of the hero before he makes his grand entrance at the court:

> He allows nothing to delay him   he who in good hour was born:
> with hose of fine cloth   he covered his legs,
> over them he put on shoes   finely adorned.
> He put on a shirt of fine cloth   as white as the sun,
> all the fastenings   were of silver and gold,
> the cuffs fit him well,   he ordered it so.
> Over these a long tunic   of finest brocade;
> worked with gold,   it shines everywhere.
> Over all a crimson skin   with golden buckles;
> My Cid Campeador   always wears it.
> Over his head a coif   made of fine linen,
> with gold it is worked   and properly made
> so none might pluck at the hair   of the good Cid Campeador;
> his beard was long   and tied with a cord,
> for this reason he did it,   he wished to protect all his person.
> Covering all   he wore a cloak of great price,
> all marveled at it   all who were there.
>
> (3084 - 3100).

Never did any actor don a more splended costume or put on his buskin and his makeup with such care.

Can the detailed, finely focused, colorful technique, the realistic touches of the above description be that of an oral poet, especially of the poet of the *Cantar de Mio Cid* whose controlled but highly charged style is usually so restrained? Does it not anticipate the elaborateness of later descriptive techniques, for example, the luxuriance of the great colorist Lope de Vega? We have become so accustomed to the tag of moderation and sobriety attached to the first masterpiece of Hispanic literature that we forget the few highly colorful descriptive passages which coincide with climactic moments of the work. The poet of the *Cantar* has gone much farther than the conventional, heraldic, descriptions of *La Chanson de Roland*. On the one hand, the live contrasting colors of his style in certain passages foreshadows that of many later ballads and, as I have suggested above, announces that of Lope de Vega in the picturesque enumerations of his traditional style. And because of its descriptive realism, which gives the impression of actuality, the epic passage we have quoted anticipates an aspect of the modern novel. Observe, for example, in lines 3094 - 3103, the details with which the juglar describes the precautions which the Cid takes before going to the Toledo Court in order to prevent his enemies from plucking his beard or pulling his hair: he ties his inordinately long beard with a cord and he covers his hair with *escarín*, a very fine cloth.

XIII   *The Cid's Beard*

In laisse 76 the poet observes:

> His beard has now grown   and keeps growing longer,
> these words My Cid has spoken of it   with his own mouth:
> "For love of king Alfonso   who has sent me into exile,
> no scissors will touch it   nor one hair of it be cut,
> and let Moors and Christians   spread the word of this."

After this vow the Cid's beard remains uncut. As we have noted, before he enters the Toledo Court it is so long that he braids it with a cord so that his enemies cannot easily pluck it. He did not cut it after the king pardoned him nor after his daughters' wedding. Undoubtedly he meant to do so on returning permanently to his home in Castile,[24] something that does not happen in the poem.

We know that the Cid of history, though pardoned twice, was not on good terms with his lord during most of his life after 1081. In the poem he enjoys the king's unreserved good will until he dies but because of the ever-present Almoravide threat he does not return to *Castiella la gentil*, ("Castile the sweet"); hence his beard remains uncut. In the last lines of the poem the juglar, when he tells us of the Cid's death calls him "My Cid, lord of Valencia." Rodrigo is still

Alfonso's vassal but not the vassal from Castile and, especially, the vassal from Vivar. The poem, therefore, does not have a completely happy ending.

The different states of the Cid's beard in the course of the poem demonstrate the singular formal significance of a physical attribute as a structural correlative. At first the juglar exclaims, "God, what a handsome beard he has!" (789); in the middle of the poem our attention is called to its growth (1238 - 42, 2059); at the end "All eyes in the court are fixed on My Cid / and on his long beard tied with a cord" (3123 - 25). In this, his final and most dramatic appearance, then, the hero's beard, grown inordinately long, becomes the cynosure of all eyes, the object of wonder. And the beard motif is not dropped at this point; it becomes even more significant. In the altercation between the Cid and García Ordóñez (laisse 40) the heated words they exchange over their respective beards bring out the merit of the hero and the mediocrity of the count. Consistent with the talent for failure which the favorite of the king frequently showed in history, he makes the mistake in the poem of attacking the Cid by making fun of his beard, a mistake he should have avoided, since the Campeador had plucked the count's beard at Cabra. Because of this humiliating incident (it is not known that it really happened but mischievous tradition records it)[25] he became known as *Conde de Cabra* (*cabra* means "goat"). The verbal clash between the Cid and the count is one of the comic high points of the poem. He who was also called *Boca-torcida* ("Wrymouth") falls into his own trap. And the irony of the situation arising from the contrast between a beard that had never been violated and one that had once been plucked is so appropriate, so fundamental in context, that its humor leaves us with the memory of a lasting aesthetic experience.

XIV *Gestures*

The physical movements described in the poem consist of certain habitual acts, facial expressions, and gestures. Like ritual motions, these formulary attitudes express more eloquently than words intense states of mind and feeling, and stamp their elemental seal on grave or happy moments of human existence. To express the pain he feels on abandoning his home the Cid turns his head back, weeping (2 - 3); he raises one hand to swear by his beard which he holds with the other hand (2476, 2829); he raises it also to make the sign of the Cross (216, 1340, 3508), and his wife, daughters, and their ladies raise theirs to thank God in prayer (1616). To express great satisfaction the hero takes hold of his beard (3280, 3713); to express great sadness he *llora de los ojos*, ("weeps with his eyes" [line 1, etc.]); to express joy *fermoso sonrrisava* (freely "he smiled happily"; glossed: "gladly smiled and looked so handsome when he smiled" [923, 2442]), or "all his body was glad and he smiled from his heart" (3184). There is much kissing of hands, which is inevitable considering that this custom was the formula for declaring vassalage, giving thanks for a gift, asking for a favor, and showing affection (*CMC*, pp. 506 - 9). The most eloquent of all the Cid's acts, biting the grass, signified abject submission[26] in the pardoning scene.

We remember the hero *animated*, emotionally charged, as it were, by his typical attitudes: turning his head as he bids a painful farewell, raising his eyes to heaven, clutching his beard, smiling, weeping, thinking and reflecting, rising to his feet before speaking, lowering his head over his horse's neck as he charged the enemy. We cannot know, we can only guess, how the juglar acted out such motions and gestures. These movements, as well as the large proportion of dialogue in the poem manifest its strong dramatic effect. Even through the printed page, the modern reader feels the impact of the juglar's histrionic skill.

XV *Formulas of Introduction to Direct Discourse*

The unrelieved repetition of formulas of introduction to direct discourse with verbs of saying would have slowed down the narrative movement of the poem. Such formulas are much more frequent in the *Roland* than in the *Cid*.[27] In the latter, excessive use of the usual introductory formula is avoided in several ways. One of them is to launch a new laisse in which the speech of a character who was already talking in the previous laisse is continued with a change of assonance but without some such formula of reintroduction as "And X continued with the following words." At other times it is only from the context of a preceding laisse that we know the identity of the speaker who begins the next laisse. This is the case, for example, between the twenty-first and twenty-second series. In many other cases an introductory line does not explicitly use a verb of saying but implies it. Through these devices the explicit use of such verbs is reduced considerably. The narrative, thus enlivened by an abundance of direct dialogue, comes close to achieving a scenic effect.[28] Among the fourteen laisses whose first line introduces the speaker, four do so with the verb "to speak" (78, 1886, 2527, 3036) and two with "to say." In the eight other instances the poet avoids, through ellipsis, the verb of saying, which is understood: "He smiled [and said] . . ." (1527); "Distressed was the king of Morocco because of My Cid don Rodrigo [and said] . . ." (1622); "This [embracing the daughters] the Cid did, their mother also, [and said] . . ." (2601 - 2); "Count don García rose to his feet [and said] . . ." (3270); "Hernando González rose to his feet [and said] . . ." (3291); "My Cid Ruy Diaz looks at Pedro Bermúdez [and says] . . ." (3301); "Martín Antolínez sprung to his feet [and said] . . ." (3361); "Then Muño Gustioz arose [and said] . . ." (3382).

Among the above elliptical formulas of introduction one is worth special mention: the verb *levantarse en pie* ("to rise to one's feet"), used four times at the beginning of four laisses, corresponds to the part of the poem in which the most heated verbal exchanges take place. These occur: during the altercation between García Ordóñez and the Cid (laisse 140); when Fernando rejects the charge of infamy (laisse 141); when Martín Antolínez challenges Diego González (laisse 146); when Muño Gustioz challenges Asur González (laisse 149).

The four repetitions of "He rose to his feet [and said]" are interrupted only once by "My Cid *looked* at Pedro Bermúdez [and said]." The interruption produces delightful comic relief. Amid the tension between opponents bursting with angry words, the Cid mischievously makes a play on the surname of Pedro Bermúdez (. . . *mudez - mudo*, i.e., "mute"), an impetuous warrior, but a man of few words. The Cid looks at him; in his eyes there is an affectionately teasing gleam: "*FABLA, Pero MUDO, varón que tanto CALLAS*" ("Speak, Peter MUTE, man who is STILL so much!"). And when, in laisse 143, Pedro Bermúdez at last speaks," the introductory formula "Pedro Bermúdez started to speak," loses its routine character and implies an amused but sympathetic comment of the narrator, who adds: "his tongue stumbles and he cannot begin;/yet once he has begun he does not hesitate." In the course of his speech Pedro Bermúdez acknowledges to the Cid that speaking is hard for him, but then, turning to the Infante don Fernando, his verbal attack is devastating, and he concludes with a spark of wit which turns around the epithet with which the Campeador had had so much fun when he called him *Pero Mudo*. Pedro finishes his answer to Fernando with the line: "Tongue without hands, how do you dare to speak?"

XVI   *Formulas of the Narrative Voice*

We will conclude our consideration of representative formulas with a few observations concerning those of the narrative voice.[29] Explicitly, by addressing his audience directly, and more subtly in other ways, the poet shows himself to be a master of the rhetoric of epic fiction.

Among the poet's formulas of direct address to his listeners the most frequent are those which arouse their attention, telling them what they would see or hear if they were eyewitnesses of the situation he is emphasizing: *veriedes tanto gozo* ("you should have seen such joy") eleven variants; *Afevos Raquel e Vidas* ("Here [you see] Raquel and Vidas") eleven variants; *odredes lo que ha dicho* ("You will hear what he has said") [eleven variants].[30] To begin a series, to emphasize the speech of an interlocutor, and, above all, to share with his listeners his intensely celebrative point of view, the poet uses the exclamation *Dios* ——! ("God ——!") as in the famous line 20, "God what a good vassal, had he but a good lord!" (seventeen variants [see de Chasca, *Registro*, pp. 18, 34]). Hart rightly says that when the poet exclaims "Dios, cómmo fo alegre! ("God, how happy he was!"), "he is not simply using a somewhat more emphatic equivalent of 'mucho fo alegre' ('he was very happy'). Rather, he is demonstrating his own sympathy for his protagonist and, by implication, enlisting his audience's sympathy for him too. It is as if he were saying 'How happy was My Cid, and how happy we all should be that it should be so!' "[31]

The exclamatory formula abounds also in nonepic literature,[32] but it is especially suited to the celebrative rhetoric of the narrative voice in epic.

The formulas of the narrative voice, then, are used to arouse the attention of the listener, to emphasize something important, and, above all, to celebrate admirable deeds. The narrative voice is as important to ancient epic as it is to the modern novel but in a fundamentally different way, for what distinguishes the literary artist of the heroic age from the novelist of our bookish age is their vision of life: the point of view of the epic poet is traditional and collective, that of the modern writer, even though he does not express himself in a traditional vacuum, is predominantly personal and individualistic.

CHAPTER 5

Structure and Form

I A Definition of Structure

IN an essay on the plot of *Tom Jones* the North American critic R. S. Crane enunciates a principle of structure or plot — the inseparability of poetic elements — which is generally applicable.[1] This principle is self-evident, but it is so frequently ignored that, with Crane, we stress its basic importance for aesthetic criticism.

Plot involves inseparably poetic components of narrative and dramatic genres, namely, action, character, and thought; it is not restricted to the framework of connected incidents. The skeletal concept of the plot is, of course, partial, since it is limited to a consideration of the connection between incidents. In its most sterile form analysis of plot degenerates into a detailed synopsis of it. Such a synopsis does not permit more than the mere mention or, at best, a superficial consideration of character.

But characters are the agents of the action, and therefore, their interactive behavior and the dramatic result of it constitute an essential element of structure. It is not enough to mention or even to describe characters, since a mere mention or description represents them only as isolated elements of the material cause; their actions and reactions must be understood as dynamic determinants of the formal cause. Considered apart from their formal function, characters are deprived of their full poetic identity, indeed they may acquire a nonpoetic identity.

For example, the relations of the Cid with his *mesnada* — members of his family and followers who became his vassals — could be judged from a nonpoetic viewpoint as a social phenomenon of eleventh-century Spain; the derogatory portrayal of the *ricos homes*, that is, members of the highest nobility like the Infantes of Carrión and Count García Ordóñez, could be taken for a manifestation of the democratic attitude of the Castilian juglar who took sides with a Castilian member of the middle nobility, namely the Cid, a mere *infanzón*; the king-vassal relationship could be considered as a sociopolitical phenomenon of the age without regard to the poetic fact that this relationship is the basis of the structure. All of these aspects of the *PMC* as a product of its times place it exclusively in its social and historical prespective and for this reason, seen in this light, it provides a rich source of authentic information for the historian.

Its *historicidad* undoubtedly gives the poem an air of verisimilitude. However, this alone does not account for its artistic excellence. The *Cantar* is an outstanding poetic specimen of its genre if by "poetic" we understand the formal working and power of the organized whole, which is compounded of fact and fiction. The historical characters, portrayed by the juglar with the modifications required by epic's celebrative form, but without detracting from the poem's verismo — these characters move in the ideal sphere of art. In that sphere the poet only suggests King Alfonso's bad side and exaggerates his good side. On the other hand, his idealization of the Cid does not violate the truth, for what above anything else characterizes both the Cid of history and the poetic Cid is his unflagging loyalty to an unjust lord. Concerning the juglar's portrayal of the hero we therefore say again, quoting Aristotle's *Poetics*, that "if it happens that he [the poet] puts something that has actually taken place into poetry, he is none the less a poet; for there is nothing to prevent some of the things that have happened from being the kind of things that can happen and that is the sense in which he is their maker."[2]

How does thought comprise an element of structure? In disposing the action and portraying his personae the poet shapes the former in sequential points of time and characterizes the latter governed by the guiding principle of his theme. The thematic complex of his composition, a complex consisting of a central idea and of complementary ideas, determines the manner in which he organizes the actions and presents his characters. The characters themselves, directly or indirectly through their actions and through their words, explicitly or implicitly carry out their creator's intention.

II *A Definition of Form*

We use the word "form" to signify not only the shaping of an organic whole but the cumulative power of its unfolding process to exert a given effect on the reader or listener. "Form" is, then, the dynamic artistic structure whose working and power are realized

when the initial complex of the signifieds and signifiers fulfill their
function through the final signifieds and signifers.[3]

All epic works of the heroic age exemplify celebrative generic
form, but within it each individual epic posesses its own peculiar
form. To understand a given epic as a typical specimen of its kind
we should be aware of the formulistic techniques, thematic
associations, and mythic necessity which are the common possession
of all epic poets since Homer. But to evaluate a particular epic as the
product of an individual poet's creative initiative, it is necessary to
determine his special way of integrating into the composition
whatever he borrows from common poetic property. For example,
one of the well-known themes of Germanic and French epic is the
magic sword. As we have noted elsewhere,[4] only one of the Cid's
two swords is remotely related to its transpyrenean counterparts.

That which most distinctly manifests the form of a specific epic is
the moral character of the protagonist, whether his deeds take place
in a mythic and marvelous world like that of Odysseus, Achilles, or
Siegfried or in a predominantly real world like that of Rodrigo. In
either case the epic hero's extraordinary powers raise him to a
transcendent sphere above mere mortals. Hence even when he suf-
fers a disastrous end, like Roland, his death, rather than a tragic
event, is the result of a heroic act that arouses admiration more than
pity and fear. The French masterpiece is, then, both celebrative
and, to a lesser degree, pathetic. *The Poem of the Cid*, however, is
wholly celebrative. There is no doubt even from the beginning,
when things look darkest, that all the Cid's efforts will be successful.
"Ride forward, My Cid, good Campeador," the Archangel St.
Gabriel says to him in a dream, "for no man ever rode forth at so
propitious a moment; / as long as you shall live that which is yours
will prosper" (497 - 99). Through these words, therefore, spoken by
a messenger of God, we know in advance that with His help and
through the hero's mighty effort, he will overcome all obstacles,
because he is superior to them; he is the master of his destiny, not its
victim.[5] The moral character of the Castilian hero is essentially
flawless, in spite of certain very human traits such as his shrewdness
in dealing with people, including his own followers.[6] He therefore
surpasses in moral excellence (Spitzer calles him a "saintly hero")
the tragic heroes of drama and epic, for these, by making a fatal mistake because of a tragic flaw, are the cause of their own destruction:
for example Achilles is destroyed by his wrath, Roland by his pride.
The Cid, on the other hand, notwithstanding the minor offense of

tricking the moneylenders, is essentially a good man. His almost flawless character combined with his military skill and an irresistible will to win save him from all harm.

III   *The Central Idea of the Thematic Complex*

In keeping with our choice to understand exterior form from the perspective of interior form,[7] our point of departure will be a consideration of the central idea of the thematic complex, the unfolding of which forms an organic whole whose consistency is produced by a system of predominantly admirable actions. For the sake of convenience we will designate the central idea with the word "theme."

We use the word "theme" then, in a broad sense, without meaning to suggest that in the *PMC* or in any literary composition theme may be reduced to a single idea. Nevertheless, among the ideas constituting a complex of nuclear ideas, one of them may be predominant, especially in works expressing collective attitudes of the same general order, in other words, works that possess a marked generic kinship. Heroic poetry is the most noteworthy in this respect, for all of the specimens of this genre celebrate the great deeds of a national, legendary hero. Therefore in the broadest sense of the word, the theme of this kind of epic is heroism; but this statement only suggests the most basic idea of the thematic complex; it reduces the concept of theme to an oversimplification which distinguishes one whole genre from other genres, but it does not distinguish one individual heroic epic from another. This distinction can be made by determining the unique character of a given epic hero and by understanding how his character determines his actions.

The poetic Cid's distinctive traits — like those of the Cid of history — are loyalty and magnanimity. Because he is loyal and magnanimous, that is, willing to sacrifice his personal interest to the interest of the king and of Christian Spain, notwithstanding that the law and custom of his times entitled him to make war against his lord, he progressively earns the good will of the hostile king. The latter's "pardon" restores his honor. The poem's most important central idea, therefore, is the restoration of Rodrigo's lost honor. It begins with his exile and ends with his triumph at the Toledo Court. And everything that happens between this beginning and this ending contributes to the hero's aggrandizement: the series of victories from Castejón to Valencia spread his fame even *alent mar* ("beyond the sea"); through the spoils he acquires in these victories, he becomes enormously rich; the highborn Infantes of Carrión honor him by wishing to marry his daughters even though they are motivated by covetousness of his wealth; and paradoxically, his greatest dishonor, the affront to his daughters, foreshadows his greatest honor, the second marriage of the young women, this time to the princes of Navarre and Aragón, a marriage through which the Cid becomes a kinsman of the kings of Spain.

IV *The Hero*

There is no praise so authentic as that of an enemy. Ten years after the Cid died, Ibn Bassam, author of *Treasury of Excellencies of the Spaniards* (he was referring to the Spanish Moslems), wrote: "The power of this tyrant [the Cid] became increasingly unbearable; its terrible weight was felt in the coastal regions and in the high plateaus, and he made tremble with fear all men, both near and far. . . . Yet this man, who was the scourge of his age, was, by his unflagging and clear-sighted energy, his virile character, and his heroism, a miracle among the great miracles of the Almighty" (quoted by MP, *EC*, 605). After quoting the above words Menéndez Pidal comments: "Thus, like Manzoni in his famous ode on the death of Napoleon, the Moslem enemy bowed reverently before a creative genius that bore the imprint of God" (*EC*, 605). Thus, though dipped in venom, Ibn Bassam's pen inscribed for history the most hyperbolical praise ever vouchsafed Rodrigo Díaz of Vivar.

As for the poet of Medinaceli, who celebrates the hero on his knees, he never stresses the terrible violence of which the Cid was capable toward those who did not play fair with him. He shows us only the Cid's good side, notably his loyalty and moderation; the only severe punitive measure the Cid of the poem takes is to order the hanging of deserters (1254), and this not on his own initiative, but upon the advice of his chief lieutenant, Álvar Fáñez (1251 - 54).

In the poem the Cid, through thick and thin, exemplifies the highest chivalric virtues: manliness, loyalty, devoutness, courtesy, and, above all, moderation and self-control. Therefore his behavior consistently arouses in our sensibility the proper effect of epic: admiration. The power to produce the force of this effect is exerted by the unfolding form of the poem, which celebrates the greatness of the hero. Having lost his honor, the Cid recovers it by degrees through a series of increasingly resounding victories. His greatest success is the reward of his phenomenal achievement: the marriage of his daughters to two princes.

In general terms, this or something like this is the heart of the structure of the *Poem of the Cid* and explains how it exerts the power of its epic form. In more specific terms of narrative technique the structure unfolds through a series of organically connected incidents and episodes within the principal action and through the characters who carry it out.

V *The Quintessential Action*

The principal action consists of a total system of incidents arising from the Cid's need to regain his honor. The determining factor is the relationship between King Alfonso and his vassal, Rodrigo Díaz of Vivar. The principal action, therefore, consists of the exploits which the protagonist carries out to rehabilitate himself through two grave crises: the disgrace of his exile and the affront of his daughters at Corpes. This action is not simple but complex, for it consists of two great discrete systems of incidents, one warlike, the other domestic. These systems are artistically linked; the poet avoids the danger of producing a dichotomous effect because he succeeds in making the domestic crisis the logical result of an incident in the warlike action. Throughout the complex action one theme predominates: the Cid's constant effort to vindicate himself. Corollary to the Cid's initiative is King Alfonso's reaction to it, first as an unjust lord on a mean human plane and then, at the lofty level of his office, as the instrument of justice.

VI *The Relative Value of Incidents*

To take any given incident, however important it may be, for the principal action, is to take the part for the whole. Milá holds that the principal action of the poem is the wedding and that every other incident is accessory to it.[8] It would be more exact to say that the wedding is the most decisive event in the structure, the most important of the intermediate incidents, that is, those which result in the aggrandizement of the Cid, because it connects the first series of warlike incidents with the second series of domestic incidents. If the wedding were the "principal action," as we understand the term in an inclusive sense, the other particular actions would be part of it. However, the structural function of the wedding is precisely to prepare the way for the work's culminating peripeteia. For this reason there is much talk about its probably bad consequences before it takes place, and therefore much argument about who was to blame for its disastrous result.

Additional textual proof of the wedding's transitional, not

culminating or inclusive importance, is the scant attention paid to it as a sumptuous occasion. The account of the preparation for the wedding feast is reduced to a mere four lines (2205 - 8). It is true that the civil ceremony is described at some length and with a certain degree of solemnity, but what the poet emphasizes is that the Cid is not pleased by the whole affair. The religious ceremony which by its very nature was bound to be more solemn, could have given the poet the opportunity to describe its undoubted[9] magnificence with ringing lines. However, he does not even mention it. Why? In our opinion because the poet did not wish to divert our attention from the protagonist. By omitting it he leaves fresh in our minds the Cid's previous disapproval of the match, and thus subtly suggests that it will turn out badly. Thus, by understating the wedding itself, the poet succeeds in making the disapproving father dominate its celebration negatively and at the same time also succeeds in conveying the idea that it is the greatest honor the father has received so far. The wedding guests, the flower of peninsular nobility, recognize this honor through their presence and by accepting the Cid's magnificent presents. From the viewpoint of structure, merely *suggesting* the magnificence of the wedding is a masterstroke of understatement; enough but not too much is said to make us aware of its positive and negative importance.

VII   *"God, What a Worthy Vassal, Had he But a Worthy Lord!"*

Since the king and the Cid are the key characters, tracing the stages of their relationship will give us a clear idea of the structural development in the poem.

We are indebted to Gustavo Correa for a penetrating analysis of the honor theme in the *Poema de Mio Cid*.[10] Only with respect to one point, a rather important one, do I find myself not in complete agreement. Our difference may be reduced to the following questions: Is Alfonso a perfect king? Is the Cid a model vassal? Correa answers both questions in the affirmative. Only to the second do I give an unequivocal yes. The correct solution of this problem is all important for an understanding of the *Poema* as a work of art, because, as Correa himself has so well shown, the king-vassal relationship is the basis of its structure.

The fact that the epithet "bueno" is used seven times and "ondrado" five to characterize the king is not enough to establish his perfection. Neither can a subtle dialectic eleminate from that pregnant verse *Dios, que buen vasallo si oviesse buen señore!* ("God what a good vassal, had he but a worthy lord!''), whether we accept Amado Alonso's[11] or Leo Spitzer's[12] gloss, its unmistakale anti-Alfonsine and pro-Cidian sentiment, a sentiment resulting from the unfavorable opinion which the citizens of Burgos have of the king's conduct.

It is true that Rodrigo himself does not hold Alfonso responsible for his personal disaster: *Esto me an buolto mios enemigos malos* (''This is what my bad enemies have schemed against me'' [9]). Neither does his wife, Jimena: *Por malos mestureros de tierra sodes echado*, (''Because of evil schemers you are banished from the land'' [267]). But it is not proper for the perfect knight nor for any of his followers or relatives to blame the king even if he is not blameless; neither is it fitting for the people to give open expression to their disapproval, although their censure does not fail to make itself felt indirectly. The king can do no wrong; but what a pity that he should not be as perfect as his vassal!

Certain characteristics of the ideal, generic, king of the medieval *patria grande* (''great [spiritual] fatherland'') can undoubtedly be seen in the complex personality of Alfonso. But we must not close our eyes to his local side, to the Alfonso of this particular epic and of the *patria chica* (''his [local] motherland''), to the Leonese-Castilian king (perhaps more Leonese than Castilian), to the idiosyncratic human being. If we see his individual as well as his generic aspect it is not difficult to reconcile the apparent contradiction between the clause *si oviesse buen señore*,[13] suggesting that Alfonso was not exactly a model king, and the almost idolatrous cult of which he is the object as the representative of kingship, a cult implicit in the tone of the *Poema* as a whole but definitely evident in the ritualistic gesture of abject submission with which the Cid, groveling before Alfonso, bites the grass when they meet for the pardoning scene on the banks of the Tagus (2021 - 24). But even if we fail to see individual characteristics in the king as an agent in the poem and insist on considering him a representative type of his exalted state, his initial ill will toward the Cid can be considered as the symptom of a disease which at that time afflicted the Spanish monarchy as an institution.[14]

It is not fitting to the epic form, the typical effect of which is to awaken admiration for the hero, to set up a more admirable person as a model for the protagonist. Above all is it not fitting to the *Poema de Mio Cid*, whose protagonist is the model hero par excellence — he has even been called, as we have noted, a saintly hero — for the king to be portrayed as a paragon to whose level of ex-

cellence the vassal must rise, as Correa suggests when he affirms
that the Cid "has achieved the same stature as his lord."[15]

The achievement of such equality is not evident in the poem.
Right or wrong, the king is always the master of his subjects' fate; he
is never a sharer of honor on equal terms but rather the arbiter who
confers it or takes it away. If his arbitrary acts are right, his personal
merit rises to the level of his radiant kingship; if not, his kingship
becomes tarnished but never seriously impaired. As king, Alfonso
dwells in a sphere which is inaccessible to the vassal; as a human being Rodrigo rises above him. This complicated situation is brought
out by the text of the *Cantar*. Alfonso's injustice imposes an awed
respect, and especially when he demands the unwilling cooperation
of the people in order to enforce his decree. When the exiled Cid
departs from Burgos under the black cloud of the royal interdict,
however much the Burgalesans may love and admire him (*grande
duelo avien las yentes cristianas*, "all Christian people with grief
were stricken" [29]), they do not dare help him:

> *Conbidar le ien de grado,   mas ninguno non osava:*
> *el rey don Alfonsso   tanto avie le grand saña*

> They would have invited him gladly,   but did not dare;
> for King Alfonso   was so wroth.

                                                            (21 - 22)

We may suppose that when the juglar recited these lines he
communicated through the inflection of his voice the collective
regret that the king should be so severe toward a blameless subject.
One feels throughout the entire fourth laisse a humble and resigned
popular censure together with the general attitude of unquestioning
acceptance of the royal will. The prestige of the king is so great that
even his unjust decrees are taken as the whims of fate, as those
mysterious irregularities of an imperfect world.

The honor of the Cid never reaches nor can it ever reach *la misma
altura de la de su señor* ("the same height as that of his lord"), not
even when the second marriage of his daughters makes him a
kinsman of the kings of Spain, because a king-emperor, like a star,
dwells apart in awesome loneliness, as may be seen by the words
which Correa himself quotes from don Juan Manuel's *Libro de los
estados*. Even in a negative sense the king exists on a superior level,
since if a vassal is affronted on his account the king's affront is

greater — greater, because any dishonorable act becomes magnified if it touches the royal person. When after the Corpes incident the Cid sends Muño Gustioz to the king to demand justice, the latter says to Alfonso: *Tienes* [i.e., the Cid] *por deshondrado, mas la vuestra es mayor* ("He [the Cid] holds himself dishonored, but your dishonor is greater" [2950]). And the king agrees with him:

> *e verdad dizez en esto,   tú Muño Gustioz,*
> *ca yo casé sus fijas   con infantes de Carrión;*
> *fizlo por bien,   que fosse a su pro.*
> *Si quier el casamiento   fecho non fosse oy!*

> And you speak the truth,   you, Muño Gustioz.
> I arranged the marriage of the daughters   to the heirs of Carrión;
> I did it for the best,   for his benefit.
> Oh, that such a marriage   had never been arranged!

(2955 - 58)

Later the Cid reports his wife as saying:

> *desto que nos abino   que vos pese, señor*
> about all this that happened to us   may you grieve, my lord

(3041)

and

> *por mis fijas quem dexaron   yo non he desonor,*
> *ca vos las casastes rey,   sabredes qué fer oy.*

> I am not dishonored   because they abandoned my daughters,
> for since you, king, married them,   you will know what to do now.

(3149 - 50)

Under the circumstances it behooves the king to be the instrument of justice. Only through a trial at law which he himself and no one else can authorize may the matter be adjudicated — unless he should prefer to act arbitrarily, which he does not choose to do, having by now grown in moral stature. An affront indirectly affecting the king on the part of persons *de natura tan alta* ("of such high estate") as are the Infantes of Carrión is a national issue justifying the summoning of the grandees of Spain. Rodrigo is vindicated at the Cortes of Toledo as is also the king, because if the latter shared the dishonor of the affront he also shares the honor of the victory which the plaintiff's champions win in the judicial duel. In this sense king and vassal are coparticipators in honor and dishonor, but on an unequal plane, since the Cid can theoretically be ruined by a legal defeat, whereas the king remains fundamentally immune. It is true that the Cid's defeat would have been a blow to Alfonso, but not a serious one. In any event such a defeat is impossible to conceive. The right is clearly on the side of Rodrigo. Moreover, the defendants are so inferior physically and morally that we know quite well beforehand who the victors are going to be. The chief purpose of the fictitous trial is to bring into bold relief in a grand climax the human dignity, the moral greatness, and the juridical virtuosity of the Cid.[16] As the action of the Cortes unfolds we also learn to admire the acquired greatness of a now just-minded king, so different from the grudging tyrant of the first Cantar.

In a sense it is the Cid who honors the king because Alfonso honors himself by honoring him. If the standard by which we determine honor is intrinsic human merit and not birth, Rodrigo is the true object of homage. In this deceivingly simple but deeply ambivalent poem the fundamental complication arises from the clash between two sets of standards, the personal and the political. The citizens of Burgos sympathize with the Cid, who is right according to every human standard; but they must do violence to their feelings when their mores oblige them to comply with a royal act which cannot be questioned regardless of its justice or injustice. Hence the king's pardon, which is indispensable for the restitution of the hero, may be seen as a formidable technicality which cannot be denied the petitioner without lessening the human worth of the bestower.

An analysis of the structural significance of the king-vassal relationship would tend, I believe, to confirm what I have said. The dividing line between the two main parts of the poem comes at the moment when the relative position between the king and the Cid subtly changes. This happens when Rodrigo no longer is a petitioner and Alfonso finds himself in a defensive position. The change occurs precisely in the middle of the poem (line 1892), twenty-seven lines from the mathematical center, when king Alfonso says in a soliloquy: *Del casamiento non sé si [el Cid] abrá sabor* ("I do not know if he [the Cid] will be pleased with this marriage"). The king, then, once bound to destroy Rodrigo, and until recently the recipient of propitiatory gifts, *now* finds himself having qualms lest he should displease his vassal. And rightly so. For henceforth the Cid will never fail, whenever the occasion arises, to show his displeasure with the projected marriage before it takes place, and after it is solemnized he disclaims all responsibility for its evil consequences and blames the king for them.

What is the step-by-step process through which Alfonso one day finds himself in an inferior position with respect to his vassal, a position graphically defined by the line *la conpaña del Çid creçe, e la del rey mengó* ("the Cid's followers increase and those of the king diminish [2165]")? The first step in this transition was the king's change of heart toward the exile, a change which makes the pardon possible. The pardon, however, is not the result of a magnanimous benevolence. The Cid's character and abilities have won for him a success so imposing that Alfonso cannot help but recognize it.

The progression of the moral action takes place on two planes, that of the Cid, active and volitional, in the foreground; that of the king, passive and responsive, in the background. The Cid *acts* and the king *reacts*. And this system of actions and reactions progresses in three stages which correspond to the three warlike actions of the first two Cantares: the action at Alcocer, the defeat of Fariz and Galve, and the action at Valencia. After each victory the Cid sends a present to Alfonso and the importance of the victory may be gauged by the worth and size of the gift: first thirty horses, then a hundred, and finally two hundred, topped by a bonus of thirty palfreys and thirty high-spirited war horses. The degree of increasing benevolence (with a corresponding decrease of ill will) on the king's part may also be gauged by the worth of the presents, not only with respect to their material value (in this case Alfonso would be no more than a comic king of spades), but even more, because they are concrete signs of the honor which the hero, *ganándose el pan* (freely translated: "by gaining sustenance conquering the enemy") is winning for himself. With the defeat of the invading Almoravide hosts after the capture of Valencia the Cid has done all he can for himself, and this is more than what is needed to bring about the king's pardon.

The royal prize that goes with the pardon, namely the marriage of the hero's daughters to the highborn Infantes of Carrión, brings with it dire consequences which Alfonso deplores and on account of which he finds himself, as noted, in a defensive position. Again the monarch is the instrument, if not the cause, of Rodrigo's disgrace, but with the difference that on the first occasion, bearing him ill will, he was only too ready to listen to the slanders of the scandalmongers and not unhappy to see his subject in deep trouble;

while now, being kindly disposed, he sincerely regrets the unfortunate results of which he was the unwitting cause. There is a more significant difference: the Alfonso who decreed the exile identified himself with the forces of evil as represented by the envious slanderers, forces which he abets with all the arbitrary power of his office at its worst; but the Alfonso who arranged the match with good though ill-fated intentions rejects these forces and brings them to justice with all the majesty of his office at its best. The difference in the king's moral position makes a great difference also in the way he is able to repair the damage he has done. The honor of the Cid no longer depends only on his master's arbitrary will. An authority superior to that of the king, the Law, rules on the matter of the vassal's second disgrace. It is true that the machinery of the law must be set in motion and administered by the monarch, since he is the only one who can summon or refrain from summoning the Cortes and since he is also the chief judge who during the trial may grant or fail to grant the pleas of the contending parties. The Cid could conceivably be still at the mercy of a prejudiced king who might maladminister justice. Under the changed circumstances that possibility does not, of course, exist. The tyrant who listened to the Cid's enemies has been replaced by the just representative of exalted kingship. He who decreed the exile was prompted by an ugly passion. He who presides over the Cortes is motivated by a high sense of duty. The envious and unfair king becomes the fair and upright king.

It would be a mistake to assign to the Alfonso of the first phase the part of an opponent, and to the Alfonso of the second that of a champion of the Cid. The king is traditionally above the contending parties. His is the role of Fate, first frowning and then smiling on his subject. This abstract agent, however, functions through a human being who for human reasons favors at first the forces of evil as a result of a generic weakness of the kings of those semibarbarous times, the weakness of being acutely susceptible to the insinuations of intriguing courtiers. Did the citizens of Burgos have this institutional rather than individual weakness in mind when they expressed their regret that the perfect vassal should not have had a model lord? If so, there is justification for Spitzer's subtle statement to the effect that "the vassal is good, the king is good . . . ; what is lacking is an adequate relationship between a good vassal and a good lord, because of the imperfections of human life on earth, which is not exactly paradisiacal."[17] Perhaps something may be added to these words: the goodness of the king is relative, that of the Cid absolute. The fomer exemplifies the norm of his class; the latter transcends the norm of his. Alfonso's position, is, therefore, morally inferior to that of his vassal. Nevertheless, his royal authority makes it possible for him arbitrarily to determine the fate of the Cid and of his people. Herein lies the dramatic power, the psychological tension of the poem, that is, in the opposition of the arbitrary power of the monarchy to the moral greatness of an individual, the former imposing itself through an unjust decree, the latter triumphing over it by means of a phenomenal material success and of an unexampled integrity.

VIII *The Cid's Enemies*

Since the protagonist is a model hero, it is fitting that his unalloyed goodness and valor should be projected in bold relief against the unmitigated wickedness and cowardice of the villains in the work, namely, his sons-in-law, the Infantes of Carrión. The Infantes, as Spitzer has noted, represent the forces of evil which an ironic fate, personified by the unwitting king, pits against the hero in the second half of the poem, where at the Toledo Court the clash between him and the Infantes, abetted by the Cid's enemies, is dramatized. This conflict is not clearly brought out in the first part, in which the dramatic interest is provided by the unhappy initial phase of the king-vassal relationship; however it is foreshadowed at the very beginning when the Cid says: "This is what my evil enemies have schemed against me" (9). Jimena also says, in line 267: "Because of evil schemers you are banished from the land." Undoubtedly, one of these meddlers was Count García Ordóñez, the chief of the band of scandalmongers who poisoned Alfonso's receptive mind against Rodrigo. It was these enemies who, at first behind the scenes, caused the first critical incident, namely, the decree of expatriation. Later, in the second part, the opposed forces clash openly at the Toledo Court. This culminating conflict is caused by the most violent and heartrending incident of the whole poem: the outrage at Corpes. There the monstrous cruelty of the sons-in-law vents itself against the helpless innocence of their young wives. In the end when the affronted father and his champions confront the offenders at the court, good triumphs over evil and heaven rewards the hero magnificiently: two princes ask for his daughters' hands.

IX *The Cid's Daughters and His Wife*

The Cid's daughters are kept in the background except on the occasion of the civil wedding ceremony and at Corpes. Nevertheless, they are to be counted among the prime movers of the action. In the first place because, once the king has deprived their father of his honor, one of his chief motives is to find honorable marriages for his daughters: "May it please God and Santa Maria/one day with my own hands I may give my daughters in marriage" (282 - 282b). And also because later, when the marriage which the king arranges fails because of Corpes, the husbands' conduct there determines all that happens in the last part of the poem.

As for the relations between Rodrigo and his wife, Jimena, there is not much to add to the analysis of Pedro Salinas,[18] the best on the subject. Perhaps the only objection that might be made is that he does not take into account Jimena's connection with the central theme of the poem, that is, the Cid's honor, a theme about which Salinas had written an excellent study previously.[19] In the second study he limits his view to "that intimate zone in which the protagonists are the innermost feelings of the characters."[20] But Jimena feels more than the personal suffering of separation from her husband. In her own feminine way she shares the disgrace of the exile with him, for he has left her relatively poor within the walls of Cardeña and at the mercy of a displeased king who, as we have noted (p. 34), once went to the extreme of putting her and her children in prison. What dignity could a woman have, widowed by her husband's exile, dependent on the hospitality of friends, with two unmarriageable daughters if her husband should fail? The exile lasted three years. During this period which must have seemed interminable, Jimena and her children had to live confined in Cardeña. She probably was afraid to communicate with her friends and they with her. The juglar permits us to assume all this when he has Jimena say to the Cid upon rejoining him: "Grace, Campeador, who in good hour girded sword! / You have delivered me from much vile shame" (1595 - 96). These words identify Jimena with the political situation in the poem and make her an integral part of its theme.

Much can be said about the other characters. For the moment we refer the reader to the excellent analysis of Dámaso Alonso.[21]

X *Variety in the* Poema de Mio Cid

The fundamental variety of the poem is the result of the contrast between what Américo Castro calls sense experience and moral experience.[22] Broadly speaking, this contrast is observed between the first part which narrates a series of military incidents, and the second part dealing with the Cid's domestic troubles. In both parts the two kinds of experience noted by Castro take place more or less simultaneously, but their relative importance is inverted. In the first part a great moral victory, the Cid's magnanimous decision not to fight his king, serves as the spiritual background for a series of military actions; in the second part the military action continues up to a certain point with the battle against Búcar, in which the behavior of the Infantes is as cowardly as it had been in the lion incident. Angered by their humiliation, they cruelly take out their spite on their wives at Corpes, and to right that wrong the Cid seeks justice at the Toledo Court.

In each of the two parts, furthermore, there is an ascending gradation culminating with a climax: in the first the military action reaches its highest point in the battle against Yusuf in which the Cid spectacularly exercises his invincible generalship so that his wife may witness it at its best; the action of the second part culminates at the Toledo Court, where the imposing presence of the Cid and his eloquence, as well as the greatness to which the king at last has risen, present an unforgettable moral spectacle.

The three major incidents forming the "architectonic masses" noted by Menéndez y Pelayo[23] are each of a different kind. The expatriation is a political event; Corpes leads to a family quarrel; the Toledo Court is a spectacular judicial assembly. There are also differences between the important military actions of each of the three cantars. In describing at length and with considerable detail the taking of Alcocer the poet shows an expert knowledge of the Cid's strategy and tactics; the battle against Yusuf in the rich Valencian countryside is a spectacular exhibition of bold courage; and in the battle against Búcar, as we have already indicated, one of the juglar's chief formal aims is to bring out the cowardice of the Infantes.

This rather specific variety of the military actions unfolds within a more general and subtle variety of emotional tone. The first cantar is pathetic and warlike; the second, warlike, spectacular, and triumphant; the third, violent, dramatic, and triumphant. There is also a contrast between two zones of interest: that which Pedro Salinas calls the "intimate zone," and that which we call the political zone. In the first, the Cid and his family are involved; in the second, King Alfonso and Rodrigo.

Through the above contrasts the poet achieves simple differentiation. More subtle are the contrasts produced by processes that unfold in contrary directions. The most basic of these becomes progressively apparent in the king-vassal relationship, which we have already analyzed. The same kind of contrast results from the relationship of the Cid and his sons-in-law.[24]

In addition to the kind of psychological development noted above, two kinds of physical movement are combined. This is one more aspect of variety through which interest is maintained. Without contrasting peace-seeking actions, the unrelieved narration of one military clash after another would have been monotonous. Our poet avoids satiating his listeners with uninterrupted battle accounts by having Minaya Álvar Fáñez, his right-hand man, undertake conciliatory missions to King Alfonso after each of three important victories. While the Cid, never back-tracking, continues on his route, Minaya zigzags back and forth. Three crucial victories, then, are followed by three momentous embassies.

The most striking contrast in the narrative movement as a whole is to be noted between the first 2,526 and the last 1,206 lines, that is, between the first two-thirds and the last third of the poem. In the first great division military operations predominate: marches, raids, battles, and sieges. The last third of the poem deals exclusively with the Cid's family affairs. These are climaxed by the announcement of the second marriage of his daughters.

The warlike operations merit special attention, so varied are they in the poem, so uniform in certain French chansons.[25] Castejón is taken by stealth; the Cid and his men lie all night in ambush before attacking. At Alcocer the Cid also takes the Moors by surprise, but the encounter between the Christians and the enemy is more violent. Here the loud clash of arms in the open is presented *agitato* and *fortissimo* in two parallel asyndetic series (laisses 35, 36), the most resounding in the whole formulisitc repertory of the juglar. In describing the battle of Tévar, the poet makes fun of the way the Catalans fight. The battle against the unnamed Moorish kings of Valencia is like an echo of the encounter at Alcocer. The battle against Yusuf is spiced by a dash of fictionalization — the juglar wants to make a good story of it — through the obviously invented device of having the Cid's wife and daughters watch his victory from the lofty "balcony" of the alcazar of Valencia. In the last battle of the poem, the juglar presents King Búcar in a delicately ironic light. This comic devaluation of a Moorish enemy balances the derogatory humor vented at the expense of a Christian enemy, the count of Barcelona, at Tévar.

Among the large contrasts minor ones abound. Contrasts, large and small, enliven the narration throughout the poem and may be found at random even in the hemistiches of a given line.

XI *Tempo*

As we have noted, through the long military phase of the poem, the movement in space is, on the whole, straightforward on the part of the Cid and back and forth on Minaya's part. Because the straight and zigzagged lines give the impression of being traced simultaneously, the movement during the military phase is complex. And the tempo, especially that of the Cid's strenuous progress, is rapid. From the moment the king issues his decree of exile until three years later, when the Campeador takes Valencia, he never stops anywhere for long, except to lay an ambush, and to wait for the besieged enemy to surrender. He and his men sleep briefly; they arise each day at dawn. The most frequently heard sounds are the matutinal crowing of cocks and, between the lines, the sound of hoofbeats, rhythmic and regular during marches, thunderous in battle. Especially in the first cantar the *leit motif* is the sound of hoofbeats.

Frequently the poet accelerates narrative movement by rapidly enumerating the names of places. These flash past the reader with cinematographic velocity:

> *Salieron de Medina,   e Salón passavan,*
> *Arbuxuelo arriba   privado aguijavan,*
> *el campo de Taranz   luégol atravessavan,*
> *vinieron a Molina,   la que Avengalvón mandava.*

> They left Medina   and passed Jalón,
> up the river by Arbuxuelo   they spurred without pausing,
> then they passed   by the plain of Taranz,
> they came to Molina   where Abengalbón was lord.   (1542 - 45)

These four lines lose a good deal of force in translation, for it cannot render the assonance *a-a* of the final imperfects, the cumulative force of which gathers momentum. The translation can only suggest movement by means of the enumerations of five place-names in four lines and, less successfully, through the use of six uniform past tenses of verbs of movement for the original's two preterites (*salieron* and *vinieron*) and four imperfects (*passavan, aguijavan, atravessavan, mandava*). The perfective initial preterite, *salieron*, imposes its predominant notion of rapidly finished action on the four final imperfects, thus confirming the fact that the imperfect is a "camaleonic" tense, the tense which most readily yields to the dominant notion of a given verbal context, especially the preterite and the vivid present.[26] It should be noted finally, that the first and fourth lines of the four we have quoted are swiftly launched by the rhyming preterites (*salieron, vinieron*). These preterites, the endings of which designate the third person plural, are not burdened by the weight of the subject pronoun *ellos* ("they"), which cannot be omitted in English.

The above example must suffice to illustrate one aspect of the fast-paced technique of the poem, especially in its initial phases. From the moment the Cid leaves Burgos until he encamps before Alcocer, rapid progress is almost continuous and the places along the way are specified with the exactness of a timetable.

XII *Time*

In the *Poem of the Cid* the actualization of past time is inseparable from palpable movement in space; in many parts we feel time in its most immediate and real form, the passing of each day: "The day went and night came in" (311). Time in the Cantar is presented in terms of day-to-day experience:

> The dawn goes gray   and the morning comes,
> the sun came forth,   God, how fair was the dawn!
> All began to stir   in Castejón;
> they opened the gates   and went out of the town
> to look at their fields   and all their property.

(455 - 58)

The nights are very short. Sometimes night and day are turned around: "They rode forward by night without resting" (434). The Cid, after riding hard a good part of the night, arrives at San Pedro de Cardeña to bid his family farewell when "the cocks quicken their song and dawn is breaking." This strident song of roosters proclaims the haste of the Campeador and his men. The moneylenders, Raquel and Vidas, do not hurry enough for the impatient Martínez Antolínez who says to them urgently that "Mio Cid must depart before the cock sings" (169). Once the Jews agree to make the loan, Martín, afraid they will be too deliberate in handing over the six hundred marks, says: "You see the night is falling, the Cid has no time" (137).

The duration of a given period of time is precisely stated almost in every part of the poem, but this precision is most notable in the first cantar which gives the impression of a comprehensive journal covering three years of the Cid's life, from the moment the juglar tells us that "Six days of grace are already past, / three days remain and afterwards none" (306 - 7), until the conquest of the whole Valencian region. This time-span is summed up in the three lines of the extremely brief laisse 71:

> Seizing and despoiling,   riding at night,
> sleeping in the daytime,   taking those towns,
> My Cid spent three years   in the lands of the Moors.

After these three years two more pass before the poem ends. The wedding having taken place shortly after the taking of Valencia, the Infantes remain there with their wives nearly two years (2271). If we add to these two years the seven weeks' time limit which the king sets for the court to assemble after the Corpes outrage, and the three weeks until the judicial duel takes place, we calculate that five years passed from the time the Cid left Burgos until his champions represented him on the dueling field. Thus the thirteen-year historical period, 1081 - 1094, that is, from the year of the first expatriation to the taking of Valencia, is reduced in the poem to five years. During the historical thirteen-year period the Cid suffered the king's severest displeasure at least twice and was pardoned twice, the second time briefly, but in the poem the vassal is expatriated only once, forgiven once and for all, and the king changes his attitude permanently. Obviously, the compressed time, the still complicated but less extended king-vassal relationship in the poem, do not correspond to what truly happened in history but to what was required by the juglar's poetic intention.

XIII   *Psychological Development*

To fit into a narrator's neat conception of the character development of a person who breaks with another person, the changing
state of mind of one or the other may unfold simply in a certain psychological direction following the incident or incidents that
produced the break. This kind of uncomplicated process is exemplified by King Alfonso whose ill will against the Cid is gradually
dissipated by the latter's loyal gestures, deeds, and consistent
success. As for the Cid, he is, on the whole, a more complicated person than the king. Against his better judgment and never yielding to
a rebellious urge which is subtly suggested, he reluctantly abides by
Alfonso's well-meant wish to make a prestigious match for his
daughters. Once they are married his love for them, trapping him
into wishful thinking, blinds him to the despicable character of his
sons-in-law. Within the complexity of his character, however,
Rodrigo undergoes a simple gradual change of attitude for the
better in one respect. At the beginning of his exile he is naturally discouraged and uncertain of his future. On leaving his homeland he
says, "Now I depart Castile since the King's wrath pursues me, /
and know not if I shall return in all my days" (219 - 20). And on bidding his wife farewell: "Now we part. God knows if we shall ever
meet again" (373). At the beginning he weeps frequently but his
tears eventually turn to smiles as Heaven grants him one victory
after another. Until the first battles of Valencia (its capture and then
its first defense) he is fully aware of the obstacles to be overcome and
never underestimates them. However, it is not until the eve of the
decisive battle against the African hosts that he behaves like a proud
general swollen with the sense of his invincibility:

> Delight has come to me   from lands beyond the sea;
> I shall arm myself,   it is something I must do;
> my wife and my daughters   will see me in battle,
> in these foreign lands   they will see how we defend our houses,
> they will know fully   how we earn our bread.
>
> (1639 - 43)

XIV   *Presentation of Characters*

The timing and the manner of putting important and even secondary characters on the scene — in stage parlance one says "making a
good entrance" — may also be considered a form of narrative move-

ment. The most dynamic narrative movement in the poem springs from the almost continuous presence and actions of the Cid. It is further enlivened by the entrances of his most important followers.

The poet never jumbles the incidents, however rapidly they follow each other, nor does he fail to portray in bold relief the persons who figure prominently in them. He spaces their appearances opportunely; he is a master of economy, that is, skillful in the orderly and sparing presentation and placement of figures in time. He never crowds them, blurring the focus on the center of attention. In the first 1,307 lines the poet presents in action, besides the Cid, only his four most faithful followers, each of them sharply outlined: Minaya Álvar Fáñez, the Campeador's right arm, very loyal but also a man of independent mind who never hesistates to give advice to his master; Martín Antolínez "that most excellent citizen of Burgos," dependable, mischievous, and astute; Pedro Bermúdez, sparing of words, reckless, and impulsive; and good Bishop Jerome, the fighting cleric, "learned in letters and with much wisdom / and a ready warrior on foot or on horse" (1290 - 91).

Each of these four characters merits special attention. Therefore the poet presents them individually at the precise moment when their distinctive traits can best shine: Minaya when the tonic of his optimism is most needed by his discouraged uncle; Martín, when the need to trick the Jews requires his shrewdness and astuteness; Pedro Bermúdez, when his impulsive temper makes him disobey the Cid in the heat of battle against Fáriz and Galve, precipitating with his unauthorized first blows a military action, which, because of its spirit, impetus, and picturesque details, is the most interesting though not the most important in the poem (laisses 35 - 37); and Bishop Jerome when, Valencia having been taken, it is appropriate that the religious spirit of the Reconquest be made known as an important factor of the Cid's policy.

XV *Narrative Movement*

For the most part, the rectlilinear narration is carried forward by characters already on the scene or by persons who make their entrances without causing surprise. However, there are exceptions in the form of abrupt transitions resulting from the shifting from one action with its agents to another action with other agents. The listener or reader is then agreeably surprised and aesthetically pleased, without, for the moment, realizing what the reason for his pleasure is. His pleasure, we think, results from the clarity, suggestiveness, and unerring direction of the storyteller's exposition. His mastery of narrative art enables him to leave gaps which we ourselves may fill.

Perhaps the outstanding example of abrupt transition occurs between laisses 100 and 101. Minaya Álvar Fáñez and Pedro Bermúdez have brought King Alfonso the news of the Cid's great victory against Yusuf and presented to him the Cid's third and most generous gift: two hundred horses. The king gratefully accepts the gift and tells the messengers that good must follow *todas estas nuevas*, "all these good tidings" (1876). This is the last line of laisse 100. Then the poet abruptly shifts the scene and in the third line of laisse 101: "About the Heirs of Carrión I would now tell you." What he tells us is that the Infantes wish to marry the Cid's daughters. The transition is abrupt but entirely logical. When the juglar informs us that the heirs covet the Cid's wealth, it is natural that they should ask the king to arrange the match at the precise moment when the enormous riches the Campeador has won are most impressive both on account of the unprecedented munificence of his gift to the king and of the latter's change of heart. Transitions like the above are pleasing within the narrated action.

But even more pleasing and stirring are the abrupt transitions in the dramatic action, that is, scenes in which the juglar enacts the roles of characters engaged in dialogue. Such scenes are especially effective in the last cantar. At the Toledo Cortes The Campeador's arguments confound the defendants. The heirs naturally expect that the Cid, before anything else, will seek redress for the dishonor of his daughters; but to their surprise, he first demands that they return his swords Colada and Tizón. This is the first surprise and, for the Infantes, the only agreeable one of several. The judges appointed by the king grant the king's wish, and the heirs are elated because they believe the Campeador will be satisfied if they comply with this one request. Indeed, their belief seems to be justified, so happy is the Cid on receiving the returned swords: "All his body was glad and he smiled from his heart" (3184). Then, suddenly changing his expression, he raises one hand and stroking his beard with the other, he swears by that beard which *nadi non messó*, "which no one ever tore," that *assís IRÁN VENGANDO doña Elvira e doña Sol* "thus will doña Elvira and doña Sol be avenged STEP BY STEP" (3187). As the Infantes see that double gesture, hear that oath, and the idiomatic verbal construction we have emphasized (translated freely with the words "step by step"), we can imagine that they became pale as they suddenly realized that the Cid had trapped them. The verbal construction consisting of the future of the auxiliary *ir* followed by the present participle *vengando* indicates a gradual and progressive kind of imminent action. This verbal form is highly charged with formal significance. Had the Cid used the present perfect, "Thus have I avenged my daughters, doña Elvira and doña Sol," the Infantes would have been enormously relieved.

There is a brief lull before the Cid strikes again. His fierce expression softens as, handing Tizón to his nephew, Pedro Bermúdez, he says with a mixture of affection and irony, "take it nephew, it now has found a better master" (3190). Then, turning to Martín Antolínez, he gives him the other sword, Colada, saying that if the occasion should arise, he would gain with it honor and glory. After this show of affection to Pedro and Martín, the heirs might have believed that the Cid would leave them alone. Had he not in the past been blindly benevolent?

But their hopes are dashed a second time when, frowning again, the Campeador makes his second demand. Another surprise! Who could possibly believe that the old father-in-law, once so indulgent, would get such a diabolical idea into his head? The Cid asks the judges to rule that the heirs of Carrión return to him the three thousand gold and silver marks he had given them when they departed with his daughters from Valencia. This demand touches the sorest spot of the Infantes, who had married the Cid's daughters for their wealth. Remembering the monstrosity of their offense, we experience the punitive pleasure of seeing evildoers pressed where it most hurts. The Infantes no longer have the money, for they are wastrels who have squandered it all. Therefore they offer to pay in lands from their country of Carrión, but their offer is rejected. One of the judges orders that since they have no money they pay the equivalent in kind. The Infantes realize they cannot disobey the judge's verdict which is endorsed by the king, and they work frantically to round up their swift horses, palfreys, and mules and to gather their swords with which to liquidate their debt on the spot. But all they own in movable personal property is not enough, and to top it all, they suffer the humiliation of being forced to borrow. The Cid having won his civil suit, he accuses the heirs of infamy and crushes Count García Ordóñez in a verbal exchange. Then two of the Cid's champions, Pedro Bermúdez and Martín Antolínez, challenge Fernando and Diego respectively, and Muño Gustioz, the

Cid's third champion, challenges the brother of the Infantes, Asur González. Each accusation of infamy draws a heated and arrogant reply, but the accusers win the argument. However, the dispute is not definitively settled until the Cid's representatives defeat the three brothers on a dueling field three weeks after the Court scene.

This very old, possibly the oldest description of a trial, is also perhaps one of the best in world literature.

XVI   *Expectation and Suspense*

As we listen to a good story we may anticipate gladly or anxiously what happens next even if we know it in advance. In the poem the Archangel St. Gabriel assures the Cid in a dream that all his undertakings will be successful. Even without this assurance the medieval listener, aware as he was through tradition of the hero's invincibility, could not have any doubts about the happy outcome of his struggle against tremendous odds. Such foreknowledge, either on the part of the medieval listener or the modern reader, does not preclude the aesthetic excitement of our witnessing in a state of tension the triumphs of an epic hero, nor does it eliminate completely our anxiety on his behalf, but such anxiety is provisional. On the other hand, even with foreknowledge, we feel intense concern for a helpless and innocent person who, because of ominous circumstances, we fear is likely to be hurt or destroyed. This is what happens in the case of the Cid's daughters. The circumstances leading to Corpes are the only ones in the whole poem that distress us in this way. (This does not mean that the juglar fails to convey the gravity of the protagonist's situation.)

At the beginning the Cid is sorely grieved by his plight and that of his family ("Now we part. God knows when we shall be together again" [373]); but the pain of separation is tolerable. Minaya Álvar Fáñez assures him that "all these sorrows will yet turn to joy" (381) and, as we have noted, no one less than a heaven-sent messenger, St. Gabriel, whose promise is an absolute guarantee, tells him: "Ride forward, Cid, good Campeador, / for no man ever rode forth at so propitious a moment; / as long as you live that which is yours will prosper"(405 - 8).

An emotion is intensified when it is produced by a psychological reaction to a previous, contrary emotion. Thus, because of the great emotional suffering caused by the expatriation, the ensuing joy of the expatriate's victories is magnified. And, inversely, the Cid's heart was never so torn as when at the height of his glory he heard the news of the outrage at Corpes.

The juglar skillfully foreshadows this misfortune. From the moment the Infantes make their appearance we sense that they will cause trouble. When we first meet them in laisse 82 they themselves make it clear that their only reason for wishing to marry the Cid's daughters is their father's wealth. However, they do not confide their scheme to any one, not even to their friend and the Cid's worst enemy, Count García Ordóñez, because they are ashamed to marry beneath their station: "My Cid is from Bivar [the insignificant village] and we, of the Counts of Carrión" (1375 - 76). When much later they ask King Alfonso to arrange the match, the poet tells us that they "are taking counsel together, plotting in secret" (1880). And, after they are married, their cowardice in the lion episode and in the field of battle elicits everybody's ill-concealed ridicule. To vent their spite they secretly plan such a hideous vengeance that the juglar says to the audience: "let us have no part in what they said" (2539). Our anxiety, latent to this point, becomes intense. What do the Infantes intend to do? The juglar, a master of his storytelling art, chooses not to tell us all he knows.

The moment of greatest anxiety is imminent. The heirs ask the Cid to let them take their wives back to Carrión. The Campeador, usually such a good judge of people, suspects nothing. His blindness worries us. When an admirable person unwittingly makes a mistake that we sense will hurt him and those he holds dear, the dramatic irony of such a mistake intensifies our anxiety. Thus, when the Cid, who could have and should have kept his daughters with him, lets them go, we feel a deep foreboding.

Splendidly attired and playing at arms, the Cid and many of his men accompany the couples on horse to the outskirts of Valencia, then turn back. Only Félez Muñoz, the very young nephew of the Campeador, continues with them. Why did not the Cid send along one of his older stalwart men who knew the true character of the heirs? Muño Gustioz had witnessed their cowardice when, fearing they would die in the battle against Búcar, they tried to conceal their fright declaring they did not wish to make widows of their wives. Pedro Bermúdez had seen Fernando turn his horse around because he was afraid to face the enemy in combat. These two men, then, knew the craven side of the Infantes and probably sensed that their cowardice in the face of danger could become brutality before the weak. If one or the other had accompanied the girls they probably would have been saved. Their own father, notwithstanding his foolish obliviousness to the detestable nature of his sons-in-law, could have heeded the evil omens that warned him before leaving doña Elvira and doña Sol, "but he cannot repent," the juglar tells us, "for both of them are wedded" (2617).

On their way to Carrión the Infantes stop at Molina, where they are regally entertained by the Cid's good friend, the rich Moor Abengalbón. After showering them with presents, the Moor accompanies them to Medina. There the heirs repay his hospitality by plotting his death; but a servant who understands Spanish overhears them by chance and forewarns his master.

This is the tensest moment. Abengalbón could have saved the girls; but, ironically, he does not interfere out of respect for his friend: "If I did not desist [from punishing the heirs] because of My Cid of Vivar, / I would do such things against you [i.e., the Infantes], that every living being would know about it / and I would return his daughters to the loyal Campeador" (2677 - 80). The Moor returns to Molina oppressed by a presentiment of disaster, while the heirs spur their mounts on to Carrión with diabolical haste: "They march without rest all day and all night" (2690). In the following seven lines the horses swallow distances with the same swiftness we have noted elsewhere. The weary party finally arrives at the oak grove of Corpes. There:

> *los montes son altos,   las ramas pujan con las nuoves*
> *elas bestias fieras   que andan aderredor.*

> the mountains are high,   the branches rise to the clouds,
> the savage beasts   roam all about.

The travelers encamp. That night the heirs sleep with their wives in their arms "showing them love" (2703). Besides suggesting the depravity of making love to their wives before the outrage that was shortly to take place, the juglar first hints then says explicitly that the lovemaking is calculated to prevent suspicion of their evil intention. Next day they order their followers to go ahead of them so that none remained behind "except both their wives, doña Elvira and doña Sol," for "they wished to frolic alone with them to the height of their pleasure" (2710 - 11). Did these words fool the young women, or did they suspect that they would be left for dead in the oak grove of Corpes?

XVII *Humor*

Certain details of the Corpes incident, such as the wild beasts (2699), the lovemaking (2703), the blood running over white silks (2739) are masterstrokes of a powerful poetic imagination, as Colin Smith has said.[27] Corpes is, indeed, one of the poet's three greatest successes. The others are his description of the pardon and his dramatization of the scene at the Toledo Court. These and other climaxes of the serious action, however, would not have peaked without the underlying tension of the hero's sustained efforts over a long period of time. These high points provide the most stirring moments of the narration, which is consistently maintained at a high level of epic dignity. Without detracting from this dignity, however, the juglar introduces humorous incidents in the right places.

Dámaso Alonso was the first critic to give the comic elements of the poem their due. There is nothing essential to add to his excellent analysis. I will, therefore, only stress here the most important point of his essay. "The first contrast presented to us," he says, "is that which (up to a certain point) separates the heroic characters from those who are humorously portrayed."[28] The mixture of the serious and the comic — two poles of Spanish art, the constant, multivalent duality of the Spanish spirit — is, according to Alonso, one of the principal aspects of the variety of effects in the epic creation of the Castilian poet.

A North American professor, Thomas Montgomery, has also contributed an enlightening study of the humorous treatment of the count of Barcelona and the lion episodes and their function in the poem as an organic whole. As for the Cid's encounter with the count, Montgomery sees it as comic interlude providing amusement before the basic serious action is resumed after the intermission between the first and second cantares.[29] Montgomery also notes that another diverting incident, that of the lion, occurs between the second and third cantares. The observation is penetrating but incomplete because he does not take into account the first of three well-timed comic scenes, namely, the sand-chest incident. If this incident is also taken into consideration, the distribution of the humorous scenes (they are indicated by the dots in the diagram below) is even more striking:

I   II   III

` . . . ———————— . . . ———————— . . . ————————`

Among the poet's means for making a well-constructed plot we may include the symmetrical spacing of the incidents which are enlivened by the tonic of humor. Moreover, in addition to the aesthetic satisfaction derived from this proportionate distribution, a practical end is served under the circumstances of oral presentation: it behooved the juglar to arouse the interest of his audience at the beginning of the first session and to maintain it at its end, so it would look forward to the resumption of his performance. The second session does not end with a diverting note. In this instance the juglar leaves his hearers in suspense regarding the outcome of the marriage, for the Cid refuses to give his daughters in marriage himself and expresses his misgivings about it. The uncertain ending of the second cantar left the medieval audience and leaves the modern reader guessing how it will all end. At the beginning of the third session the poet confirms our anticipation that things will not turn out well. Here he presents the Infantes in a ridiculously shameful light as Fernando hides under a bench and Diego behind the beam of a wine press when the Cid's lion gets loose. Unlike the count of Barcelona episode but like the sand-chest incident, the lion incident is structurally indispensable, for, shamed by their humiliation, the Infantes later take out their spite on their wives. This outrage, in turn, is the cause of the Cid's culminating defense of his honor.

XVIII *The Epic Dimension*

Wolfgang Kayser in his wide-ranging disquisition on epic form[30] classifies narrative works into three categories, namely, those in which (1) an event or (2) a person or (3) space predominates. He understands "event" as a determinative psychological motivation like the wrath of Achilles. A predominant person is a protagonist like Ulysses whose Greek world is made up not only of his own peerless self but also of other persons from that world who after their wanderings come back home. Predominant space is exemplified by the Inferno of the *Divina Comedia*: in the Inferno the characters are identified with their previous existence in terrestrial space. The three formal categories, as Kayser himself rightly says, may be mixed in various proportions in the same work (pp. 564 - 65). This is certainly true of the *Poem of the Cid.*

In the poem what Kayser calls "event" is the Cid's driving motive, namely, the desire to regain his honor. Since his initiatives arising from this motive produce reactions in other characters, especially King Alfonso, in other words, since he is the primary cause in a system of actions and reactions, and since as such he towers above all others and his deeds arouse great admiration, the poem is, more than anything else, a protagonistic work.

The characters act and react in a circumambient complex of geographic, social, national, psychological, and ethnic circumstances. In this spatial complex real geography is more important in the poem than in other epics, as the unusually frequent enumeration of local place-names suggests. Physical space also encompasses a large area. The Cid's trajectory extends over more than half of the Peninsula: a stage sufficiently vast for his exploits. His deeds, furthermore, though physically confined to the particular place where they are carried out, extend figuratively to the unbounded area of fame. The fame of the Campeador has spread throughout the land, indeed beyond the sea, *d'allent del mar.*

Besides the three fundamental categories stressed by Kayser, another should be taken into account: the temporal dimension which, in epic, should be of a certain magnitude. It is impossible to conceive in epic a compact unity of time such as Aristotle observes in Greek tragedy. In the *PMC* the narrated incidents take place during a five-year period. The Campeador needed three years to reach the height of his military career. The final, most glorious victory, won after a prolonged siege in reality, but swiftly dispatched in the poem, could not have taken place without the long and arduous efforts that led to it.

Milá[31] thought that the first cantar was disproportionately long. Acutally it is about equal in length to the second cantar and about 365 lines shorter than the third.[32] The only reason it might seem unduly long is that it deals almost exclusively with the Cid's military exploits. However, as we have shown, the poet's account of them should not strain the listener's attention. Rapidity of movement, variety and contrast, and the spice of humor at the beginning and end enliven our interest. Beyond this, however, it is necessary for the poet to give a complete account of the Cid's deeds from Castejón to Tévar so that we may justly appreciate his long and indefatigable perseverance in a great enterprise. Only by accompanying him throughout his protracted itinerary; only by making all the starts and stops with him; only remembering the countless hoofbeats of the rapid marches succeeding one upon the other for three years with their many skirmishes and five pitched battles; only realizing that for almost a thousand days he has not cut his beard because of his grief over his expatriation, only then can we truly comprehend the significance of his rehabilitation when the king at last pardons him.

Notes and References

Chapter One

1. Numerals following quotations here and in the rest of the book refer to line numbers in the Poem.

2. In 1063, two years before his death, Ferdinand announced the partitioning of his realm at the General Cortes held in León. It was a step he had long contemplated. Sancho, the eldest son, was given Castile; Alfonso, the second son, León; García, the youngest, Galicia and Portugal. The two daughters, Urraca and Elvira, did not inherit any lands, but they were granted jurisdiction over all monasteries in the divided territories on the condition that they would never marry. The purpose of this condition was to prevent intrigues on the part of designing sons-in-law. Sancho was opposed to the partitioning for the following reasons: it violated the principle of an indivisible empire established by the Visigoths; it denied him his right of primogeniture; he resented the power which his younger brother Alfonso acquired as king of imperial León.

3. The *Primera Crónica General* was compiled by a group of researchers under the direction and personal supervision of the greatest patron of learning in the Middle Ages, Alfonso X of Castile (1252 - 1284), known by all Spaniards as *El Sabio*, "the Learned." (His biography and career may be read in John E. Keller, *Alfonso X el Sabio* [New York: Twayne Publishers, 1967].) The *Crónica* is of special interest to students of traditional literature because it incorporates in its prose text lost versions of a number of Spanish epics.

4. For an account of circumstances that led to the battles of Llantada and Golpejera and for a description of these battles, see *EC*, pp. 165 - 75.

5. For details of the siege of Zamora, the murder of Sancho and the complicity of doña Urraca, see *EC*, pp. 180 - 88.

6. According to two thirteenth-century chroniclers the Castilians agreed to accept the Leonese king on one condition: he must swear on oath that he had no part in the death of Sancho. This late piece of information is based on poetic sources which told of the oath long after the event that prompted it.

Menéndez Pidal thinks these sources are true to history, but Jules Horrent disagrees. The French scholar makes a plausible case for considering the oath to be the invention of a Burgos poet, c. 1200. See Horrent, "La jura de Santa Gadea. Historia y poesía," *Studia Philologica. Homenaje ofrecido a Dámaso Alonso* (Gredos: Madrid, 1961), II, 241 - 65.

7. Not the Jimena of the Romancero whose literary fame was propagated by the Spanish playwright Guillén de Castro (1569 - 1631) in *Las mocedades del Cid*, and by the most widely read of all plays in French literature, Corneille's *Le Cid* (1637). The heroine of the Spanish ballads, Jimena Gómez, is a creature of the popular imagination, as is her father, the Count of Gormaz, who is slain by Rodrigo to redress family honor.

8. A codification of the law of all Castilian dominions undertaken under the direction of King Alfonso the Wise (1252 - 84). The work is divided in seven parts, hence the title.

9. These early exploits are not recorded by sources other than the poem, but Menéndez Pidal thinks they are historically true. "Given the notable historicity of the *Cantar*," MP says, "we may accept it as a reliable source of information concerning certain events, like the Cid's stay in Castejón . . ." (*TPC*, p. 52).

10. Known as Berenguer the Fratricide because he had his brother murdered a year after the Cid made his appearance at their court. See *EC*, p. 279.

11. Moktadir, following the strife-producing custom of both Christian and Arab rulers of those times, partitioned his realm, leaving Zaragoza to his older son, Mutamin, and Tortosa, Lérida, and Denia to his younger son, Al-Hajib.

12. The *Historia Roderici* informs us that the Cid remained in Zaragoza until the death of Mutamin late in 1085 or early in 1086 and that he stayed on for some time under Mutamin's successor, his son, Mostain II.

13. The weak Toledan ruler Al-Kadir secretly abetted Alfonso's campaign against his own kingdom for three reasons: (1) he was a *mudéjar*, that is, a Moslem who, without compromising his faith, traditionally yielded to Christian domination; (2) being a weakling incapable of controlling his enemies at home, namely, those who belonged to the fanatical anti-Christian party, he desperately needed Alfonso's support against them; (3) Alfonso promised him that once Toledo was his he would set him up as ruler of Valencia.

14. The castles of Dueñas and Gormaz; the town of Lagas; Ibeas de Juarros, Briviesca, both near Burgos and, near the Santander Mountain, the valleys of Campo and Egina. See *EC*, pp. 344 - 45.

15. The Cid himself did not go to Villena. Instead he encamped at nearby Onteniente, where provisions were more abundant. However, to make certain he would not miss the king, he placed outposts not only at the meeting place agreed upon, but also farther northwest, at Chinchilla.

16. On this score Alfonso relented and allowed the Cid's family to join him later.

17. See *EC*, 437 - 94 or, in the abbreviated English translation of Harold Sunderland, *CS*, 301 - 44. For a more condensed summary see Stephen Clissold's *In Search of the Cid* (London: Hodder and Stoughton, 1965), 127 - 40.

18. According to Menéndez Pidal, Mohammed's army consisted of 150,000 horse and 3,000 foot. The poem tells us that 3,930 of the Cid's men fought 50,000 Moors. See *CS*, p. 352.

19. Was this confession, made under torture, proof enough that Ibn Jehhaf possessed the girdle? Menéndez Pidal thinks that Ibn Bassam and Ibn Alcama lead to that conclusion when they write of the treasures found in the cadi's hidden hoard as proof of his guilt in the murder of Al-Kadir. Without adducing documentary proof, Menéndez Pidal surmises that Jimena wore the girdle on solemn occasions of pomp and circumstance in Valencia, and that, after abandoning the city, took it with her back to Castile, "where," he writes, "in some way unknown to us, . . . it came to shed its luster in the palace of the Queens of Castile. There, just as it had affected Ibn Jehhaf, it excited the greed of another notorious seeker after wealth, the Constable, Alvaro de Luna. Upon the execution of the once all-powerful Constable in 1453, King John had a search made, as the Cid had done, for hidden treasure and eventually discovered, buried between two columns of the Alcazar at Madrid, the great treasure of the Kings of Castile, chief among which was the 'loin-girdle, of solid gold and studded with precious stones, that once belonged to Cid Ruy Díaz' " (*CS*, p. 398). Pidal quotes Alonso Díaz de Montalvo, who witnessed the discovery of the treasure. His source is Montalvo's version of the so-called *Cuarta crónica general*, reproduced in the *Colección de documentos inéditos* compiled by the Marquis de la Fuensanta (1893), CVI, 137.

Chapter Two

1. Ramón Menéndez Pidal, *"La Chanson de Roland" y el Neotradicionalismo* (Madrid, 1959), p. 429.

2. See Edmund de Chasca, "Pluralidades anafóricas en la estructura de *Cabalga Diego Laínez* y resumen de las técnicas anafóricas en el Romancero del Cid," *Revista de Estudios Hispánicos* (Universidad de Puerto Rico) 2, nos. 1 - 4 (1927), 21 - 32.

3. Ramón Menéndez Pidal, *Reliquias de la poesía épica española* (Madrid: Espasa-Calpe, 1951), lxxiii.

4. This subordination of the poet to the public taste is not characteristic of French jongleurs according to Pidal. "In France," he says, "the individuality of the poet frequently seeks to impose itself upon the collectivity . . ." (*PP*, p. 50).

5. Ramón Menéndez Pidal, "La épica medieval en España y en Francia," in *En torno al Poema del Cid* (Barcelona-Buenos Aires: E.D.H.S.A., 1963), p. 77. The essay was originally published in *Comparative Literature* 4 (1952), 97 - 117.

6. For a more lengthy treatment of the role of the traditional poet see Edmund de Chasca, *El arte juglaresco en el "Cantar de Mio Cid,"* 2nd ed. augmented (1967; Madrid: 1972), pp. 16 - 18.

7. Joseph Bédier, *Les Légendes epiques. Recherches sur la formation des Chansons de Geste,* 4 vols. (Paris: Champion, 1908 - 1913).

8. Colin Smith, ed., *Poema de Mio Cid* (Oxford: Clarendon Press, 1972) xcviii, 184 pp.

9. Smith, *PMC*, pp. xx - xxiv.

10. T. S. Eliot, "Tradition and Individual Talent," in *The Sacred Wood: Essays on Poetry and Criticism,* 7th ed. (N.Y.: Barnes and Noble, 1950), pp. 47 - 59.

11. Smith, *PMC*, p. xxi.

12. Paul Bénichou, *Creación poética en el romancero tradicional* (Madrid: Gredos, 1968), p. 90.

12a. The most exhaustive study of *Abenámar* . . . is that of Juan Torres Fontes, "La historicidad del romance *Abenámar, Abenámar,"* *Anuario de Estudios Medievales* 8 (1972 - 73), 224 - 56. In an addendum (p. 256) the author affirms that Bénichou's considerations do not in any way invalidate his own conclusions. Among these, the following is especially important: "The [historically verified] development of events along the frontier [that of Granada] during these years [1432 - 1436] allows us to accept the historicity of almost every part of *Abenámar* in its *Cancionero de romances* [c. 1548] version" (p. 255).

13. For a full study of *Álora* see Edmund de Chasca, "*Álora la bien cercada:* un romance modelo," *Explicación de Textos Literarios* 1, no. 1 (1972), 29 - 37.

14. Smith, *PMC*, p. xxxiii.

15. The *Poema de Mio Cid* is preserved in a manuscript dated 1307. The copyist was a certain Per Abad. All modern Cidian scholars agree that the poem is earlier than Per Abad's manuscript. However, since Menéndez Pidal dated the original *circa* 1140 arguments supporting a later date have been advanced by others. I will not add my voice to the confusion of voices regarding the problem of the dates of the *PMC* in this book, which is not addressed to specialists. Suffice it to say here that since the work is, in my opinion, an oral composition which evolved in the course of the traditional process — a process of creation and recreation — one may guess on the strength of internal evidence and of the external evidence found in the *Poema de Almería* of 1147 - 49, (this Latin poem tells us that Mio Cid was celebrated in song because he overcame the Moors and also "our counts" [Count García Ordóñez and the counts of Barcelona?]) that parts of the poem, dating to within a few years of the Cid's death are embedded in the full version which we know today, whereas other parts could have been incorporated as late as the thirteenth century, as Pattison holds.

16. These initial incidents are presumably narrated in the missing first folio

of Per Abad's manuscript. Menéndez Pidal supplies them from the *Crónica de Veinte Reyes*, the source of which is the poem. The poem itself confirms that the Cid was exiled for the reasons set forth in the *Crónica*. Martín Antolínez shrewdly says to the moneylenders Raquel and Vidas: "The Campeador was sent for the tribute:/he seized much wealth and great possessions./He kept for himself a considerable portion,/whence he has come to this, for he was accused" (109 - 112).

17. See p. 25. The *Historia Roderici* does record the Cid's raid against Gormaz.

18. In line 902 the juglar calls this promontory known today simply as *El Poyo, El Poyo de Mio Cid*, wrongly thinking that so long as the world endured the place would be associated with the hero s name.

19. See MP, *CMC*, pp. 41 - 73.

20. The Latin History referred to corresponds to the *Historia Roderici* which served its discoverer, Father Manuel Risco of the Augustinian Order, as the source for his *La Castilla y el más famoso castellano*, 1792.

21. See pp. 46 - 47.

22. See p. 44.

23. Ibid.

24. The exception is the Cid's reluctance to comply with Alfonso's well-intended offer to arrange the first marriage of his daughters.

25. Menéndez Pidal thinks there is a factual basis for this marriage in the form of a broken marriage contract. We have suggested the possibility of item 2 because, unlike Smith, we do not reject out of hand the possibility of a broken engagement represented in the poem as a marriage destroyed by the husbands' cruelty.

26. The Cid of reality was no saint, but neither was he the devil the Arab historians sometimes made him out to be as, for example, when, following the legal custom of the times, he had the convicted regicide, Ibn Jehhaf, burned at the stake. However, even the Arab historians did not withhold praise from their Christian enemy. Indeed the most eulogistic pronouncement anyone ever made about Rodrigo was that of Ibn Bassam *(EC*, p. 605).

27. Aristotle, *Poetics*, tran. Gerald F. Else (Ann Arbor: University of Michigan Press, 1967) p. 34.

28. Although the summoning of this particular court is fictitious, the role which the Cid plays as an expert in the law has an historical basis.

29. Karl Vossler, *Algunos caracteres de la cultura española* (Buenos Aires, 1942), p. 11.

30. It is used twice.

31. George Tyler Northup, "The Poem of the Cid Viewed as a Novel," *Philological Quarterly* 21 (1942), 18.

32. Leo Spitzer, "Sobre el caracter histórico del Cantar de Mio Cid," *Nueva Revista de Filologia Hispánica* 2 (1948), 112 - 13.

33. Spitzer, p. 109.

34. Northup, p. 19.

35. See. p. 25.

36. Gerald Brenan, *The Literature of the Spanish People* (New York, 1957), pp. 44 - 45.

37. The assumption is not entirely justified. The Cid was always friendly with Motamid of Seville, but after the hospitality of King Moktadir of Zaragoza enabled Rodrigo to make that kingdom his base of operations, Moktadir's son and grandson, Mutamin and Mostain, were like weather vanes who were turned for or against the Campeador by the winds of expediency.

38. Carmelo Gariano, "Lo religioso y lo fantástico en el *Poema de Mio Cid*," *Hispania* 47 (1964), 67 - 78.

39. Thomas R. Hart, Jr., "Hierarchal Patterns in the *Cantar de Mio Cid*," *Romanic Review* 53 (1962), 161 - 73.

40. Marcelino Menéndez y Pelayo, *Antología de poetas líricos castellanos*, Vol. XVII of *Obras Completas* (Santander, 1940 - 43), p. 125.

41. See John H. R. Polt's review of my *Estructura y forma en el PMC*, in *RPh*, 11 (1958), 307. Polt declares that the Cid's economic motive is so dominant that we cannot eliminate it by denying it. We have not denied such an obvious motive but have sought to explain it as an inescapable means to a laudable end. To hold that the obsession for gain is the hero's dominant motive is to identify him with the ruthless freebooters to whom the now outdated followers of Dozy compare him.

42. Polt does not take into account the elementary linguistic phenomenon of the semantic variability of a given word in different contexts. Thus *christianos* may refer to a person who professes the religion of Christ. In lines 1300 and 1546 it is applied in this sense very emphatically to bishop Jerome. In the context of the poem the plural expressions *yentes christianas*, "Christian people," or *essos christianos*, those "Christians," designate the Cid's followers (745, 1700, 1799); in a more limited sense *yentes christianas* (29) refers to the citizens of Burgos; in a general sense *christianos* refers to all Christendom (566, 1033); in an indefinite sense the plural means "all living souls" (93, 1295). The frequently used expression "*moros e christianos*" sometimes distinguishes between the two people (968, 988, 2493); at other times the expression refers to "every living being," "everybody"; the negative "*moros ni christianos*" is used to mean "nobody."

43. Quoted by Menéndez Pidal, *EC*, p. 608.

44. Northup, p. 18.

Chapter Three

1. C. M. Bowra summarizes the findings of A. F. Gilferding and P. N. Rybnikov in Russia, of Mathias Murko in Yugoslavia, and of V. Radlov in the Kara-Kirghis region. See, C. M. Bowra, *Heroic Poetry* (London, 1952), pp. 216 - 19.

2. Albert B. Lord, *The Singer of Tales* (New York: Antheneum, 1965), p. 79.

3. See R. Menéndez Pidal, "Los cantores épicos yugoslavos y los occidentales. El *Mio Cid* y dos refundidores primitivos," *Boletín de la Real Academia de Buenas Letras de Barcelona*, XXX (1955 - 56), 212.

4. See Menéndez Pidal, "Los cantores épicos yugoslavos . . . ," p. 212.

5. See E. de Chasca, "Toward a Redefinition of Epic Formula in the Light of the *Cantar de Mio Cid*," *HR* 38 (1970), 251 - 63.

6. Lord, *Singer of Tales*, p. i of foreword.

7. Milman Parry, *L'Epithète Traditionelle dans Homère* (Paris, 1928), p. 16.

8. Jules Cornu, "Études sur le Poème du Cid," *Romania* 10 (1881), 75 - 99; continued in *Études Romanes Dédiés à Gaston Paris* (Paris, 1891), pp. 418 - 58; "Beiträge zur einer künftigen Ausgabe des *Poema del Cid*," *Zeitschrift Rom. Phil.* 21 (1897), 461 - 528. Menéndez Pidal discusses Cornu's thesis in his ed. of *CMC*, pp. 82 - 86 and that of G. Paris (favorably) in *Romania* 22 (1898), 153 - 54.

9. Rudolf Beer, *Zur Ueberlieferung altspanischer Literatur-denkmäler* (Vienna, 1898).

10. P. M. Russell, "Some Problems of Diplomatic in the *Cantar de Mio Cid* and their Implications," *Mod. Lang. Rev.* 48 (1952), 340 - 49.

11. "It would be . . . an error to conclude that the special interest of the *Cantar* in legal matters or in lay documents can be taken as evidence against the possibility of monkish authorship." Russell, "Some Problems," p. 349.

12. P. M. Russell, "San Pedro de Cardeña and the Heroic History of the Cid," *Medium Aevum*, 27 (1958), 57 - 59.

13. MP, *PJ* (Madrid, 1957), p. 369.

14. Six editions: 1924, 1942, 1945, 1949, 1956, 1957.

15. R. Menéndez Pidal, "Los cantores épicos yugoslavos . . . ," p. 199.

16. It is only fair to say that Menéndez Pidal noted as early as 1924, in the first edition of his *Poesía juglaresca y juglares*, the excellent memory of many juglares. However, he did not then give sufficient weight to the memory factor. On p. 378 of the sixth (1957) edition of this indispensable work he informs us about plagiarism among juglares. He says: "Undoubtedly there were many juglares like the character named *"El Memorilla"* (freely translated "Mr. Memory"), who in the seventeenth century pirated plays memorizing them after one single performance and then had them printed with the glaring faults one may imagine."

17. C. M. Bowra, *Heroic Poetry*, pp. 240 - 41.

18. Lord, *Singer of Tales*, p. 129.

19. R. Menéndez Pidal, "Los cantores épicos yugoslavos . . . ," p. 212.

20. Ibid., p. 214.

21. See P. N. Dunn, "Theme and Myth in the *Poema de Mio Cid*," *Romania* 83 (1962), 348 - 69.

22. E. de Chasca, *El arte juglaresco* . . . , pp. 209 - 10.

23. Orest R. Ochrymowycz, *Aspects of Oral Style in the "Romances juglarescos" of the Carolingian Cycle*, University of Iowa Studies in Spanish Language and Literature, no. 17 (Iowa City: University of Iowa Press, 1975), pp. 132 - 44, 172 - 73.

24. For a detailed analysis of enjambment in the *PMC*, in the *Alexandre*, and in Yugoslav songs see E. de Chasca, "Composición oral y escrita en el *Poema de Mio Cid*," *Filología* 12 (1966 - 67). This article is reproduced in the second appendix to the second edition of E. de Chasca, *El arte juglaresco* . . . , 320 - 36.

25. To fit the irregular versification of the *PMC* "under the same" should be changed to "under similar."

26. Verbal: formulas of style, i.e., stylistic patterns; parallel series; transitional repetitions. Nonverbal: direct discourse without a verb of saying, abrupt changes of scene, etc.

27. See Ruth House Webber, *Formulistic Diction in the Spanish Ballad* (Berkeley: University of California Press, 1951).

28. E. de Chasca, *Registro de fórmulas verbales en el "Cantar de Mio Cid"* (Iowa City: University of Iowa 1968).

29. R. Menéndez Pidal, *Poesía juglaresca* . . . , p. 30.

30. Ibid., p. 102.

31. Ibid., p. 55.

32. R. Menéndez Pidal, "Dos poetas en el 'Cantar de Mio Cid,' " *Romania* 82 (1961), 145 - 203. Reprinted in *En torno al Poema del Cid* (Barcelona-Buenos Aires: E.D.H.A.S.A, 1963), pp. 109 - 62.

33. See de Chasca, *El arte juglaresco*, 2nd ed., p. 201.

34. R. Menéndez Pidal, *En torno* . . . , p. 161.

35. W. S. Merwin's translation, *Poem of the Cid* (New York: Mentor "Classics", 1962), pp. 232 - 36.

36. R. Menéndez Pidal, *En torno* . . . , pp. 2 - 6.

37. See E. de Chasca, *El arte juglaresco* . . . , pp. 270 - 310.

38. See A. B. Lord, "Composition by Theme in Homer and Southslavic Epos," *Transactions and Proceedings of the American Philological Association* 82 (1951), 75, n.9. See also A. B. Lord, *Singer of Tales*, p. 79.

39. W. S. Merwin's translation.

Chapter Four

1. See *El arte juglaresco* . . . , 2nd ed., for an exhaustive examination of internal rhyme (pp. 219 - 36); of the use of numbers (pp. 237 - 69), and of temporal forms (pp. 270 - 310).

2. *Singer of Tales*, p. 47.

3. See Franklin M. Waltman, "Unity of Authorship in the 'Poema de Mio Cid,' " *H* 56 (1973), 575. The author, in note 14 of this study, lists twenty-seven lines that string elements in three.

4. An expression is called a verbal formula or a stylistic pattern if it occurs three or more times. The letters A and B designate the first and second halflines.

778A: 815A, 914A, 1009A, 66A, 1599A, 2628A, 2154A; *778B:* 1967AB, 2394B; *779A:* 1617A, 1806A; 2448A, 2485A, 2906A, 1273A, 1939A; *779B:* 472A, 2386B, 2425A, 2475B; *781AB:* 501AB, 762AB, 1724AB, 2453AB; *782A:* 49A, 136A, 139A, etc. (this half-line belongs to a large formula family — 128 occurrences — of direct discourse with a verb of saying which besides the verb *decir* ["to say"], includes formulas with the verbs *responder* ["to reply"], *fablar* ["to speak"], *conpeçar de fablar* ["to start to speak"] and *dixo, dixieron* ["he said," "they said"] with *essora* ["then"]); *782B:* 826B, 1034B, 1054B, 1296B, *783AB,* 954AB, 956AB, 1107A, 1301AB, 2445AB, 2480AB, 2718AB, 2826AB, 3526AB; *784A:* 613A, 759A, 1237A, etc. (the twenty-four occurrences of this expression belong to the largest group of formulas in the *PMC,* namely epithets, of which there are 360, or 24 percent of all the formulas); *784B:* 793AB, 814AB, 1849B, 2485AB; *785AB:* 618AB, 2752AB; *786A:* 772AB, 776AB, 1147AB, 1679AB, 2403AB; *786B:* 758B, 403A, 943B, etc. (the core of a large family, 24 occurrences of stylistic patterns, consists of the inflected verb *ir* + the present participle, forming a compound verb and indicating progressive action, as in line 791B of our sample, *commo se van allegando,* "how they keep on coming"); *787A:* 2012A, 2156A, 2252B, 2262A, 2643A, 3568A, 3603A; *787B:* 202B, 245B, 294B, etc. (58 occurrences); *788A:* 248A, 613A, 1197A, etc. (11 occurrences of this stylistic pattern); *788B:* 498B, 749B, 778B, etc. (12 occurrences); *789A:* 2437A, 3094A, 578B; *789B:* 20A, 243A, 926A, 930A, 1305A; *790A:* 578A, 578B, 608A; *790B:* 756B, 1722B, 1745B, 2413A, 3642B, 3648B, 3662A; *791A:* 873A, 1494A, 1673A, 2293A, 2440A; *791B:* 967B, 2276B, 262B, etc. (see 786B); *792AB:* 8AB, 2455AB, 3281AB, etc. (the first half-line occurs with slight variations thirty-eight times); *793A:* 1751AB, 2831AB; *793B:* 814B, 1849B, 2485B.

5. Metrical irregularity is not peculiar to the *PMC,* nor to Spanish epic in general. It occurs also in other literatures. See MP, *CMC,* (1956 ed.), III, 1175 - 76 of the "Adiciones," and E. C. Hills, "A Comparative Study of the Metre of the 'Poem of the Cid' and of certain Anglo-Norman, Franco-Italian, and Venetian Epic Poems," in *Homenaje a Menéndez Pidal,* I, 759 - 77.

6. Lord, *Singer of Tales,* pp. 65 - 66.

7. I have counted 360 simple and compound epithets. See *Registro de fórmulas verbales en el "Cantar de Mio Cid,"* pp. 11 - 19, or *El arte juglaresco* . . ., pp. 331 - 48.

8. See E. de Chasca, "Rima interna en el *Cantar de Mio Cid,*" in *Homenaje a Antonio Rodríguez-Moñino* (Madrid, 1966), pp. 133 - 46; idem., *El arte juglaresco* . . . , pp. 217 - 35.

9. Rita Hamilton, "Epic Epithets in the *Poem of the Cid,*" *Revue de Littérature Comparée* 36 (1962), 161 - 78.

10. P. E. Russell, "San Pedro de Cardeña and the Heroic History of the Cid," *Medium Aevum* 27 (1958), 70.

11. Parataxis: The placing of related clauses, etc., in a series without the use of connecting words.

12. See J. A. Notopoulos, "Parataxis in Homer," *Transactions of the American Philological Association* 80 (1949), 7, 9. Also H. M. Chadwick and N. K. Chadwick, *The Growth of Literature* (Cambridge, 932 - 40), quoted by Notopoulos, pp. 1502ff., 2134ff., 413ff., 593ff., 746ff., 3161ff.

13. Notopoulos, p. 15.

14. *El arte juglaresco . . .*, pp. 29 - 32.

15. Samuel Gila Gaya, *Curso superior de sintáxis española* (Barcelona, 1935) pp. 239, 247.

16. Other laisses so linked are 15 - 16, 34 - 35, 43 - 44, 117 - 18, 129 - 30.

17. See *El arte juglaresco . . .*, pp. 183, 207, n. 15.

18. J. Rychner, *La Chanson de Geste*, p. 57, quotes two recommencement formulas in *Le Moniage*, lines 301 and 302.

19. The felicitousness of this transition is emphasized on p. 150.

20. See Lord, *Singer of Tales*, p. 65.

21. *Interpretación de la obra literaria* (Madrid: Gredos, 1954), pp. 560 - 87.

22. A. Castro, "Poesía . . .," p. 13.

23. The role of Felix Muñoz and his bat are examined at length in *El arte juglaresco . . .*, pp. 112 - 18.

24. See Menéndez Pidal, *CMC*, (ed. 1911), II, 495 and his note on line 1241 in his *Clásicos Castellanos* edition.

25. In *CMC*, II, 704, Pidal conjectures that "perhaps García Ordóñez had been so called, because he had possessed Cabra at some time." However, in *La España del Cid*, ed. 1969, p. 261, n.1, he says: "I renounce the conjecture I proposed formerly. Sometimes the name of a place was given to a person who had had good or bad fortune there."

26. See *El arte juglaresco . . .*, p. 139.

27. In the 641 lines of the first fifty laisses of the *Roland* eleven of them (4, 9, 19, 21, 24, 29, 30, 40, 41, 42, 46) begin with a line which introduces the speaker with a verb of saying. In the Cid, in 1,086 lines of the first cantar only five such formulas are used to open a series.

28. The best commentary on the scenic technique of the poem is that of Dámaso Alonso in *Ensayos . . .*, pp., 71 - 72.

29. An excellent study of the function of the narrative voice in the *PMC* is that of Thomas R. Hart, "The Rehetoric of (Epic) Fiction: Narrative Technique in the *Cantar de Mio*," *PQ* 51 (1972), 23 - 35. Far from limiting his study to the explicit expressions of the narrative voice, Hart probes beneath the surface and perceives the narrator's implicit attitudes, thus confirming the words of Wayne Booth in *The Rhetoric of Fiction* (Chicago: University of Chicago Press, 1961), p. 20, which Hart quotes: "The author's judgment is always present, always evident to anyone who looks for it . . . though the author can to some extent choose his disguises, he can never choose to disappear."

30. See E. de Chasca, *Registro* . . . , p. 34 - 35.
31. Hart, p. 33.
32. MP, *CMC*, Vol. II, 629.

Chapter Five

1. R. S. Crane, "The Concept of Plot and the Plot of '*Tom Jones*,'" in *Critics and Criticism* (Chicago: University of Chicago, Press, 1952), pp. 616 - 47.

2. Aristotle, *Poetics*, trans. Gerald F. Else, (Ann Arbor: University of Michigan Press, 1967), p. 34.

3. The "signified" (Fr. *signifié*, Sp. *significado*) and "signifier" (Fr. *signifiant*, Sp. *significante*) are terms used by the Swiss linguist Ferdinand de Saussure in his famous work, *Course in General Linguistics* (c. 1915). In everyday terms the signified is the meaning and the signifier the sound which conveys the meaning. Signified and signifier are inseparable; together they produce the "sign," i.e., the word. The "initial signified-signifier," is that of the speaker or writer; the final "signified-signifier" is that of the listener or reader.

4. *El arte juglaresco* . . . , pp. 211 - 12, 329.

5. According to Américo Castro, *La realidad histórica de España* (Mexico, 1954), p. 244, the Cid exemplifies a typically Spanish polarity in being governed both by the will of God and his own will.

6. See Jules Horrent, *Historia y poesía en torno al "Cantar de Mio Cid"* (Barcelona: Ariel, 1973), p. 339. Horrent cites me as an example of those who insist too much on the uniform and exclusive moral excellence of the Cid. To support his statement he refers to an article (*HR* 21 [1953], p. 191), which in its expanded and revised form *(El arte juglaresco)* does take into account the hero's human traits, thus correcting the oversimplification Horrent refers to.

7. "Interior form" corresponds to meaning, that is, the signified; "exterior form" to the verbal means of expressing that meaning, that is, the signifier. Hence exterior form is the acoustic materialization of interior form or, to put it in ordinary terms, the Word. (We spell *Word* with a capital W (a) because it is all-encompassing, from the phoneme, to the total signifier which constitutes the whole verbal structure of a work and (b) because of the complexity and multivalence of both the signified and the signifier.

8. Manuel Milá y Fontanals, *Obras completas* (Barcelona, 1888), II, 242.

9. We base our assumption of the magnificence of the omitted religious ceremony (Bishop Jerome must have presided, the ladies present must have worn their most dazzling finery, and the knights their most luxurious attire), because after two weeks of feasting all the guests returned to their homes loaded with gifts of furs and cloaks and so much money that "they went back rich to Castile, those who attended the wedding" (2261).

10. Gustavo Correa, "El tema de la honra en el *Poema del Cid*," *HR* 20 (1952), 185 - 99.

11. Amado Alonso, "¡Dios, qué buen vasallo! ¡Si oviesse buen señore!" *RFH* 6 (1944), 187 - 91.

12. Leo Spitzer, "¡Dios, qué buen vasallo si oviesse buen señor!" *RFH* 8 (1946), 132 - 36. See also Martín de Riquer's contribution to the discussion in *Revista bibliográfica y documental* 3 (1949), 249. The most authoritative discussion of the line in the light of its poetic and historical context is Menéndez Pidal's in his 1940 University of Valencia lecture printed in *Castilla, la tradición y el idioma* (Buenos Aires, 1945), pp. 162 - 64.

13. Spitzer takes this clause to be the protasis in a contrary to fact condition and glosses: "What a wonderful vassal the Cid would be [everything would be perfect] if he had a good lord." According to Amado Alonso it is a main optative clause with the *si* equivalent to *así* with the meaning of *ojalá* ("would that"): "¡Dios, qué buen vasallo! ¡Si oviesse buen señore!" In either case the implied comparison is in the Cid's favor: absolutely so in Alonso's version, indicating that the vassal is perfect but that the king is not; relatively so in Spitzer's version, suggesting that the vassal is not perfect because his lord is not, nothing being perfect in this imperfect world.

14. See MP, *EC* (1969 ed.) pp. 268, 293, 404, 621 - 22; also 1929 ed., p. 295.

15. Correa, p. 196.

16. The Cid's Cortes speech is, in Robert Southey's words, "perfect eloquence of its kind." Quoted by Erasmo Buceta in "Opiniones de Southey y de Coleridge acerca del *Poema del Cid*," *RFE* 9 (1922), pp. 52 - 57. "The Cid," writes Menéndez Pidal, "was an expert in law. We see him assume the responsibilities of a lawyer on behalf of the monastery of Cardeña, of a judge in Oviedo, capable of citing Gothic laws; we see him casuistically make fine distinctions in the quadruple drawing up of a formula for making a legal oath. And the Cid of poetry coincides with the Cid of history, when he methodically claims his rights at the Toledo Cortes" *EC* (1929 ed.), pp. 638 - 39.

17. Spitzer, *NRFH* 2 (1948), 110.

18. Pedro Salinas, "La vuelta al esposo: ensayo sobre estructura y sensibilidad en el *Cantar de Mio Cid*," *BHS* 24 (1947), 79 - 88.

19. Pedro Salinas, "*El Cantar de Mio Cid, Poema de la honra*," Universidad Nacional de Colombia, vol. IV (1945), pp. 9 - 24.

20. Salinas, "Vuelta . . . ," p. 80.

21. Dámaso Alonso, *Ensayos* . . . , especially the paragraphs concerning character contrast (p. 83); humor (p. 90) and the Cid's fellow heroes (p. 99).

22. "Poesía y realidad el Poema de Mio Cid," *Tierra Firme* (Madrid) 1 (1935), 23.

23. Marcelino Menéndez y Pelayo, *Tratado de romances viejos*, (Madrid, 1903), I, 347.

24. Dámaso Alonso has penetratingly studied this relationship in *Ensayos* . . . , pp. 84 - 89.

25. See MP, *PMC*, p. 80.

26. For an extended study of tense, especially the preterite and imperfect in the poem, see E. de Chasca, *El Arte juglaresco* . . . , 2nd ed., pp. 270 - 310.

27. Colin Smith, ed., *Poema de Mio Cid* (Oxford: The Clarendon Press, 1972), p. xxiv.

28. D. Alonso, *Ensayos*, p. 90.

29. Thomas Montgomery, "The Cid and the Count of Barcelona," *HR* 36 (1960), 9.

30. Wolfgang Kayser, *Interpretación y análisis de la obra literaria*, trans. Maria D. Mouton and V. García Yebra (Madrid: Gredos, 1954), pp. 560 - 87.

31. Manuel Milá y Fontanals, *Obras Completas* (Barcelona, 1888), I, 245.

32. We do not know the exact number of lines in the complete first or third cantares because of lacunae in each.

Selected Bibliography

PRIMARY SOURCES

1. Editions
MENÉNDEZ PIDAL, RAMÓN. *Cantar de mio Cid.* 3 vols. 3rd ed. Madrid: Espasa-Calpe, 1956. Vol. I: Crítica del texto, gramática; vol. II: vocabulario; vol. III: texto del cantar y adiciones (the edition of the text is paleographic). Pidal's epoch-making edition has been used as the standard tool for *Cid* scholars since its first publication in 1911.
———. *Poema de mio Cid.* Madrid: Clásicos castellanos No. 24. 12th ed., emended as in the first, 1911 ed.
SMITH, COLIN. *Poema de Mio Cid.* Oxford: The Clarendon Press, 1972. The text, edited from Menéndez Pidal's paleographic edition and from a photographic edition of the unique MS, is very conservative. In his extensive introduction the editor challenges Pidal's views.

2. English Translations
SOUTHEY, ROBERT. *Chronicle of the Cid.* London: Longmans Green, 1879.
HUNTINGTON, ARCHER M. *Poem of the Cid.* 3 vols. Vol. II English translation. New York: Hispanic Soc. of Am., 1907 - 8.
ROSE, R. S. and BACON, L. *The Lay of the Cid.* Berkeley: University of California Press, 1919.
SHERWOOD, MERRIAM. *Tale of the Warrior Lord.* New York: Longmans, Green, 1930.
MERWIN, W. S. *The Poem of the Cid.* New York: Mentor Classics, 1962. A good verse translation accompanying the Spanish text of Menéndez Pidal's *Clásicos Castellanos* edition.
SIMPSON, L. B. *Poem of the Cid.* Berkeley: University of California Press, 1962. Prose.

SECONDARY SOURCES

1. Textual Studies
MENÉNDEZ PIDAL, RAMÓN. *Cantar de Mio Cid.* See entry under "Editions."

Part I of vol. II contains 136 pages of textual criticism; Part II a 281-page study of the grammar; vol. II has 481 pages of vocabulary entries.

HORRENT, JULES. "Crítica textual sobre el 'Cantar de Mio Cid.'" In *Historia y poesía en torno al Cantar de Mio Cid*, pp. 197 - 241. Barcelona: Ariel, 1973.

CHASCA, EDMUND DE. *Registro de fórmulas verbales en el "Cantar de Mio Cid."* Iowa City, Iowa: University of Iowa, 1968). Reprinted in *El arte juglaresco*, 2nd. ed., 1972, pp. 331 - 82.

————. "Registro comparativo de los números en el Romancero del Cid y en el *Poema de Mio Cid*." *Filología* 16 (1972), 53 - 59.

WALTMAN, FRANKLIN M. *Concordance to the PMC.* London and University Park, Pa.: The Pennsylvania University Press, 1972.

2. Critical Studies

ALONSO, AMADO. "¡Dios que buen vasallo! ¡Si oviesse buen señore!" *RFH* 6 (1944), 187 - 91.

ALONSO, DÁMASO. "Estilo y creación en el *Poema del Cid*." In *Ensayos sobre poesía española*. Madrid: *Revista de Occidente*, 1944. 2nd. ed. Buenos Aires, 1946. One of the best aesthetic evaluations in *Cid* criticism.

————. "El anuncio del estilo directo en el PMC y en la épica francesa." In *Mélanges . . . Rita Lejeune.* Pp. 379 - 93. Gembloux: J. Duculot, 1969.

AUBRUN, CHARLES VINCENT. "Le *Poema de Mio Cid*, alors et à jamais." *PQ* 51 (1972), 12 - 22.

BANDERA GÓMEZ, CESÁREO. *El "Poema de Mio Cid": Poesía, Historia, Mito.* Madrid: Gredos, 1969.

BUCETA, ERASMO. "Opiniones de Southey y de Coleridge acerca del Poema del Cid." *RFE* 9 (1922), 52 - 57.

CASTRO, AMÉRICO. "Poesía y realidad en el Poema del Cid." *Tierra Firme* 1 (1935), 7 - 30.

CHASCA, EDMUND DE. "The King-Vassal Relationship in the *PMC*." *HR* 21 (1953), 183 - 92.

————. *Estructura y forma en el "Poema de Mio Cid"* (Iowa City: Univ. of Iowa Press and Mexico: Editorial Patria, 1955).

————. *El Arte juglaresco en el "CMC."* 2nd. ed. Madrid: Gredos, 1972.

————. "Toward a Redefinition of Epic Formula in the Light of the *CMC*." *HR* 38 (1970), 251 - 63.

CORBATÓ, HERMENEGILDO. "Sinonimia y unidad del *Cid*." *HR* 9 (1941), 327 - 47. The author refutes the arguments of E. C. Hills against the unity of the poem.

CORREA, GUSTAVO. "El tema de la honora en el *Poema de Mio Cid, HR* 20 (1952), 185 - 99.

DEYERMOND, A. D. *Epic Poetry and the Clergy: Studies on the "Mocedades de Rodrigo."* London: Tamesis, 1968. In this, one of the best recent books on a particular epic poem, the author considers it in relation to epic poetry in general, including the *PMC*.

————, and CHAPLIN, MARGARET. "Folk-Motifs in the Medieval Spanish Epic." *PQ* 51 (1972), 36 - 53.

DUNN, P. N. "Theme and Myth in the *Poema de Mio Cid*." *R* 83 (1962), 348 - 69.

GARIANO, CARMELO. "Lo religioso y lo fantástico en el *Poema de Mio Cid*. *H* 47 (1964), 67 - 78.

GILMAN, STEPHEN. "The Imperfect Tense in the *PMC*." *Comparative Literature* 8 (1956), 291 - 366.

————. *Tiempo y formas temporales en el "Poema del Cid*." Madrid: Gredos, 1961.

————. "The Poetry of the 'Poema' and the Music of the 'Cantar.' " *PQ* 51 (1972), 1 - 11.

HILLS, E. C. The Unity of the 'Poem of the Cid.' " *H* 12 (1929), 113 - 18. The author notes certain stylistic and metrical differences between the first and second parts of the poem. Therefore, contradicting the title, Hills argues against its artistic unity.

HUERTA, ELEAZAR. *Poética de Mio Cid*. Santiago de Chile: Ediciones Nuevo Extremo, 1948.

HAMILTON, RITA. "Epic Epithets in the *Poem of the Cid*." *RLC* 36 (1962), 161 - 78. An outstanding study of the poetic function of epithets.

HART, THOMAS R. "The Infantes de Carrión." *BHS* 33 (1956), 17 - 24. A good analysis of the structural function of the Cid's sons-in-law.

————. Hierarchal Patterns in the Cantar de Mio Cid." *RR* 53 (1962), 161 - 73.

————. "The Rhetoric of (Epic) Fiction: Narrative Technique in the *Cantar de Mio Cid*." *PQ* 51 (1972), 23 - 35.

HORRENT, JULES. *Historía y poesía en torno al "Cantar del Cid*." Barcelona: Ariel, 1973. This important book includes, in Spanish translation, the following previously published studies: "Sur le *Carmen Campidoctoris*." *Studi in onore di Angelo Monteverdi* (Modena, 1959); "Tradition poétique du *Cantar de mio Cid* au XIIe siècle," *Cahiers de Civilisation Médiévale* 7 (1964), 451 - 77; "Notes de critique textuelle sur le *CMC*," in *Mélanges . . . M. Delbouille* (Gembloux: J. Duculot, 1964), II, 275 - 82; "Localisation du *CMC*," *Mélanges . . . R. Crozet* (Poitiers: Société d'études médiévales, 1966), I, 609 - 15. The book contains a valuable eighty-five-page introduction on the Cid of history, and it reproduces "La jura de Santa Gadea. Historía y poesía," *Studia Philologica. Homenaje ofrecido a Dámaso Alonso* (Madrid: Gredos, 1961), II, 241 - 65.

HATHAWAY, ROBERT L. "The Art of Epic Epithets in the 'Cantar de Mio Cid.' " *HR* 42 (1974), 311 - 21.

KULLMANN, EWALD. "Die dichterische und sprachliche Gestalt des *Cantar de Mio Cid*." *RF* 45 (1931), 1 - 65.

LAPESA, RAFAEL. "La lengua de la poesía épica en los cantares de gesta y en el romancero viejo." In *De la Edad Madia a nuestros días*, pp. 9 - 28. Madrid: Gredos, 1967.

Menéndez Pidal, R. *Castilla, la tradición y el idioma.* Buenos Aires: Austral, 1945.

———. "Poesía e historia en el 'Mio Cid.' " *NRFH* 3 (1949), 113 - 29.

———. *La Chanson de Roland y el neotradicionalismo.* Madrid: Espasa-Calpe, 1959.

———. "Dos poetas en el 'Cantar de Mio Cid.' " *Romania* 82 (1961), 109 - 69.

———. *En torno al Poema del Cid.* Barcelona-Buenos Aires: Editora y Distribuidora Hispano-Americana, 1963. A convenient compilation of seven of the author's *Cid* studies of 1913 - 1962, including a study of monographic length, "Dos poetas en *El Cantar de Mio Cid,*" previously published in *Romania* 82 (1961), 109 - 62.

———. "Los cantores épicos yugoslavos y los occidentales. El *Mio Cid* y dos refundidores primitivos," *Boletín de la Real Academia de Buenas Letras de Barcelona* 31 (1965 - 6), 195 - 225.

Menéndez y Pelayo, Marcelino. "Tratado de romances viejos." Vol. II of *Antología de poetas líricos castellanos.* Madrid: Consejo Superior de Investigaciones científicas, 1962. In one of his extensive digressions the author elaborates one of the first and best critical expositions of the structure of the *PMC.*

Michael, I. "A Comparison of the use of Epic Epithets in the *PMC* and the *Libro de Alexandre.*" *BHS* 38 (1961), 32 - 41.

Milá y Fontanals, Manuel. *De la poesía heroico-popular española.* Edited by Martín de Riquer and Joaquín Molas. Barcelona: Consejo Superior de Investigaciones Científicas, 1959. Milá's original *Obras completas* were published in Barcelona by A. Verdaguer in 1888. His commentary on the *Cid* is found in vol. I.

Montgomery, Thomas. "The Cid and the Count of Barcelona." *HR* 30 (1962), 1 - 11. A penetrating study of the formal function of the last incident in the first Canto of the *Poema.*

Northup, George Tyler. "The Poem of the Cid Viewed as a Novel." *PQ* 21 (1942), 17 - 22.

Ochrymowycz, Orest R. *Aspects of Oral Style in the "Romances juglarescos" of the Carolingian Cycle.* University of Iowa Studies in Spanish Language and Literature, no. 17. Iowa City: University of Iowa Press, 1975. In pages 132 - 44, 172 - 73 the author analyzes enjambment, that is run-on lines, in the *Poema de mio Cid.*

Pardo, Aristóbulo. *Los versos 1 - 9 del "Poema de Mio Cid."* Bogotá: Inst. Caro y Cuervo, 1972. 32 pp.

———. *La trayectoria de Mio Cid y la armadura del Poema.* Bogotá: Inst. Caro y Cuervo, 1973. 40 pp.

Pattison, D. G. "The Date of the 'Cantar de Mio Cid': a Linguistic Approach." *MLR* 62 (1967), 443 - 70.

Salinas, Pedro. "El *Cantar de Mio Cid,* Poema de la honra." *Universidad Nacional de Colombia* 4 (1945), 9 - 24.

————. "La Vuelta al esposo: ensayo sobre estructura y sensibilidad en el *Cantar de Mio Cid.*" *BHS* 24 (1947), 9 - 24.

SINGLETON, MACK. "The Two Techniques of the *Poema de Mio Cid.*" *RPh* 5 (1951 - 52), 222 - 27.

SPITZER, LEO. " '¡Dios, qué buen vasallo si oviesse buen señore!' " *RFH* 8 (1946), 132 - 36.

————. "Sobre el carácter histórico del Cantar de Mio Cid." *NRFH* 2 (1948), 17 - 22.

VOSSLER, KARL. "Spanischer Brief" to Hugo von Hofmannsthal. In *Algunos carácteres de la cultura española,* pp. 11 ff. Buenos Aires: Espasa-Calpe, 1942. The eminent German romanist expounds his "personalist" views on the *PMC,* according to which the Cid's driving motive was not patriotism but to achieve personal glory and honor.

WEBBER, RUTH HOUSE. "Narrative Organization of the *Cantar de Mio Cid.*" *Olifant* 1 (1973), 21 - 34.

WOLF FERNANDO. *Historia de la literatura castellana y portuguesa.* Translated by Miguel de Unamuno. Notes and additions by Menéndez y Pelayo. Madrid: España Moderna (1895). Wolf's original German version was published thirty-six years earlier (Berlin: A. Ascher, 1859). He was the first critic to evaluate with sensibility and penetration the organic unity of the Poem.

3. The Cid of History

DOZY, R. "Le Cid: textes et résultats nouveaux." In *Recherches sur l'histoire politique et littéraire de l'Espagne pendant le Moyen Age.* Leyden: E. J. Brill, 1849.

————. *Le Cid, d'après nouveaux documents.* Leyden: 1860. Reproduced in 3rd ed. of *Recherches.* . . . (Leyden-Paris: E. J. Brill, 1881). More than any other investigator the brilliant Dutch Arabist propagated the Cid black legend based largely on the prejudiced Arab sources which he used.

PUYOL, J. "Le Cid de Dozy." *RH* 23 (1910), 424 - 79. A rigorous critique of Dozy's cidophobic work.

MENÉNDEZ PIDAL, RAMÓN. *La España del Cid.* 2 vols. 7th ed. Madrid: Espasa-Calpe, 1964. A monumental reconstruction of eleventh-century Spain. For a fair evaluation of Pidal's prodigious accomplishment see S. Clissold, *In Search of the Cid* (London, 1965), pp. 19 - 20.

————. *The Cid and His Spain.* Abbreviated translation of *La España del Cid* by Harold Sunderland (London: Frank Cass, 1934).

LÉVI-PROVENÇAL, E. "Le Cid de l'histoire." *Revue Historique,* 180 (1937), 58 - 74.

CIROT, G. "Le vrai Cid." *BH* 41 (1939), 86 - 89, 178 - 80.

CLISSOLD, STEPHEN. *In Search of the Cid.* London: Hodder and Stoughton, 1965. In this excellently written book addressed to the cultured public, the author relies heavily on the *PMC* itself as a historical source.

4. Epic Form

SCHLEGEL, FRIEDRICH. *Sämmtliche Werke*, I, 318 - 19. Vienna: I. Klang, 1821. With his usual sensibility and depth Schlegel observes the less-serious side of epic, that is epic humor. His general view encompasses the humorous elements in the *PMC*, especially the sand-chest episode. Schlegel was the first foreign critic to acknowledge the merit of the *PMC*.

BÉDIER, JOSEPH. *Les Légendes épiques*. 4 vols. 3rd. ed. Paris: Champion, 1926 - 29.

BOWRA, C. M. *Heroic Poetry*. London: Macmillan, 1952.

CASTRO, AMÉRICO. *La realidad histórica de España*. Mexico, D.F.: Porrúa, 1954. According to Castro the exemplarity of the Spanish epic hero was a blend of sins and virtues (p. 259).

CHASCA, EDMUND DE. *El arte juglaresco en el "Cantar de Mio Cid,"* pp. 22 - 59. 2nd. ed. Madrid: Gredos, 1972.

5. Oral or Written Composition

MENÉNDEZ PIDAL, RAMÓN. *Poesía juglaresca y juglares*. Publicaciones de la *RFE*, vol. VII (1924), pp. 26, 36, 45 - 46, 60, 66 - 69, 71 -72, 74, 81, 103 - 4, 116 - 18, 120, 137, etc. These pages contain reproductions of il-luminations of *juglares* and *juglaresas* playing many kinds of in-struments and singing.

PARRY, MILMAN. *L'Épithète traditionelle dans Homère*. Paris: Les Belles Let-tres, 1928.

———. "Studies in the Epic Technique of Oral Verse-Making." *Harvard Studies in Classical Philology*, vol. 51 (1930).

REYES, ALFONSO. *La experiencia literaria*, pp. 10 - 15, 48 - 49. Buenos Aires: Losada, 1942.

WEBBER, RUTH HOUSE, *Formulistic Diction in the Spanish Ballad*. Berkeley: University of California Press, 1951. A considerable number of verbal formulas in the ballads also occur in the *PMC*.

RUSSELL P. M. "Some Problems of Diplomatic in the *Cantar de Mio Cid* and their Implications." *MLR* 48 (1952), 340 - 49.

RYCHNER, JEAN. *La Chanson de geste*. Geneva-Lille: Droz, Girard, 1955.

RUSSELL, P. M. San Pedro de Cardeña and the Heroic History of the Cid." *Medium Aevum* 27 (1958), 57 - 79.

LOUIS, RENÉ. "Qu'est-ce que l'Épopée Vivante." *La Table Ronde* 132 (1958), 9 - 17.

LORD, ALBERT B. *The Singer of Tales*. Cambridge: Harvard University Press, 1964. Paperback reprint. N.Y.: Atheneum, 1965. Through this fun-damental book, the author, following in the footsteps of his teacher, Milman Parry, has become the most influential scholar of the oralist school.

MENÉNDEZ PIDAL, RAMÓN. "Los cantores épicos yugoslavos y los occidentales. El 'Mio Cid' y dos refundidores primitivos." *Boletín de la Real Academia de Buenas Letras de Barcelona* 31 (1965 - 1966), 195 - 225.

CHASCA, EDMUND DE. "Composición escrita y oral en el *Poema del Cid.*" *Filología* 12 (1966 - 67), 77 - 94.

6. Versification

HILLS, E. C. "Irregular Epic Meters. A Comparative Study of the meter of the *PMC* and certain Anglo-Norman, Franco-Italian and Venetian Epic Poems." In *Homenaje a Menéndez Pidal*, I, 759 - 77. Madrid: Hernando, 1925.

STAFF, E. "Quelques Remarques concernant les Assonances dans le Poème du Cid." In *Homenaje a Menéndez Pidal*, II, 417 - 29. Madrid: Hernando, 1925.

MORLEY, S. G. "Recent Theories about the Meter of the *PMC.*" *PMLA* 48 (1933), 969 - 80.

MENÉNDEZ PIDAL, RAMÓN, *Cantar de Mio Cid*, I, 76 - 124, and "Adiciones" to 2nd ed. (1956), III, 1173 - 85. Pidal's analysis is definitive with respect to the assonance of second hemistitches. He reviews previous studies of meter. For a discriminating select list of studies on the subject see Colin Smith's edition of the *PMC*, pp. 181 - 82.

HARVEY, L. P. "The Metrical Irregularity of the *CMC.*" *BHS* 40 (1963), 137 - 43.

MALDONADO DE GUEVARA, F. "Knittelvers, 'Verso nudoso.' " *RFE* 48 (1965), 39 - 59.

CHASCA, EDMUND DE. "Rima interna en el 'Cantar de Mio Cid.' " *Homenaje a Rodríguez-Moñino*, I, 133 - 46. Madrid: Castalia, 1966. Reproduced in chapter II of *El arte juglaresco. . . .* Until the appearance of this study the considerable proportion of assonant first half-lines had remained unnoticed.

MYERS, OLIVER T. "Assonance and Tense in the Poem of the Cid.' " *PMLA* 81 (1966), 493 - 98.

MONTGOMERY, THOMAS. "Narrative Tense Preference in the *Cantar de Mio Cid.*" *RPh* 21 (1968), 253 - 73.

Index

This index includes references to passages which are quoted from works by Ramón Menéndez Pidal; but it does not include, in Chapter I, references to a given work of his from which no quotation is taken. In this case a given Menéndez Pidal work is referred to in the text itself within parentheses and designated by an abbreviation. For example, MP, *EC*, stands for "Menéndez Pidal, *La España del Cid*."

Almoravides, 28 - 29, 31, 32, 37, 40, 41, 42, 43, 44, 46 - 47, 75, 77, 78, 79
Alonso, Amado, 20, 135, 174
Alonso, Dámaso, 83, 108, 142, 155, 174
Alonso, Martín, ensign of Alfonso VI, 22
Álora la bien cercada, frontier ballad, 57
Alpuente, 32
amplification of epic songs, 98
anaphora, 116
Aristotle: Poetics, 67 - 68; 129, 157
Aubrun, C. V., 174
Authorship of the Poema de Mio Cid, 82
Álvar Fáñez, 29, 31, 32, 37, 49, 119, 144, 149, 150
Al-Wacashi, 45
Anzúrez, Pedro, 22
Asur González, brother of the Infantes de Carrión, 61, 152

Bacon, I., 173
Bairén, 49
Ballads, frontier, their news bearing function compared to modern journalism, 58
Bandera Gómez, Cesáreo, 174
Battles, distribution of, in the PMC, 63
Beard of the Cid, 123 - 24, 150, 158
Bédier, Joseph: his individualist theory of epic, 52 - 53; the role of clerics in the composition of chansons de geste, 53; unhistoric form of chansons de geste, 53; 178
Beer, Rudolph, 82
Benicadell (also Peña Cadiella), 38, 49
Bénichou, Paul, 57, 162n12
Beni-Gómez family, The, 22
Beni-Wejib family, The, 43, 44, 45, 48
Berenguer II of Barcelona, Count, 26, 32, 35, 36, 60, 63, 117, 145, 155, 160n10, 162n15
Booth, Wayne: The Rhetoric of Fiction, 168n29
Bowra, C. M.: Heroic Poetry, 164n1, 178
Brenan, Gerald, 54
Búcar, King, 60, 63, 64, 79, 142, 145
Buceta, Erasmo, 174
Buriana, 36

Cabra, 24, 39, 62
Cancionero llamado Flor de Enamorados (Song Book Called Flower of Those in Love), 97
Cardeña, Monastery of, its purported influence in composition of the PMC, 82, 90
Carmen Campidoctoris (Poem of the Campeador), 84
Castejón, 25, 60, 63, 122, 131, 144, 146
Castellón, 60
Castro, Américo, 121, 143, 174, 178
"ceñir la espada en buena hora" ("to gird on one's sword in a happy hour, contextual modification of its meaning, 107
Ceuta, 46
Chanson de Roland, 53, 55, 68, 69, 74, 96, 116, 123, 168n27
Chaplin, Margaret, 175
characters, their presentation, 148
Chasca, Edmund de, 89, 162n13, 164n41, 166n24, 166n28, 167n7, 174, 178, 179
Cid, The, of history: date and place of birth, 19; his ancestry, 20; early training; knighted, 20; participates in expedition to Graus, 20; becomes supreme commander of royal army, 21; defeats Jimeno Garcés in single combat, 21; at the siege of Zamora, 23; becomes vassal of Alfonso VI, 23; falsely accused by his enemies, 24, 25; his first exile, 25; refrains from fighting his king, 25; ally of the kings of Zaragoza, 26; restored to royal favor, 30; allowed by Alfonso to wage war in the East through a "sealed privilege," 31; regains the East for Alfonso, 31 - 32; his second exile, 32 - 36; again becomes master of Valencia, 35; his tactics in defeating Berenguer Pine-Wood of Tévar, 35 - 36; the only predominant force in Moorish territory after Alfonso loses Andalusia, 37; abandons the East to help Alfonso at Granada, 37; returns to the Levant after incurring Alfonso's displeasure, 38 - 39; invades lands of García Ordóñez, 39; his dealings with the usurp-

epic poet, The, his anonymity and reasons for it, 51 - 53
epic poetry: fulfills the function of history according to Menéndez Pidal, 50;
veristic stage, 50; its fictionalized and
decadent stage, 50, 51; creation and
recreation, 51; considered by oral epic
poets as their common property, 52;
epic and history, 66 - 68
epic, traditional life of, 80
epic techniques: traditional, thematic
and narrative, 80
epithets, poetic function of, 104 - 109
Ermengol, Count, 35
Escarpe, Castle of, 26
expectation and suspense, 152 - 55
exterior form, 169n7

Félix Muñoz, 60, 119, 153
Ferdinand I, 20, 21, 159n2
Fernán González, 72
Fitzmaurice-Kelly, James, 75
form, definition of, 129 - 30
formula of recommencement, 117 - 19
formulaic style, definition, 81; in the
PMC, 81
formulary style, definition, 81
formulas of introduction to direct discourse, 125 - 26
formulas of narrative mode, 80, 99, 104,
165n5
formulas of the narrative voice, 127
formulas, verbal, 80, 89, 100, 101 - 103,
104 - 109, 120, 165n5, 167n7
formulistic style, definition, 81
fuero de Castilla (code of laws of Castile), 25

García of Galicia, 22
García Jiménez, 32
García Ordóñez, Count, 24, 39, 49, 62,
71, 124, 128, 141, 151, 168n25
Gariano, Carmelo, 74, 77, 175
Genoa, republic of, 39
Gestures, 124 - 25
Gilferding, A. F., 164n1
Gilman, Stephen, 175
Golpejera, battle of, 21 - 22
Gormaz, 25, 62
Granada, 37

Hamilton, Rita, 106, 175
Hart, Thomas R., 75, 76, 168n29
Harvey, L. P., 179
Hathaway, R. L., 175
heroic age, 50
Hills, E. C., 175, 179
Historia Roderici (History of Rodrigo),
20, 24, 44, 61, 62, 63
Homer, 56, 81
honor of the Cid. See thematic complex
Horrent, Jules, 59, 169n6, 174, 175
Huerta, Eleazar, 175
Huesca, 49
humor, 155 - 56
Huntington, Archer M., 173

Ibn Alcama, Arab historian, 43, 44, 46 -
47, 49, 63, 77 - 78
Ibn Al-Faraj, the Cid's vizier in Valencia,
41
Ibn Ayesha, Yusuf's son, 40, 41, 42, 44,
45, 49
Ibn Bassam, Arab historian, 27, 132,
163n26
Ibn Jehhaf, The usurper, 41, 42, 43, 44 -
46, 47 - 48, 161n19
Ibn Rashik of Murcia, 32, 33
Infantes of Carrión, 22, 60, 61, 71, 119,
128, 131, 137, 141, 142, 151, 153, 154,
156
infanzón (member of the middle nobility), 20, 21
interior form, 131, 169n7
internal rhyme, 100, 166n1, 167n8

Jaén, battle of, 40
James I of Aragón, 79
Játiva, 34, 63
Jerome of Périgord, bishop of Valencia,
75, 78, 149
Jimena Díaz, the Cid's wife, 23, 34, 142,
143, 160n7
Jimena Gómez, 160n7
Juan Manuel, Don: Libro de los estados
(Book of the Estates [Classes]), 136
juglares (oral poets), 90
jura de Santa Gadea (Oath [at the church]
of Saint Agatha), 159n6
juxtaposition: of like elements, 110; of
normal opposites, 110; of antithetical

Index

185

elements, 110; agglomerated twinning, 110 - 11

Kayser, Wolfgang, 120, 156
king-vassal relationship, *134 - 41*
Koran, 29, 36
Kraus, Friedrich, 97
Kullmann, Ewald, 175

Laín Calvo, ancestor of the Cid, 20
Lapesa, Rafael, 175
Lérida, 36
Lévi-Provençal, E., 177
Libro de Alexandre, 88
linked lines between one laisse and the next, 16
lion incident, The, 60, 66, 142, 156
Liria, 37
Llantada, battle of, 21 - 22
Lorca, 32
Lord, Albert B., 55, 80, 87 - 88, 97, 100, 104, 108, 178
Louis, René, 178

Maghreb, 28
Maldonado de Guevara, F., 179
Martín Antolínez, 149, 151
Masdeu, Francisco, 74
Memorilla, El (Mr. Memory), 165n16
Mena, Juan de: *Laberinto de Fortuna*, 57
Menéndez y Pelayo, Marcelino, 76, 142, 176
Menéndez Pidal, Ramón; on the Cid of history: 20, 23, 25, 26, 29 - 30, 35, 42, 47; his traditionalist views on epic, 50 - 52 and 161n4; on news-bearing ballads, 57; on the *PMC* as consisting of a succession of coalesced poems, 59; accepts the *PMC* as a dependable source of historical information, *60 - 61*, 62 and 160n9; traces the Cid's route, 63 and 163n19; his nationalist views on the *PMC*, *69 - 70*, 73; importance of his *La España del Cid (The Cid and His Spain)*, 74; his reconstruction of eleventh-century Spain, 75; refutes Dozy, 77; dates the composition of the *PMC* c. 1140, 82;

equates written and oral composition in his earlier writings, 83 - 84, 90; subscribes theory of oral composition and transmission in a later study, 84, 90; his thesis of dual authorship, 91; observes differences of style in first and second parts of the *PMC*, 91; affirms continuity of inspiration in the *PMC*, 91; compares earlier poet of San Esteban to later poet of Gormaz, 96; thinks there is a factual basis for the first marriage, 163n25; on the derogatory nickname of García Ordóñez, 168n25; on the Cid's legal expertise, 170n46; his editions of the *PMC*, 173; other works, 176, 177, 178; on versification in the *PMC*, 179
Merwin, W. S., 173
mester de clerecía (manner of the clerical poets), 88
mester de juglaría (manner of the minstrel [oral] poets), 88
mesura, definition of, 19
metrical irregularity, 104, 169n5
Michael, I., 176
Milá y Fontanals, Manuel, 157, 176
mills, the Cid's, 20
Mocedades de Rodrigo, Las (The Youthful Deeds of the Cid), 51, 55, 56
Mohammed Ibn Al-Haj, 49
Mohammed Ibn Teshufin, Yusuf's nephew, 46 - 47, 64, 66
Moktadir of Zaragoza, 26, 65, 160n11
Molina, 33, 160n15
monastic influence in epic, theories of, *81 - 82*
Moniage, French chanson, 97
Montalbán, 118
Montgomery, Thomas, 155, 176, 179
Monzón, Castle of, 26
Morella, 27, 34, 60
Morley, S. G., 179
Morocco, 44, 60, 119
Mostain of Zaragoza, 26, 31, 32, 35, 37, 38, 45, 49, 65
Motamid of Seville, 24, 25, 28, 29, 33, 37, 60
Motawwakil of Badajoz, 37
Muño Gustioz, 151, 153
Murcia, 37